Freda Utley

THE HIGH COST OF VENGEANCE

Body of a woman who died in an air-raid shelter during the bombing of Dresden

OMNIA VERITAS

Freda Utley

The High Cost
Of Vengeance

1949

This book was made possible by a research grant from the
FOUNDATION OF FOREIGN AFFAIRS, WASHINGTON, D.C.

Published by
Omnia Veritas Ltd

www.omnia-veritas.com

1.	9
Road to War	9
2.	31
The Spirit of Berlin	31
3.	69
The Material Cost of Vengeance	69
4.	125
Tragedy in Siegerland	125
5.	153
German Democracy between Scylla and Charybdis	153
6.	191
The Nuremberg Judgments Is Germany our Colony?	191
7.	214
Our Crimes against Humanity	214
8.	247
Our Un-American Activities in Germany	247
9.	270
How Not to Teach Democracy	270
10.	314
The French Ride High	314
11.	349
Conclusion	349
Other titles	359

To My Dear Friends

John and Joan Crane

Whose Help and Encouragement

Have Been Invaluable

In the Writing of This Book

Do not be seduced by the prospect of a great alliance. Abstinence from all injustice to other powers is a greater tower of strength than anything that can be gained by the sacrifice of permanent tranquility for an apparent temporary advantage.

—THUCYDIDES, The Peloponnesian War.

Freda Utley

1

ROAD TO WAR

Following World War I France and Britain refused to listen to the statesmen who said that you can have peace or vengeance, not both. They broke their armistice pledge to Germany that peace would be made on the basis of President Wilson's Fourteen Points and "the principles of settlement enunciated" by the American President.[1] They continued the starvation blockade of Germany for six months after the Armistice, in order to force the German democrats who had taken over the government to sign a dictated peace. Having promised a peace without annexations or indemnities, they deprived Germany of territory and imposed a crushing reparations burden on the newly established Weimar Republic. Having promised general disarmament they disarmed Germany without disarming themselves. The victors refused even to discuss the terms of peace with the vanquished who had surrendered on stated conditions which were not fulfilled, and in general discredited democracy in German eyes by associating it with broken pledges, national humiliation, and economic distress.

The Nazi movement, born from the dragon seeds planted at Versailles, and brought to monstrous growth by the world depression

---

[1] Referring to the Armistice, Maynard Keynes in 1919 wrote in his prophetic book *The Economic Consequences of the Peace:* "The nature of the contract between Germany and the allies is plain and unequivocal. The terms of the peace are to be in accordance with the addresses of the President, and the purpose of the peace conference is 'to discuss the details of their applications.' The circumstances of the contract were of an unusually solemn and binding character; for one of the conditions of it was that Germany should agree to Armistice Terms which were to be such as would leave her helpless. . . . The honor of the allies was (thus) peculiarly involved in fulfilling their part, and if there were ambiguities, in not using their position to take advantage of them."

which raised the total number of unemployed in Germany to six million, took power at the moment of Europe's and America's greatest economic crisis. Inevitably, the Second World War followed the first after an interval of only twenty years.

Instead of learning that you cannot build confidence and security, democracy and prosperity, on a foundation of hatred and vengeance, the victorious allies this time have torn Germany apart, deprived her of all possibility of existence without exterior aid, and while unable to agree among themselves on a peace treaty, have jointly reduced the defeated enemy country to the status of an African colony.

History is repeating itself with results likely to be even more tragic for Europe than the events which led up to World War II. Once again the victorious allies are making it impossible for the Germans to place their faith in democracy and justice, since they find justice denied and democracy mocked by the occupying powers. Once again the German democrats are in danger of yielding right of way to the totalitarians because legal methods and appeals to justice are again failing to obtain a fair deal for the German people. Last time we produced Hitler; this time we may succeed in giving Stalin hegemony over all Europe.

If France, following World War I, had been prepared to treat Germany as generously and intelligently as England had treated France after Napoleon's defeat, Europe might have known another century of peace. The long conflict between Germany and France could have ended on terms as advantageous to both, and as conducive to European peace, as the Anglo-French collaboration which succeeded centuries of rivalry and war between England and France. Instead, France sought a fictitious security by disarming the Teutonic giant while giving him every reason to plot for revenge. The crushing burden of reparations the Germans were required to pay, and the denial to Germany of a secure and honorable status among the nations of Europe, so enfeebled German democracy that the Nazis won power and France was overwhelmed by the forces she herself had created.

It may be true that the lesson to be learned from history is that mankind learns nothing from it. But the explanation for the failure of the

Western democracies to read the lesson of the immediate past seems mainly due to the effect of war propaganda and the ignorance or lack of integrity of the molders of public opinion.

The pen is still mightier than the sword and responsible for more human misery when unscrupulously employed in "psychological warfare." As Samuel Johnson wrote in the eighteenth century: "I know not whether more is to be feared from streets filled with soldiers accustomed to plunder, or from garrets filled with scribblers accustomed to lie."

War propaganda, and the falsification of history indulged in by a multitude of journalists, authors, professors, and politicians has convinced the American public that the Germans have a peculiar aversion to democracy and are an innately aggressive people who will always attempt to rule the world unless kept down and taught to love democracy by a long period of instruction in a reformatory.

Only those who have studied the history of Europe know that Germany did not become a militarist nation until centuries of French aggression, from the days of Richelieu to Napoleon's conquests had caused a reaction which enabled Prussia to forge the modern German state out of the disunited and powerless congeries of kingdoms, principalities, and free cities, which constituted "the Germanies" before the French Revolution.

Americans who have had it dinned into their ears for years that Germany has attacked France three times within living memory will be astonished at reading what was said at the time in Britain and the United States about the Franco-Prussian War.

The *London Times* on July 16, 1870, wrote as follows:

The greatest national crime that we have had the pain of recording in these columns since the days of the First French Empire has been consummated. War is declared—an unjust but premeditated war. The dire calamity, which overwhelms Europe with dismay, is, it is now too clear, the act of France, of one man in France. It is the ultimate result of personal rule.

There can be no doubt as to the side on which the world's sympathies will be enlisted, and, whatever may on former occasions have been the offenses of Prussia, she will in this instance have on her side all that moral support which is seldom denied to those who take up arms in self-defense.[2]

George Bancroft, the U. S. Minister in Berlin, reported as follows:

The leading statesmen as well as public opinion in America regard the present war essentially as an act of self-defense on Germany's part, and the outstanding task is to insure Germany permanently, by a better system of frontiers, against new wars of aggression on the part of her western neighbors, of which the past three centuries have brought so large a number.

The tragedy of modern history is that the Germans have always been kicked around when they were pacifically minded, with the natural result that the apostles of violence have again and again won the leadership of the nation, following the failure of the democrats and antimilitarists to win a fair deal for the German people, or protect them from attack.

Having finally girded their loins to resist French aggression and forced France to abandon her centuries-old ambition to establish her hegemony over the Continent, the Germans proceeded, once Bismarck's influence was withdrawn, to follow in France's footsteps. Nevertheless the popular conception of the Germans as the cause of all recent wars is erroneous. In the half century which elapsed between the Franco-Prussian War and World War I, Germany was at peace, whereas Britain and France conquered most of Africa and extended their Asiatic colonial empires; Russia fought Turkey and Japan; and the United States acquired new territory by wars with Spain and Mexico.

Having both studied and taught history at London university in the twenties, when war passions had cooled, and having had the privilege of knowing the eminent British historian, Dr. G. P. Gooch, who with other scholars was establishing the facts concerning the causes of World War I, I

---

[2] Cited in Gustav Stolper, *German Realities* (New York, Reynal & Hitchcock, 1948), p. 218.

am also aware that Germany cannot be regarded as solely responsible for the first act in the Tragedy of Western Civilization. Diplomatic documents made public by the Bolsheviks, together with those from the Vienna archives, proved that Tsarist Russia and the Hapsburgs were more responsible for the outbreak of the war than Germany.

As Gustav Stolper has written:

> Not one historian of international repute of any nationality during the twenties and early thirties maintained that Germany alone was responsible, while several outstanding historians, particularly British and American, went far in establishing Germany's comparative innocence.[3]

The facts of history were overlaid by propaganda during World War II and are today forgotten. But no one can deny that after their defeat in World War I, the Germans for a time swung back and embraced pacifism and democracy with the same fervor as they had formerly followed their militarists. The Constitution of the Weimar Republic guaranteed so many freedoms that it allowed license to both Communists and Nazis, first to undermine and finally to destroy the German Republic.

The Weimar Republic might have survived its own inner weaknesses if France had been willing to bury the hatchet and pursue as enlightened a policy toward Germany as the British, who soon after the war's end realized the stupidity of stifling the democratic forces in Germany by the full implementation of the Versailles Treaty.

In 1923 the French, against British advice, occupied the Ruhr in their efforts to squeeze blood out of a stone and obtain the huge reparations the German Republic could not possibly pay. The Germans countered this high-handed action by a general strike in the Ruhr which, although it eventually forced the French to retreat, toppled Germany over into bankruptcy. The runaway inflation which resulted ruined the middle classes and laid the basis for the Nazi movement. At the same time the misery of the working classes drove many to abandon Social-Democratic leadership and follow the Communists.

---

[3] *Ibid.*, p. 221.

The intervention of America postponed the crisis for a decade. American loans and credits rescued the Weimar Republic and enabled Germany to pay a scaled-down annual indemnity, while also presenting an appearance of prosperity. There remained a hard core of unemployment amounting to about two million, but German industry was re-equipped and rationalized with the help of American loans.

Germany's hope of meeting her obligations depended on expanding world trade and continuing American credits. The world economic crisis drastically reduced German exports, brought an end to American credits, and destroyed any possibility of Germany's being able to pay either reparations or interest on her loans.

The Smoot-Hawley Tariff Act in the United States and the 1931 Ottawa Conference which raised a tariff wall around the British Empire, completed the ruin of German democracy. Germany's export trade was reduced by half, and unemployment, bank failures, and bankruptcies produced such desperation on all sides that the extremists on the right and the left were able to destroy the democratic parties which had strained so hard, and under such tremendous handicaps, to make the German people reject militarism and place their trust in a rational and peaceful world order.

President Hoover endeavored to prevent the crisis in Germany and all Europe by his moratorium on international debts. President Roosevelt, by torpedoing the London Economic Conference and devaluating the dollar, gave a further mighty impetus to the economic warfare which was the curtain-raiser to the tragedy of World War II.

In desperate economic distress, disarmed and denied equal rights with other nations, with half its industrial population unemployed, and possessing no such imperial revenues as Britain, France, Holland, and Belgium to support its workless millions, Germany succumbed to Hitler. The false Messiah who promised "work and bread," and a free strong Germany in place of the impotent Weimar Republic, extinguished German democracy.

The Nazis not only took advantage of economic distress. They played upon national resentments and fears. As H. A. L. Fisher, the eminent British historian, wrote in his *History of Europe*:

> The disarmament imposed on Germany by the Treaty of Versailles had never willingly been accepted by a nation of soldiers; and the Germans were entitled to claim, either that they should be allowed to rearm, or that a reduction of armaments should be seriously undertaken by their neighbours. With a rare unanimity of passionate emotion, the youth of Germany claimed equality of treatment, and protested against the continuance of a system which left them helpless before the airplanes, the tanks and the heavy artillery of Poles, Czechs, and Frenchmen. The long delays of the League militated against the authority of the Social democrats who stood for fulfillment of the treaties, and had been prepared to make sacrifices for European peace. For seven years Germany had wooed Geneva, and wooed in vain.

To the Germans, for a few years, it seemed that Hitler was eminently right and the German democrats profoundly wrong. For everything that had been denied to the latter was given to Hitler without a struggle. From 1933 to 1939 the truth of the maxim that "might makes right" and that justice is always denied to the weak, was proved over and over again. The union with Austria, denied to the German democrats when it could have alleviated the economic crisis which was rendering their positions untenable, was permitted to Hitler. The right to self-defense, denied to the Weimar Republic, was not questioned till long after the Nazis had extended it to mean the right to attack others. After Hitler came to power the Germans found themselves able to win every right denied to them when they were democratic.

The German "common man" who had stood idle at street corners or looked vainly for work, and felt himself an outcast in a society which had no use for his labor, now had permanent employment, and a sense of security so long as he obeyed orders.

Whereas the world's markets had been shut to German exports under the Weimar Republic, Dr. Schacht opened the gates to German trade by his barter treaties concluded outside the international monetary system controlled by London and New York. The Germans, who had suffered great privations when they followed the lead of the Social Democrats, had good jobs and comfortable homes under the Nazis. The price was the loss of freedom but a starving man will always sell his birthright for a mess of pottage.

Hitler is dead and the Nazi bid for world empire has ended in overwhelming defeat and universal hatred of the German people who followed after their false star, and are still held responsible for their crimes. Equally disillusioned by the Nazis and by democracy, the German people today are adrift and hopeless. If democracy could inspire them with hope as strong as that once inspired by the false Nazi prophets, all Europe might be saved. But we, the victors, treat them as a pariah people, and by giving little or no support to the German democrats, demonstrate that the latter are as incapable today as two decades ago, of winning for the Germans the right to work for their own support and be accorded an equal status with other European nations.

Only a little knowledge of history is required to refute the popular belief that the Germans are naturally more aggressive than the French or the English or any other people. Each of these peoples has, in turn, been the aggressor, according to its power, its opportunities, and the ambitions of its rulers.

It serves no purpose to apportion blame, since almost all nations at one time or another, have been aggressors in Europe, Africa, or Asia, and even Americans have waged wars of conquest on their continent. The survival of Western civilization now depends on our ability to forget old injuries, rise above national prejudices, and heal the scars of war. Unless the internecine feuds of Europe are ended and we start acting according to the principles we profess to believe in, the Communists will conquer. The first bad peace produced Hitler; the second is giving us Stalin.

Only a revived faith in the principles we profess to believe in and our determination to put them into practice can preserve Western civilization.

The insidious influence of totalitarian doctrine, and the decay of democratic principles is reflected in the changing attitude of the United States between the two world wars.

During World War I, President Wilson endeavored to make America's allies listen to the voice of reason and humanity, and appealed for a peace without "annexations and indemnities" to "make the world safe for democracy." But during and after World War II, the President of the United States became the foremost exponent of the policy of "all spoils to the victors," and took no account of the Atlantic Charter he had himself drawn up.

It was President Roosevelt who sold out Poland and China at Yalta and delivered Eastern Europe to the Communist terror. It was President Roosevelt who agreed with Stalin that "reparations in kind" should be exacted by the use of Germans as slave laborers. It was also the Democratic President of the United States who sponsored the Morgenthau Plan for the death by starvation of millions of Germans, and agreed to the expropriation and expulsion of millions of Germans from Silesia, East Prussia, the Sudetenland, and the Balkans for the sole crime of belonging to the German "race."

It was Churchill, the Tory imperialist, not Roosevelt, the American democrat, who stood up to Stalin at Yalta when the dictator of all the Russias proposed the massacre of thousands of German officers after victory.[4] It was Churchill, not Roosevelt or his "liberal" aides, who tried to save Europe from Communist domination and terror by advocating a strategy which would have kept the Russians out of Eastern Europe, and could have prevented the sacrifices of the war from resulting in nothing but the substitution of one totalitarian tyranny for another.[5]

---

[4] This is not intended as a defense of Winston Churchill who was too shortsighted, or too exhilarated by his own eloquence, to realize the disastrous consequences of all-out aid to Stalin's Russia. As compared with Franklin D. Roosevelt, however, Churchill can claim to have been a statesman.

[5] According to the account given by Elliott Roosevelt in *As He Saw It* (New York, Duell, Sloan & Pearce, 1946).

President Wilson was broken, and died, after his failure either to persuade America's allies to agree to a just peace, or to get the support of Congress for The League of Nations, which he thought would compensate for the concessions he had been forced to make at Versailles to the greed, fears, and ambitions of the victors.

President Roosevelt died before the consequences of his repudiation of moral values in the treatment of the defeated enemy peoples and his readiness to sacrifice principles and interests in furtherance of his "Great Design" had become fully apparent. But before his death he must have known that Stalin would not honor the commitments won from him at the cost of betraying Poland and China, delivering Eastern Europe to Communist rule, and putting the Soviet dictator in a position to menace all Europe while taking over China.

Both Democratic Presidents failed; but Wilson had fought for justice, whereas Roosevelt had sacrificed it to expediency and staked the future of the world on what he himself admitted was a "gamble" and on his faith in his ability to charm the Soviet dictator.

The consequences of Roosevelt's "successes" were more disastrous than Wilson's failures. The United Nations proved from its inception to be a greater failure than Wilson's League of Nations and has already in effect been discarded in favor of the Atlantic Pact with the enemies of Soviet Russia.

The contrast between the attitude and aims of Wilson and Roosevelt was a reflection of the changed philosophy of the liberals. During and after World War I the liberals had pleaded for a just peace, eschewed national and racial prejudices, and endeavored to combat the influence of nationalism and war-fostered hatred among peoples. But during and after World War II, so-called liberals and progressives took the lead in demanding the crucifixion of the whole German people.

If the forces of Western democracy have been weakened by the influence of totalitarians masquerading as liberals, or corrupted by Communist influence, the Communists have lost part of their strength by having divested communism of its original humanitarian content and international appeal.

None but the ignorant, the blind, and a few self-seeking men of large ambition and little talent now believe, that communism offers mankind a more just social order or greater equality between men, nations and races.

The difference in the attitude and policies of the Communists today and twenty years ago is best illustrated by their behavior toward Germany. Here the contrast between past and present attitudes, and professed ideals and present practices, is most clearly displayed.

In 1917 Lenin proclaimed the unity of the "workers of the world," denounced the war as an imperialist struggle, and offered the hand of friendship to the German people while repudiating the nationalist war aims of both the Tsarist and Kerensky governments. Under his leadership the Communists were internationalists in both theory and practice. They had no more enmity toward the German people than toward any other because they regarded "the masses" in every country as the victims of "capitalist tyranny" and "imperialist ambition."

A quarter of a century later, Stalin, having built on the foundations laid by Lenin, but with a totally different conception of the structure which was to be erected, had transformed Russia into a national-socialist state, and was wreaking a terrible vengeance on the whole German people for having followed its own National Socialist leaders instead of Russia's. And whereas Lenin had renounced all the territorial ambitions of the Tsars, Stalin was demanding all and more than they had ever dreamed of acquiring in Europe and Asia.

The degeneration of Communism and of democracy having proceeded on parallel lines, it was natural that the Western Powers and Soviet Russia could agree only upon one thing: vengeance upon their defeated enemies. Communism having become a synonym for the interests of the rulers of Russia and democracy having succumbed to the insidious poison of national hatred, the victors of World War II combined to despoil and enslave the Germans.

Whereas hatred is a powerful weapon in the hands of the Communists, it debilitates the enemies of tyranny. Our hands have been tied by our intimate association with the tyrants whose only quarrel with Hitler was his refusal to make common cause with Russia's national socialists.

Communism has lost the liberal savor which once gave it moral force. But its appeal has not yet been nullified by its inhuman acts and its prostitution in the interests of Stalin's dictatorship. Stalin was wiser than Hitler, who ignored Machiavelli's precept that to succeed a tyrant must either kill off all opposition or conciliate his enemies. Whereas the number of victims consigned to Soviet concentration camps who have escaped is infinitesimal, many Jews and democrats who had either suffered in Hitler's prisons or had friends or relatives in them, were allowed to go abroad and tell the world about Nazi atrocities. Hence the widespread knowledge of Nazi crimes and the little information in democratic countries concerning the torture and death of the millions of victims of Communist tyranny.

Because Hitler was a little less ruthless, or efficient, than Stalin in exterminating his enemies, the atrocities committed by the Soviet Government are far less widely known than the record of Nazi crime. This is the one reason why the echo of communism's original humanitarian and international appeal still evokes a response among idealists who know nothing, and refuse to learn anything, about Stalin's Russia. But the main appeal of communism today is to the most irrational and destructive impulses to which human nature is heir. By playing upon our hatreds and passions the Communists foster and inflame class, racial and national antagonisms, and cause us to act against our own interests and the cause of freedom. Since the war's end they have been successful in propagating the idea that mercy, justice, charity, and goodwill are signs of "fascist" sympathies.

Years ago, when I went to live in the Soviet Union, the Communist attitude toward *Menschlichkeit* (humane behavior) was first revealed to me by the notice I read in Sevastopol under the portrait of a certain Russian general who commanded the Tsar's troops in the Crimean War: "General X was a most dangerous enemy of the working class; by treating his soldiers kindly he sought to dull their class consciousness."

Since the Communist aim is to perpetuate or create the conditions of chaos and misery which alone can give them the opportunity to seize power, it is natural that they should not only oppose the Marshall Plan but also exert their influence to exacerbate the old hatreds and resentments which keep their enemies divided.

The best and wisest of the Jewish people cannot be seduced by the Communist appeal to the natural but irrational desire to exact retribution from *all* Germans for the murder and torture of their race by the Nazis. Intelligent and liberal Jews have been among the leading opponents of the Communists and have rejected the Communist conception of collective guilt and punishment of innocent and guilty alike. But, being human, many Jews are as putty in the hands of the Communists, who appeal to their desire for revenge in order to soften up Europe for Soviet conquest.

The Communists have likewise successfully appealed to the hatred of the Poles, the Czechs, and others who suffered at German hands, using this passion as a means to deliver the "liberated" peoples into Stalin's hands. Thus the Czechs, who expropriated and expelled the three million people of the Sudetenland, are today themselves being converted into Stalin's serfs in their own country.

If the influence of the Communists today were confined to those who still believe that the Soviet Union is a "peace loving democracy," it would be negligible. It is the cleverness of the Communists and their sympathizers and dupes in appealing to our irrational and destructive impulses which is weakening the democratic world.

Stalin is in the enviable position of having two hands to use for the destruction of the free world. As head of the Russian State he is offering the German people the opportunity to revenge themselves on the West by allying themselves with Soviet Russia. Hoping to harness German nationalism to his chariot, he gives former Nazis honorable and well-paid positions in the German Communist "police" forces which are in fact an army, and in the Communist universities and administrative offices of the Soviet zone. Soviet Russia's appeal today in Germany is mainly addressed to former Nazis who are welcomed into the ranks of their ideological brothers in the Communist party.

At the same time, as "pope" of the Communist "church," which is supposed to transcend national barriers, Stalin instructs the faithful in other lands to demand the implementation of policies calculated to drive the Germans to side with Soviet Russia because they despair of ever being allowed to earn a living under Western military occupation.

This double game would be too obvious to be successful, were it not for the influential writers, radio commentators, professors, and other molders of public opinion who have allowed themselves to be influenced by the Communists, either because they are ignorant, or because they are ambitious, or because of the skill of the Communists in playing upon national and racial hatreds and keeping alive the passions engendered by the recent war. The American people would by now have learned the self-defeating nature of United States policy toward Germany, were it not for the influence of Communist sympathizers, spread in manifold and subtle ways in newspapers, periodicals, and books; by popular lectures and the teachings of university professors; among Senators, Congressmen, and businessmen fearful of the stigma of red-baiting attached to those who question the Communist definition of "liberalism" and "progress."

The Communists and their hangers-on have succeeded in convincing a large number of Americans that justice and mercy are "reactionary," and sympathy for the underdog a sign of "fascist sympathies." They almost succeeded in convincing a majority of Americans that vengeance on the defeated, even at the cost of imposing a crushing burden on the American taxpayer, is the way to secure peace.

Communist influence, so strong in the Roosevelt era, has been largely responsible for our treatment of Germany, and our repetition in exaggerated form of the mistakes made by France and England after World War I. Nor is this influence now dead, in spite of the growing awareness of the American people of the danger it constitutes.

French influence has reinforced that of the Communists to convince the American people that Germany should be kept disarmed and deprived of liberty and sufficient industrial capacity to exist without American subsidies—a policy which must eventually succeed in forcing the Germans to side with Soviet Russia.

We have not only, once again, imposed a crushing reparations burden on the German people. This time we have also deprived an already overpopulated Germany of the territory without which her people cannot be fed, and of the industries which could produce the exports with which to buy the food otherwise unobtainable. Not satisfied with having put Russia in direct control of Eastern Germany which formerly supplied Western Germany with food, we agreed to the expulsion of more than twelve million Germans from Silesia, which we gave to Poland; from the Sudetenland inhabited by Germans for centuries past; and from Yugoslavia and other East European countries with minorities of German "racial" origin.

If ever the history of our times comes to be written by scholars free of national prejudices, the "crimes against humanity" committed by the victors of the second World War of the twentieth century A.D., will appear as equal to those committed by the Nazis. For an objective observer of the "crimes, follies, and cruelties of mankind" cannot deny that the expropriations and expulsion from their homes of millions of people for the sole crime of belonging to the German "race" was an atrocity comparable with the extermination of the Jews and the massacres of the Poles and Russians by the Nazis. The women and children who died of hunger and cold on the long trek from Silesia and the Sudetenland to what remained of the German Reich, may have thought that a quick death in a gas chamber would have been comparatively merciful.

Nor will that mythical person, the historian of the future, when he comes to draw up the balance sheet between Nazi crimes and those of their conquerors, fail to register against the democracies our decision to halt our armies on the Elbe in order to allow the Red Army to sack and ravish Berlin.

If imitation is the sincerest form of flattery no one ever paid a higher compliment to the Nazis than their conquerors.

Instead of acting according to the democratic principles we had gone to war to preserve, we tore up the Atlantic Charter and copied the Nazis in our repudiation of international law.

Instead of demonstrating our belief in the Christian and liberal principles which had made America the strongest power in the world, we reaffirmed the Nazi doctrine that "might makes right." Instead of showing the Germans that Hitler's racial theories were both wrong and ridiculous, we ourselves assumed the role of a master race. Instead of establishing a rule of law according to which individuals are punished only for the crimes they themselves have committed, and only after proof of their guilt has been established, we have indicted the whole German nation for Hitler's crimes.

We told the cold and hungry Germans in the cities shattered by our "obliteration" bombing that they could expect neither justice nor mercy, but that although we had disenfranchised them as punishment for Nazi crimes, we would teach them to love democracy.

Instead of recognizing that their "unconditional surrender" put us under a moral and legal obligation to ensure a fair deal for the German people, we did exactly the opposite. We proclaimed at Nuremberg that we no longer considered ourselves bound by the Hague or Geneva conventions because Germany had surrendered unconditionally, but that we would punish all Germans for having similarly disregarded international law when they were the victors.

The original directives, given to the United States occupation forces ordered them to do nothing to revive the German economy, and disclaimed all responsibility for the feeding of the conquered, although we had ourselves insisted during the war that Germany must provide enough food for the people of the countries she had occupied, however impossible this was, owing to our blockade. And it was agreed at Potsdam that the victors were entitled to exact reparations in kind in the form of forced labor—a provision taken full advantage of by the Russians who have held millions of prisoners of war as slave laborers and conscripted men and women in their zone to work in chain gangs or concentration camps.

The soldiers of the United States were told that they were entering Germany not as liberators but as conquerors. The task of the occupation forces was conceived of as entirely negative. It was to demilitarize, denazify, decentralize, and deindustrialize the defeated enemy country.

Nothing was to be done to make the Germans believe that the victory of the democracies offered freedom, hope, or justice. Instead, we proceeded to teach the Germans that their dead Führer had been right in saying that if Germany failed to conquer she would be destroyed. "Woe to the vanquished" was our motto as it had been Hitler's.

For three years after their unconditional surrender we kept the Germans on rations little or no larger than those in Nazi concentration camps. All Germans, even those who emerged from Hitler's prisons, were starved and humiliated.

Germans were forbidden on pain of imprisonment to criticize the Soviet Union or complain of its inhuman treatment of those we had delivered over to the Communist terror. American and German Communists and fellow travelers were installed in influential positions in the Military Government, in the German state and town administrations, on denazification boards, and as newspaper editors and managers of radio stations. We did our best to convince the Germans that we had no objection to totalitarian doctrines and practices so long as they served the interests of Soviet Russia instead of those of German nationalism.

We not only made a mockery of our democratic professions by the power and influence we accorded to both American and German Communists, we also taught American youth to abjure the principles the American people had been told they were fighting to preserve.

American soldiers on entering Germany were given indoctrination courses in hatred, and taught to have no mercy or pity in dealing with the wicked German "race," just as young Nazis had been taught to hate and abhor the Jews. "The Morgenthau Plan," approved of by President Roosevelt at Quebec, was the basis of the Army's notorious order JCS 1067 which laid down the pattern of our original occupation policy. The Morgenthau Plan for the pastoralization of Germany, had it been carried out, would have constituted the greatest act of genocide perpetrated in modern times. The Germans would have been deprived of almost all their industries, and, since their soil is incapable of supporting more than the present agricultural population, at least thirty million people would have died of starvation.

The humanitarian scruples of the American people prevented the execution of this infamous plan. Unfortunately, however, JSC 1067 remained as the textbook of our occupation forces until 1947. According to this Army order issued to General Eisenhower in April 1945, "no steps looking toward the economic rehabilitation of Germany or designed to maintain or strengthen the German economy" were to be taken. Military Government was explicitly instructed to "prohibit and prevent" production in a long and comprehensive list of industries.

The food consumption of the German people was to be held down to a minimum, with "surpluses" made available to the occupying forces and displaced persons. With a total disregard of the fact that a Germany deprived of her eastern bread basket by the Russian occupation and by the Polish seizure of Silesia had no possibility of feeding herself even at a near-starvation level, it was decreed that ration scales should be set low enough to permit the use of "net surpluses" for the sustenance of the occupation forces and displaced persons and for export.

Army order JCS 1067 explicitly states that "Germany will not be occupied for the purpose of liberation, but as a defeated enemy nation." It went on to say that reparations and restitutions were to be exacted, and no political activity permitted. "Fraternization" with the enemy was strictly forbidden. We were determined to out-Nazi the Nazis in our own treatment of the conquered.

American soldiers were threatened with punishment should they behave like Americans and aid the destitute and helpless. Kindness, even to German children, was held to be a misdemeanor. GI's were forbidden to take a morsel of food off their plates to give to the starving, and mess sergeants were instructed to throw away food left over, not to let any Germans have it. Even the gift of coffee grounds to the Germans was forbidden.

Not only was charity forbidden and pity regarded as un-American, GI's and officers, if not positively encouraged to loot, were in no way discouraged from committing the same excesses as the Russians and French. Today the verb "liberate" has become an army colloquialism for stealing.

Since every army contains a percentage of gangsters and criminal elements, there is always some looting in an occupied enemy country and a certain amount of brutal mishandling of the civilian population. The instructions given by Washington to the United States Army positively encouraged the licentious and brutal minority and penalized the decent, law abiding, and humane majority.

It is to the credit of the American people that in spite of the Roosevelt-Morgenthau directives, put into operation by General Eisenhower without protest, large numbers of American soldiers insisted on behaving like Christian gentlemen. Many succored the hungry and defenseless Germans in spite of the regulations against it. Others were impelled by the impulse which in all ages has broken the barriers between conquerors and conquered.

Americans in the occupation forces might enjoy the status of "sons of heaven," but like the angels they looked upon the daughters of earth and saw that they were fair. It was impossible to prevent GI's who were far from home and sick of war to carry the demands of vengeance to the extent of rejecting association with ill-fed but neat German women or refusing candy to starving German children. Neither army regulations nor the propaganda of hatred in the American press could prevent American soldiers from liking and associating with German women, who although they were driven by hunger to become prostitutes, preserved a certain innate decency, and by responding to kindness with affection and loyalty, often won the love of American boys who had started out only to enjoy the pleasures which war affords to the victors.

Because of the natural kindness of the Americans, the call of human nature, and the qualities of German women, the inhuman and unrealistic directives given by Washington to the United States occupation forces were from the beginning more honored in the breach than in observance.

The futility of telling Americans to act like Nazis, Communists, or robots led at an early stage to the cancellation of the nonfraternization decrees.

Meanwhile, the utter absurdity of the Morgenthau Plan and the high cost of vengeance was becoming obvious in America.

Far from realizing "surpluses," Western Germany had to be supplied with American food to prevent "disease and unrest" dangerous to the occupation forces.

Americans had not been sufficiently indoctrinated with totalitarian concepts of collective punishment to be inflicted on innocent and guilty alike to enable them to condemn millions of people to death by starvation, even if this policy had not involved risks to the occupation forces. Humanitarian sentiment was reinforced by the dangers to which American soldiers were exposed. Germs disregard racial barriers or those dividing "good" and "bad" nations, and it was also realized that starving people might prefer a quick death by attacking their conquerors to a slow lingering one. So the American taxpayer was called upon to provide just enough food to keep the Germans alive and submissive and to prevent epidemics. Gradually also, the influence of so-called liberals and "New Deal" advocates of the theory that we should love Communists and hate all Germans, declined.

The original pattern of the United States occupation had been set at a time when propaganda had convinced a large number of Americans that Soviet Russia is a "peace-loving" power and an example of a "new and better" democratic way of life, and had induced the majority of Americans to believe that Stalin could be trusted to honor his commitments.

After the Soviet Government made it increasingly obvious that it was irrevocably hostile to the Western democracies and had no more intention of observing its treaties with us than those it had formerly signed with its European neighbors, the most loving "friends of the Soviet Union" were compelled to think again. Those who were not Communists were forced to admit that the assumptions on which United States policy had been based since 1941 might conceivably be false. As the menace of Soviet aggression grew, the assumption that the Germans were the root of all evil crumbled. As it became more and more apparent that the Soviet Union menaced the whole world, it became clear that what was left of Europe must be defended against Russia even at the cost of forgiving the German people for their error in following Nazi leadership, and admitting them into the community of free Western nations.

Understanding of the terrible present danger which Communism constitutes to freedom everywhere in the world, combined with the American taxpayers' realization of the cost of vengeance, combined to modify our German policy. The Marshall Plan for the reconstruction of Europe, which included Germany as the recipient of American ECA assistance, took the place of the Morgenthau Plan for "keeping Germany in chains and Europe in rags."

The need for a complete repudiation of the totalitarian concepts which originally inspired our occupation policy is not, however, recognized even today.

As soon as I arrived in Germany in August 1948 I realized that the assumption at home that the Marshall Plan has completely superseded the Morgenthau Plan is a delusion. United States policy had changed, and compared to the first years of the occupation it had become humane and intelligent. But the basic pattern remained the same.

The adherents of the Morgenthau Plan, although they no longer directed United States occupation policies, still influenced it and could be found occupying important positions in Military Government. The Communists and their sympathizers were no longer permitted to hold leading positions in Germany; but they were still able to work through so-called liberals who have been persuaded that advocacy of a humane and constructive policy in Germany is a sign of reactionary sympathies.

Waning Communist influence has been reinforced by French intransigeance and the British desire to eliminate German competition in the markets of the world. Thus dismantlement and other measures which debilitate Germany, weaken Europe, place ever increasing burdens on America, and pave the way for a Communist conquest of the world, are still being implemented.

This book does not attempt to deal with all aspects of the German problem. It aims only to show the American people the cost of vengeance, now and in the future. That cost cannot be appraised only in economic terms. The moral, political, and military consequences of denying to the Germans, not only liberty, but also the right to earn a living and the right of self-defense, may lead to the destruction of Western civilization, unless America is made aware in time of the need to implement in Europe the principles which have made her great.

2

THE SPIRIT OF BERLIN

BERLIN IN THE SUMMER AND FALL OF 1948 REMINDED ME OF Shanghai ten years ago. In China then, as in Germany now, the Americans, British, and French were living safely and comfortably while "the natives" risked their lives against the enemy who was preparing to attack us in the fullness of time. A decade ago the United States and Britain had endeavored to maintain "good relations" with the Japanese aggressors in spite of their Nanking Massacre and other "crimes against humanity"; and in spite of Japan's disregard of Western interests in China, her insults, and such hostile acts as the blockade of the British concession at Tientsin, and the bombing of the United States gunboat *Panay*. In Germany we were trying to reach an understanding with the Soviet Government in spite of the blockade of Berlin and Moscow's open proclamation of bitter enmity toward the Western "capitalist-imperialist" Powers.

In the first years of the Sino-Japanese War, when I was a correspondent in China, America and England, while seeking to preserve their own interests by appeasing Japan and sacrificing China, treated the Japanese with far greater respect than the Chinese who were fighting our battles as well as their own. In the Cold War in Europe, we were trying not to "provoke" the Russians, and were begging Stalin in Moscow to meet our envoys to discuss the Berlin Crisis with the same disregard of the interests of the German people as we had shown with regard to the Chinese. Just as we had formerly proffered the hand of friendship to militarist Japan if only she would refrain from attacking our interests in China, so now we were assuring the Soviet dictator that we would be delighted to cooperate with him once again if only he would keep his demands within reasonable limits. We still held the whole German people responsible for Hitler's crimes, while prepared to condone and abet Stalin's if only he would not attack us and our friends. We blamed the Germans for having submitted to Nazi dictatorship, but we ourselves continued to demonstrate our willingness to renew our wartime collaboration with Russia's national socialists.

While treating the representatives of the Soviet dictator with deference, and pleading with Stalin to come to terms permitting us to embrace him, we continued to regard the democratic leaders of the Berlin population as inferiors unworthy to sit down with us to discuss our mutual defense on terms of equality. General Clay and his staff who had formerly had no scruples in entertaining and being entertained by the military representatives of Stalin's bloodstained tyranny, never met the elected representatives of the Berliners except as masters giving orders to their subordinates. True a little more courtesy has been shown to the Mayor and members of the Berlin City Council, but there has been no disposition to treat them as friends.

In Shanghai there had been the International and French concessions where the white people lived in safety with all the conveniences, services, and material advantages of a master race, protected by their own soldiers and the power of their governments, while the great mass of the Chinese population fought and labored and starved in the Chinese city. The Japanese had had their own concession to use as the base for their attack on China, just as the Russians now had their sector of Berlin from which to operate.

In Berlin there was no native city; the whole town was divided up among the four "master races," all enjoying special privileges comparable to those which the Western Powers and Japan had enjoyed in China as a result of the "unequal treaties" which gave them "extraterritorial" rights on Chinese soil. We, the Western Powers, had won our privileged position in China by aggressive war and threats; the Germans whom we now treat like the "inferior" peoples of Asia had got themselves into their present situation by their failure to aggress successfully.

The whole setup in Berlin was so similar to the one I had known in Shanghai in the twenties and thirties that I found myself unconsciously referring to the British, American, French, and Russian "concessions." The

Germans, commonly referred to by the American Military Government as "the indigenous population," were as wretchedly housed and fed and as rightless and defenseless as the mass of the Chinese population; and the "conquerors" seemed as callous in their attitude toward German sufferings as the whites had been toward "the natives" in India and China in the bad old days of Western imperialism at the height of its power. Susceptibilities had been hardened by the constant sight of poverty and hunger and our belief in our own moral superiority.

In China during the war, the Westerners had shown rather more sympathy for the poorly armed Chinese attempting to resist Japan than the majority of Americans and British in Berlin showed toward the Germans, part of whose country was already under Soviet Russia's Iron Heel by our consent. Then as now we wanted to "do business" with the aggressors, but we had at least sympathized with the Chinese and cheered them on to fight. The Chinese were not "enemy nationals," so it was correct to be sorry for them and to collect money for their relief. On the other hand the Chinese are not white, so Washington and London never considered Japanese aggression against China as nearly so wicked as German aggression in Europe.

When I came from China to the United States in 1938, I found there was infinitely greater indignation over the rape of Czechoslovakia than over Japan's partial conquest of China with the aid of the American and British war materials she was permitted to buy in huge quantities.

Sun Yat-sen described the China of the nineteenth and early twentieth centuries as a "subcolony," meaning that his country was in an even worse situation than a colony, since all the Western Powers together with Russia and Japan had exploited and oppressed China, while no one of them was responsible for her defense. Today it seemed to me that Germany was in much the same situation. Her conquerors, while quarreling among themselves, jointly hold Germany down. Her people, deprived of all means of self-defense, have no guarantee that the West will defend them from Soviet aggression; and they fear that at any moment Russia and the Western Powers may resurrect the Yalta and Potsdam agreements for their mutual benefit. The Germans had ample proof in the first years of the occupation that democratic principles were of little or no importance to any of their conquerors, and that it is only Stalin's greed and openly declared hostility toward America which has caused the rift between the Eastern and Western victors.

The Germans in Berlin and in the Western zones were being permitted to raise their heads again only because their masters were at odds. They knew only too well that should Stalin choose to make concessions to the Western Powers they, the conquered, would once again be crushed, and might once again be forced by the Western occupying Powers to pretend that Communists are democrats and to admit Stalin's German stooges into a "coalition government."

In their defenseless situation the Berliners might have been expected to resign themselves fatalistically to whatever blows fate still held in store for them. Instead, they were drawing upon spiritual forces, the very existence of which had been denied during the thirteen years of Nazi domination. They were displaying greater courage and fortitude in adversity than in the days of Hitler's power and glory. Alone among the peoples of Europe close to the terrifying power of Soviet Russia, the Berliners were defying it.

Perhaps it is true on earth as in heaven that the last shall be first and the first last. France, who had once been in the forefront of the struggle for liberty, now seemed to be lagging behind Germany in the will and courage to resist tyranny. The French, who ten years ago had asked, "Why die for Danzig?" were now saying, "What, die for Berlin!" Yet the Berliners, ex-enemy nationals as they are, were surely right in believing that if the Western Powers failed this time to recognize the indivisibility of Europe, the need to defend principles as well as self-interest, and the call of the unarmed millions in Germany and Eastern Europe endeavoring to resist the Communist terror, not all the arms and atom bombs manufactured in America would later on be able to save our civilization.

Without weapons, hungry, and in rags, living in squalor in the bomb-shattered buildings of their once proud city, and well aware that the Western Powers would not risk a clash with the Soviets to protect them from "arrest" or kidnapping by the Communists even in the Western sectors of the city, the people of Berlin refused to be cowed.

They were being encouraged in their resolution by General Clay, who, although his attitude towards the Germans was still that of a conqueror, had shown a bold front toward Stalin and was credited with having prevented the State Department from giving way to the Soviets when they started the blockade. It was said that Clay wanted to run an armored convoy through at the outset but had been held back by Washington as well as by the British and French. While the Berlin Mayor and the city councilors resented the cavalier treatment they too often received at the hands of the Military Government, they realized that General Clay was mainly responsible for the air lift and the preservation of a free Berlin.

It was my impression that on the whole, American military men behaved better toward the Germans and had more sympathy and respect for them than the civilians. There was still a good sprinkling of "Morgenthau Boys" among the civilian officials in the economic, financial, and information sections of the Military Government; and it is in any case a truism that those who fight wars do less hating than the civilians who have never learned to respect a brave enemy.

Many United States officers, air-force pilots, and GI's openly proclaimed their admiration for the courage of the Berliners. Colonel Babcock, Deputy Commandant in Berlin, said to me in August: "The courage of these people is really something to wonder at. The City Council members risk their lives and liberty, each time they go to a meeting, since the *Stadthaus* ("City hall") is in the Russian sector and we can give them no protection there."

I realized how true this had become, for, the day before, I had met Jeanette Wolff, a woman Social-Democratic leader who had been manhandled by the Communists on her way home from a meeting of the Council, and been called a "dirty Jew" by Stalin's bullies. She had escaped serious injury only because a Soviet sector policeman, who had known her when they were together in one of Hitler's concentration camps, protected her and led her to safety.

As against the encouragement they were receiving from Military Government, the Berliners had to reckon not only with the anti-German sentiment still spread in America by most of the press, but also with the influence of such advocates of appeasement as Walter Lippmann and Sumner Welles. The extent of this influence was exaggerated in Germany because the *New York Herald Tribune* was the only stateside daily newspaper with a European edition, and because the German Communist press seized upon Lippmann's and Sumner Welles's columns as evidence of the lack of support in the United States for General Clay's bold stand in Berlin.

At a meeting I attended in Berlin at America House, a German newspaper editor told a joke then current in the city: A telegram had been dispatched to Washington by a mass meeting of Berlin citizens saying: "Take courage, don't be afraid and give way to Russian threats. We are a hundred per cent behind you!"

This witticism contained a substantial truth. It was in fact the courage of the Berlin population and their unwavering support of the stand against Russia at the cost of acute hardship, which had given the United States the backing it required to hold on in Berlin.

It was interesting in Berlin to witness the "conversion" of many visitors. However great their resistance to the idea on their arrival, many of them left at least partially convinced that the capital of Hitler's infamous Third Reich has been transformed into the focus of resistance to total tyranny. This seeming paradox is not only the result of the rapid tempo of history in our times. It also must be remembered that in the tragic record of Hitler's rise to power in Germany, Berlin was conspicuous for its anti-Nazi vote, and succumbed only after the Communists had made common cause with the Nazis to destroy German democracy.

It seemed to me, in August and September 1948, and even more forcibly at the end of November when darkness and cold were adding to the misery of the inhabitants, that a phoenix had arisen from the ashes of the ruined city. A new resolute, hardened, and purified democratic movement was inspiring the unarmed people of Berlin to resist Soviet Russia's armed might with a courage unequaled anywhere else in Europe. German bravery, discipline, and singleness of purpose were at last, to judge from Berlin, being directed toward the defense, instead of the destruction, of Western civilization.

The unanimity of the Berlin population, in contrast to the divisions which weaken the democratic forces in France and even in Britain, is the more remarkable because the Germans are receiving less encouragement and help from America than any other European country. Although it is true that the United States has saved the German people from mass starvation, they have been at the end of the line in the allocation of food and raw-material subsidies from America. Even more important is the fact that the Germans still lack the moral support they would derive from being accepted as fighting allies in the American-led opposition to Communist aggression. Although they are in the front line of the worldwide struggle against Communist tyranny, the Germans are still suspect for their former acceptance of Nazi leadership. While struggling to be free, they drag the chains with which the democracies have shackled them as punishment for Hitler's crimes. Nevertheless the Germans in Berlin were providing a lesson for all Europe, and in particular for divided and frightened France. They were risking their lives for liberty, while others only talked about their devotion to democracy.

The Germans, it seemed, have learned through bitter experience that the battle today is not one between different economic systems, or between classes or even nations, but one for or against the basic values of Western civilization. A nation whose best spirits recognize that it has sinned mightily was demonstrating in Berlin that it now has greater courage in resisting evil than others who have never been tempted, and have never learned what are the consequences of succumbing to a dictatorship which repudiates all moral values.

"We know, now," a young German said to me, "that in the long run power depends upon the extent to which it is based on spiritual and moral values. Everything which Germans ever won by the sword is lost; our only permanent gains have been those won by moral force. Frederick the Great, Bismarck, and Hitler gave us nothing which has not passed away, but the influence of Luther and the Reformation have been permanent."

The man who said this to me, Rainer Hildebrandt, is not a pacifist. Nor did he think that his own country was alone guilty of "crimes against humanity." To him it seemed that Western civilization as a whole was on trial, and had failed so far to meet the test of the machine age and of a world in which the misery of one people affects all others.

"The crisis in Berlin," he said, "is an explosion of all the evils which evoked the previous totalitarianism and now threatens us with the endless night of Communist domination."

Hildebrandt was one of several Germans I met whose ancestry was partly Jewish. They were treated as secondor third-class citizens by the Nazis and never shared, nor, wished to share, in the fruits of Hitler's victories, but they have identified themselves with the German nation in the hour of its defeat and humiliation. He combined an abiding love for the country of his birth with the international and humanitarian outlook of the most idealistic Jews. Thin to the point of emaciation, with classically perfect features and eyes which are both brilliantly intelligent and kind, Rainer Hildebrandt has a vision which transcends nationality and race, burning energy and a zeal for "righteousness" in the Biblical sense of that almost forgotten word.

Hildebrandt had been a friend of the younger Haushofer who was executed for his part in the July Twentieth plot against Hitler and he has written a book for a Swiss publisher on the German resistance movement. He told me that prior to the Soviet occupation he had been among those Germans who had imagined that the Russians would liberate them. Today, having met the Communists face to face, having witnessed the horrible atrocities they committed when they took Berlin, and knowing all about the concentration camps in the Eastern zone and in Russia, he is one of the most fearless and active anti-Communists in Germany. He is in constant touch with the resistance movement in Russian-occupied Germany and has organized help for the neglected victims of Communism who escape to Berlin from the lands under Soviet domination. When I first met him Hildebrandt was trying to get permission from the Military Government to organize an international league to help the victims of Communism on the same lines as the associations formed to help the victims of Nazi terror in prewar days. Failing to obtain American or British support, withheld presumably in the interests of lingering hopes of an accord with Stalin, Hildebrandt has on his own initiative started an organization called *"Kampfgruppe gegen Unmenschlichkeit"* ("Action Group against Inhumanity").

The following is an extract from a speech he delivered in Berlin:

Decency requires that we take up this fight. We have a responsibility toward ourselves and toward the millions of people in Soviet concentration camps. We want peace, but we do not speak the word peace if it means a continuation of the Cold War. We want a peace which presupposes freedom and respect for human values; a peace which will eliminate the internal as well as external causes of war. The two great motive forces of history are, on the one hand, fear, a bad conscience, and lust for power; on the other hand, responsibility, confidence, brotherhood. These two motors cannot run side by side. The road grows ever narrower, the course which humanity takes will be determined by whichever car takes the lead. If the first car draws ahead, the other will never be able to pass it; a curtain will descend upon us heavier than the Iron Curtain, and the darkest word in the history of the world will have been spoken: "Too late."

The reaffirmation of spiritual values, faith in the spirit of man, and readiness to die for liberty; in a word, recognition of the importance of the intangibles which decide the fate of civilizations was, it seemed, the explanation for the spirit of hope which pervaded the besieged city of Berlin.

Reading the stateside press was as depressing as the bombed and fire-gutted buildings of Berlin which stretch mile after mile in every sector of the city. One had an unhappy feeling that the role of the Germans and that of the victorious and powerful democracies had been reversed. For, to judge by most of the American and British newspaper reports and commentaries, the conflict in Berlin was regarded in terms of pure power politics; as if the city where West meets East was just a point on the map, worth so much or so little as a bargaining counter in an American-Russian conflict.

It was more than a little ironic to read the comments of Walter Lippmann, Sumner Welles, and others whose writings were quoted almost daily in the Russian-licensed German press. The same writers who were advocating a deal with Russia which would involve extinction of the lamp of freedom lighted in Berlin, were reproving General Clay for standing up to Russia instead of "concentrating upon the conversion of the German spirit to individual freedom and democracy"!

How was it possible, one thought in Berlin, that anyone could still imagine that the punishment of opinion by denazification courts and penalties, "decartelization," land reform, or the *preaching* of democracy would decide the issue in Germany? How was it that these and many other writers failed to see that it was example, deeds, our own attitude in the face of totalitarian aggression, and our support and protection of the fighting democrats in Berlin which were all-important? That if we should decide to retire from the battle for the sake of a temporary truce in the Cold War, and leave the Berliners to be overwhelmed by the Soviet Union, it might never again be possible to enlist the German people on our side; and that the resistance movements in Poland, Czechoslovakia and other Soviet satellite countries would be dealt a mortal blow.

If we should once again appease Russia and betray those who trusted in our promise not to abandon Berlin, the unholy alliance of Communists and Nazis—so evident in Berlin where even the Chief of the Russian Sector Police, the notorious Markgraf, is a former prominent Nazi—would be able to destroy the democratic movement of infinite promise born in this ruined city. Germany might then once again be driven to repudiate Western civilization instead of becoming a bulwark for its defense.

As one woman Social Democrat said to me during the Moscow negotiations, "You can't treat *people* like pawns in a chess game to be moved forward, encouraged to fight for freedom against tyranny while America is at odds with Russia, and then sacrificed in another move to appease Russia. If you once again come to terms with Stalin over our heads and at our expense, you will never again be able to evoke the spirit which is now keeping us on your side in spite of Russia's greater strength and the hunger and terror Communism uses to break men's spirits."

As in a performance of Hamlet without the Prince of Denmark, the role of the chief protagonists in the drama was omitted in much of the American comment on Berlin. Occasional tributes were paid to the courage and endurance of the Berliners who were daily risking their liberty or their lives by defying the Soviets in the Eastern sectors of the city. But the effect on them and all the Germans of the decisions being arrived at over their heads in Moscow, Washington, London, or Paris, was barely mentioned. The elected representatives of the Berliners in their City Council were not even allowed to participate as advisors in the abortive currency negotiations which began in Berlin in September. We were still the conquerors and the Germans the conquered. While still vainly proffering the hand of friendship to the Russian dictator, we still refused to treat as allies even those Germans who were daily proving the reality of their democratic professions.

The German people have suffered too much not to be realists. Ready as many of them were at the beginning of the occupation to atone for the sins of the Nazis, they naturally refuse to accept the thesis that other nations should be allowed to commit crimes against humanity with impunity. They have begun to ask questions about our deals with the dictators, and *our* failures to take action against the Communists.

The Berlin weekly, *Sie*, stated on August 22:

We do not understand why the Communists are allowed to act according to the old maxim, Might is Right, which they have reformulated as, Arrogance Wins. We do not understand why Lübeck (in the British zone) continues to supply the Communist zone with electricity while tormenting darkness reigns in the Western sectors of Berlin. We do not understand why the gangster Markgraf who is wanted by the prosecutor (for war crimes) can arrest people while his employees are not arrested when they come into the Western sectors. We do not understand why what was regarded yesterday as the collective guilt of the German people, namely tolerance of SA-like gangsterism, today passes as "conciliation."

When I returned to Berlin at the end of November, more questions were being asked. Why were the British exporting planes and machinery to Soviet Russia and even repairing the Red Army's transport in the British sector of Berlin? Why were the French surreptitiously exporting machinery from Berlin to Russia? Why was the United Nations in Paris failing to condemn the Soviet blockade of Berlin—surely an obvious "crime against humanity"? Why was machinery still being dismantled and sent to Czechoslovakia and other Soviet satellite countries from the Western zones?

I had never thought of the Olympic games as of great importance, but Germans of all classes in Berlin in August 1948 asked me how we justified the exclusion of German athletes from the games being held that summer in England, although the very same people, Lord Vansittart among them, who today held *all* Germans responsible for Nazi atrocities had themselves come to Berlin in 1936 to participate as Hitler's guests in the Olympiad of that year.

To the Berliners our former readiness to "fraternize" with the Nazis was on a par with our more recent willingness to accept the Soviet Union as a "democratic" state and join hands with Stalin in depriving all people of German race of liberty, property, and the pursuit of happiness. Why should only Germans be punished and others go scot free?

In spite of all the questions and doubts about our good faith, the Berliners were still holding on. Indeed the most remarkable and significant fact, it seemed to me, was that neither our long-continued appeasement policy toward Russia, nor our treatment of the Germans as a conquered people without rights, nor our original identification of Communism with democracy, had failed to destroy all faith in Western professions and principles.

Here among the ruins and the rubble, among a great people brought down to an Asiatic level of subsistence by war and defeat and the universal abhorrence of Nazi crimes which has led us to treat all Germans as deserving of punishment; here where the children went ragged and barefoot and left cold schoolrooms to wait in dark homes for their mothers to return from work—work like that of Chinese coolies—stacking bricks, pulling heavy loads along the streets, and doing a man's heavy labor on the airfields; here, in spite of hunger and humiliation and back-breaking labor, one found, not despair, hatred of the East and West alike, and a futile lust for revenge, not nihilism or a cynical defeatism and self-seeking, but a stubborn faith in the values of Western civilization which the Nazis had denied and Western occupation policies have done little to revive.

In the city where the anti-Nazis had fought hardest, but not hard enough, to prevent Hitler's coming to power, one sensed in every word and deed, not only of the Mayor and the City Council, but of the mass of people, a determination never to let it happen again.

A student from the port of Rostock in the Russian zone, who came to see me in Berlin in September, said that the German workers there would prefer war, even if it meant death, to the misery of their life under the Communists. He also told me how depressing it was to hear every night on the radio that the Western Powers were still negotiating in Moscow, although they had said originally that they wouldn't negotiate until the Berlin blockade was lifted. "We are allowed no other papers but the Russian-licensed ones," he said, "and it is not encouraging to see the headlines about 'The great defeat of America' and to read how you are begging Stalin to talk to you and come to terms."

I talked to many other visitors and refugees from the Soviet zone, to returned prisoners of war from Russia, and to several people who had escaped, or been released, from the concentration camps at Buchenwald and Sachsenhausen in the Soviet zone, where hundreds of thousands of Germans are today even worse treated than Hitler's victims in the same camps. I met others who were ostensibly free, but to whom life in Russian-occupied Germany seemed little better than prison. One and all they echoed the saying I heard everywhere in Berlin: "Better a horrible end, than horror without end."

In America, "Give me liberty or give me death," is only an echo from the past, without urgent appeal for people who take freedom for granted. But the liberties men fought and died for a century and a half ago are felt to be worth more than life by those who live in or near the Russian zone, and have experienced a servitude far more terrible than any which formerly existed in Europe under its Kings.

The word democracy has been too debased by identification with communism for it to be heard often in Berlin. An older, cleaner word is used by the people and their leaders: freedom. At the great demonstration I witnessed on August 26, held outside the gaunt, fire-gutted Reichstag building after the Communist storm troopers and police had driven the City Council out of the Stadthaus in the Russian sector, the keynote of all the speeches was "freedom." This was the word which roused tumultuous applause among the hungry, shabby multitude.

The faces of all the people around me showed signs of privation and sorrow. Everyone, from the skinny children to the women old before their time, might have been expected to care more for promises of bread and peace. But it was not until a speaker said, "The fight is not only for Berlin but for freedom everywhere," that the tired sad faces lit up and the applause rang out.

"We are unarmed but our spirit is stronger than theirs," said Ernst Reuter, the elected Mayor of Berlin who was prevented from taking office by the Russians. And the eyes of the crowd turned toward the Russian soldiers standing guard close by at the Soviet War Memorial.

The cynic may say that the Berliners are not democrats, that they are merely fearful of the Russian terror which every one of them has experienced in one form or another. True, that tragedy has touched every German one speaks to in Berlin, whether it is the women raped by the Soviet soldiers; the mothers whose husbands or sons were massacred in the Russian sack of the city or are still held as slave laborers in Soviet mines or factories; the families whose homes were burnt over their heads by the Russians; or those who have recently had someone arrested by the Communists and sent to the dread concentration camps at Buchenwald and Sachsenhausen. Yet Reuter that day had the crowd with him when he said: "If the Russian people were free to speak, they would be fighting together with us for liberty."

Another popular speaker, the lovely and gracious Frau Annadora Leber, whose Alsatian husband was killed by the Nazis, declared at an open-air meeting I attended in Spandau: "Not every Russian is responsible for the crimes of those who rule over him. We all know that some Russians have shown us kindnesses. They are victims of the same system which oppresses us in the Eastern zone and now threatens all Berlin. Germany must become part of the Western world again. To win freedom, we must endure starvation and face death."

And she continued with these words of warning: "In the depresssion years many of you said: 'it couldn't be worse,' but you found out later that under the Nazis it eventually became far worse. Now in spite of our terrible difficulties with food—no Berlin woman knows from day to day how she will be able to feed her family— we *know* that it would be even worse than now if the Russians ruled over us. We know that we would be taken away to slave labor camps and be ruled over by the same methods the Nazis used. The new PG's[6] (Communists) are the same as the old PG's (Nazis)."

Every speech I heard and every talk I had with Germans of all kinds in Berlin, convinced me that it is not only the close and ever present fear of Russia which inspires the German resistance to communism. It is as much their experience under the Nazis, and their realization that communism means a repetition of it, which holds the Germans on our side of the Iron Curtain.

Those who have experienced life under a totalitarian dictatorship are better aware of the supreme value of liberty than others who have never known servitude. This perhaps explains why the Germans, in spite of their aptitude for a century past in submitting to authority, are less susceptible today to Communist propaganda than Americans who have accepted liberty as their birthright and cannot even imagine what it means to be without it.

The Berliners are regaining their self-respect and that of the whole German nation by their courage in resisting the Communist threat to themselves and all Europe. The former enemies of democracy have become its foremost defenders.

---

[6] Short for *Partei Genossen* ("Party Comrades")

"Berlin is not Prague" is more than a patriotic slogan. It expresses the German determination to show the West that those whom we fought yesterday are more to be relied upon in today's world-wide struggle against the totalitarians than some former allies in whom we put our trust, but whose leaders succumbed without a struggle to Communist pressure.

In a long talk I had with Ernst Reuter in his house in Berlin, he said that the feeling in the city was that by a certain kind of behavior the Germans could redeem themselves and "make it impossible for the West to treat us any longer as 'natives.'"

When I asked how it was that, after all they had experienced, not only under the Nazis, but also under Western occupation, the Germans had not all become nihilists, Reuter replied: "Today we have a chance to do something to help ourselves; to struggle in our own defense even though we are unarmed. The most effective remedy for despair is action. Our life has been given meaning again by our struggle against Communism. Berlin today is proud of itself. We have won back our self-respect, and we are confident that eventually we shall also win your respect."

The war was, however, still too recent for the United States and Britain to accept the Germans as allies. If the courage of the Berliners had convinced American military men, from generals to GI's, that the Germans could become our best allies on the Continent, sentiment at home, French fears and blindness, and the original pattern of behavior set by our occupation policies, precluded a radical change in our attitude toward the Germans. We had made a half turn since we began to understand that "you can't do business with Stalin"; we had begun to revive Western Germany and to set our faces against further dismantling; and friendly relations with the German people were now encouraged rather than discouraged. But we still failed to treat the Germans as equals. We were still obsessed by the totalitarian concept that some nations are "good" and "peace-loving" and others wicked and aggressive. We still refused to recognize the fact that people are people everywhere, and that our primary purpose should be to encourage and support the truly liberal forces to be found among all peoples.

In besieged Berlin American and British buses, reserved for Allied personnel, still drove around town almost empty, while the Germans trudged on foot or waited in long queues for the few and overcrowded streetcars and buses allowed by the Russian blockade. We "the conquerors" still occupied the best houses, reserving ample space for ourselves, while the majority of Berliners lived in squalor in cellars and bomb-wrecked apartments. We still ate to repletion, drank well, and even had fresh milk imported by air from Denmark, while Berlin babies had none, and no Germans except black-marketeers had enough to eat. The demarcation line between the occupation forces and the "natives" was still applied even to the lavatories in Military Government offices—some were labeled only for use by Americans, and others were permitted to German personnel. We had electric lights eight hours out of twenty-four, while the Germans had only two hours' use of current and only enough gas to boil a kettle of water a day. In some parts of the Western sectors of the city electric light and gas were available only at 1 A.M. and tired women who had worked all day had to rise to cook and wash in the middle of the night; but we could still dance by electric light till 11 P.M. When winter came our houses or apartments were warm night and day, but the Germans had no coal. German hospitals overflowing with patients were in darkness and lacked medicines and even bandages, but almost empty American and British hospitals had their lights burning all night.

The automobile and jeep drivers, and all other Germans, from clerks to experts, employed by the Military Government were not only receiving their wages six weeks in arrears, thanks to the control over the Berlin banks which we had originally given to the Russians in 1945. They were also receiving only a quarter of their wages in the new Western marks introduced after currency reform. The other three-quarters were paid in the Russian marks which were worth only a fourth of the Western marks we had halfheartedly brought into Berlin. Appeasement, or what was more politely called the desire "not to provoke" the Russians, had led us to penalize all the Berliners, including those working for us, by using the Russian marks as legal tender.

The June currency reform will be discussed in a later chapter. It is, however, necessary to comment here on the curious policy of the Finance Office of the Military Government. Having first given the Russians an excuse for their siege of the city by introducing the new Western mark, it then refused to bring in a sufficient quantity to permit the city administration and the Military Government to pay wages and salaries in *Deutsche* (D) marks. While flying food into Berlin at tremendous cost, we accepted Russian marks in payment for it, thus effectively supporting the value of the Russian sponsored currency.

The Communists had the whip hand over the city administration, since the banks are in the Russian sector, and the Communists could withhold the funds necessary to pay wages. They were also in a position to block the accounts of every factory owner and business enterprise in the city.

On the other hand, if more D marks had been flown in, more of them would have fallen into the hands of the Russians to use for the purchase of the goods they needed from the Western zones. For, whereas we accepted the Russian mark in payment for the supplies we flew into the city, the free, or black, market was controlled by the Russians, and D marks were demanded for most unrationed supplies, such as the meager quantities of fresh fruit and vegetables and coal which entered the Russian sector of the city. D marks were also required for the purchase of the clothing and household goods which had appeared in the shops following currency reform. The trouble was, of course, that there was little of anything to be bought in the Russian zone, which the Soviets were stripping for their own use. Such few goods, or raw materials to make them, as could be brought into Berlin through the blockade had to be paid for with D marks. Naturally the Russians would not sell anything they controlled for their own paper marks.

In these circumstances it would have been more sensible to give the food ration free to all workers in the Western sectors than to take Russian marks in payment for it.

The day I left Berlin on the air lift I was provided with a small, but symbolic, example of how our attitude toward the Germans hampers us in the Cold War for Berlin.

While I stood watching the German workers unloading the plane on which I was to fly to Frankfurt, the United States Air Force pilot waiting beside me said: "We'll be delayed at least half an hour longer beyond our scheduled time, because our cargo, as you see, is airstrips, and the Germans can't handle the stuff fast, not only because it's so heavy, but because they haven't got gloves."

The United States was spending millions of dollars each week to supply Berlin. "Operation Vittles" is a miracle of American organization, as I realized to the full while I listened in on the radio operator's headphones to the instructions being given every few seconds to each of the Big or Little "Willies," which take off and land at two to three-minute intervals. A second's mistake or miscalculation of time, altitude, or position could be disastrous. Yet operations can be slowed down, and tired American pilots compelled to work a fifteen, instead of a normal twelve-hour shift, because a hundred or so dollars have not been spent to provide the Germans who load and unload the planes with gloves!

Obviously this omission was not due to the practice of petty economies, although in effect cents were being saved and dollars wasted. It was the hardening of our sensibilities through the accustomed sight of hungry, cold, and ragged people, through three years of occupation of a conquered country, which had, no doubt, induced this costly disregard for the human needs of the Germans working with us in Berlin. Not that the GI's and pilots and American mechanics I talked to on the airfield and during this and subsequent flights had a "master race" attitude toward the Germans. On the contrary, they called my attention to the barefooted women strewing sand on the runway and exclaimed: "Did you ever see anything like it! Aren't those German women wonderful?" And my pilot said: "I used to think that it was only in China you could see women working like that; I never imagined white people could do it. I admire their guts."

I admired them too, but I also wondered how it must feel to go home at night to cook and wash and care for children after doing a man laborer's heavy work all day. I also wondered how these ragged women would be able to work in the cold of winter.

The women are the silent chorus, the unsung and weary heroines of the struggle dramatized by the spectacular air lift. The women outnumber the men by more than two to one in Berlin, and it is upon them that the chief burden of the struggle rests. Many of them have lost their husbands, or wait in vain for them to return from Russian prisons. They are the sole support of their children and often also of a grandmother or some relative crippled or blinded in the air raids. Day after day they must not only earn their living but also tend to and comfort their cold and hungry children, while never getting enough to eat themselves.

The ration in Berlin is now 1,800 calories; before the blockade when the Allies could have provided enough food, it was even lower. One wondered in Berlin how human flesh and spirit could stand the long ordeal of the women whose life is one continuous round of drudgery and want without any pleasures ever, or any future hope of a happy married life. Yet the Berlin women knew that there was one thing left they had not yet lost: and they would endure to the end to preserve it for their children: freedom. A greater proportion of women than men had voted in the October 1946 elections which defeated the Communists in Berlin; and in December 1948, 86 per cent of the population was to register its vote for the democratic parties. In the happy West such a large proportion of voters has never gone to the polls, although we have streetcars and subways and automobiles and plenty of leisure.

I visited the "homes" of several German workers and their families, and marveled that the women, somehow or other, managed to keep a cellar, or one or two patched-up rooms in a bombed tenement house, clean and neat in spite of overcrowding and the lack of hot water and sufficient soap. Their children, who in most other countries would be dirty and unkempt in such circumstances, are still kept looking respectable by their mothers' continual darning and patching of clothes.

Instead of the extraordinary industry of German women evoking sympathy and respect, it too often only results in Americans' thinking that the Germans are quite well off. Mrs. Roosevelt, for instance, after spending a day or so in Berlin reported that she saw no destitute and hungry children, and that the Germans did not seem to be as poor as the French and other former victims of Nazi aggression. She cannot have had time to see more of Berlin than Dahlem and Zehlendorf where the United States occupation forces live—suburbs inhabited by the former well-to-do which we never bombed with the same intensity as the working-class districts of Berlin. But even if she had taken the time to visit the poorer parts of the city, Mrs. Roosevelt might not have revised her opinion. To win the pity of some people it is necessary to imitate those beggars, who although they may be "earning" a good living by appealing to the charitable for alms, appear in rags and dirt to evoke sympathy.

I wished that all the complacent visitors and residents from the victor countries could see what I had seen, and that they had the imagination to put themselves in the situation of the majority of Berlin's women and children.

There were some Military Government officials who felt as I did. Elizabeth Holt, for instance, wife of a State Department official and herself assistant to the head of the Educational and Religious Affairs branch of the Military Government, was in constant contact with German women and was wearing herself out, not only because of the help and encouragement she gave them, but also because she could not rest or enjoy life thinking of the suffering all around her. Thanks to Mrs. Holt, I made my first contacts with German women active in the social work conducted by all three parties: Socialists (SPD), Christian Democrats (CDU), and Liberals (LDP).

Ursula Kirchert, a Socialist, took me to spend a morning at a medical clinic, where I watched a procession of the sick, the crippled, the undernourished, and the old receiving what help could be given them by the doctor, in the absence of many medicines and the even greater need of nourishing food. One patient had a huge abscess on his neck, which after being lanced had to be bound up with paper, since the Germans had no cotton bandages, no absorbent cotton or lint. The doctor told me that his great difficulty was that medical supplies could be bought only with D marks, since the Russian zone could not supply them. Consequently socialsecurity funds, which are under Russian control, are useless in obtaining them, and his patients whose wages or pensions consisted mainly of Russian marks could not buy them.

The saddest and hardest-working people in Berlin are the women with children whose husbands fell in the war, or are still prisoners. The expellees from Silesia thrown out of their homes and driven westwards with nothing but what they could carry on their backs are in an even more destitute condition.

I visited one woman from Silesia, Frau Scheibner, whose husband was, she hoped, a prisoner of war in Russia and not already dead. She had three young children and they had all walked to Berlin, the mother carrying the youngest child. Her mother and father were Berliners and until a week before my first visit they had all lived with her parents in two tiny rooms. Now she was "happy" because by great "good fortune" she had obtained possession of a not-too-damp cellar in the same building. She had of course no linen and her furniture consisted of two mattresses and a packing case used as a table. Her eldest child, a girl of twelve, looked after the two youngest while the mother worked as a "trimmer"—the German word used in Berlin to describe the thousands of women who collect, stack, and cart the bricks from bombed-out houses.

The youngest child, a pretty girl of five, was playing on the stone cellar floor with a little friend from next door, while her brother, a boy of eight, did his school homework, sitting on one of the mattresses. When I gave her a can of dried milk, Frau Scheibner told me what upset her most was the little girl begging for more milk every day. Of course these children, like the rest of those in Berlin, never received any fresh milk, but there was a small ration of dried milk. Their mother felt that if she could only get enough food for her children, she would be content in their new "home."

Upstairs in the same house, I found a couple who considered themselves among the luckiest people in the world because the husband, missing for five years, had returned from Russia a few days before. Frau Woltherz had had no news of her husband since 1943 and had given him up for dead. Her joy was indescribable when he suddenly appeared, having been freed because he was too ill to work any more. I wondered how he would ever be able to get well on the inadequate ration on which the Berliners somehow exist, but his wife was so happy to have him back that she thought nothing of their hardship. Woltherz said to me: "If the

Russians had behaved differently, they would have won us. It is too late now. After the treatment we have received we will never go along with them. I shall probably be an invalid for the rest of my life, but if I could fight again I would join up with America against the Soviets."

Another day I visited a widow with two children whose husband had been killed on the Russian front. She had just been joined by two younger sisters who had spent three years as Russian slave laborers in the Urals. One had been a seamstress and the other a worker on a farm, and both looked to be typical "proletarians." But in March 1945, they had been arrested, put in a cellar and beaten until they "confessed" to having been members of Hitler's *Jung Mädel*. Apparently the Red Army soldiers who had arrested them had been ordered to round up a certain number of Nazis, and the simplest way to do this was to take anybody they could lay their hands on and torture them until they would say they had been Nazis.

After signing a paper written in Russian which they could not understand, the two girls, whose name was Graubusch, had been placed in cattle trucks and transported to the Urals. There had been forty-three people in the car and several had died of suffocation and thirst. They had been given only one cup of water each two days. On arrival at the prison camp they had been set to work making bricks. They had been forced to take the hot bricks out of the ovens with bare hands, and to push loads of them in wheelbarrows for fourteen hours a day.

Many of the German women in the camp had died—in one year, more than half of the original number. Typhus had carried off many in spite of a German doctor prisoner who had tried to help them. The manager of the camp had been a *Volksdeutsche* and very brutal. Presumably he had saved his own life, which would have otherwise been forfeit on account of his race, by taking the position.

The prisoners had to sleep on wooden benches without blankets. They were fed on cabbage soup and a small bread ration, but had been told to say how good it was in Russia and that only Germans behaved like devils. They were never allowed any contact with the Russian population, being led out to work under armed guards and returned to their prison after their day's labor. A few of the guards had been kind but most of them were brutes. One "bitch of a woman" had forced the prisoners returning from work to stand at the prison gates for an hour or more in the cold with their clothing damp from perspiration and their dresses "burning on their bodies."

Atrocities are now "old stuff." No one cares what innocent Germans suffer, although still ready to make them pay for Nazi atrocities. But I think that if Americans at home could see and hear what the Germans have gone, and are going, through we might begin to help the people of Berlin and the released or escaped victims of Communist cruelty and oppression. It was with a sense of impotent pity that I learned that only one of these two German sisters was permitted to remain in the United States sector of Berlin. The other was forced to live in the Russian sector, where she might at any moment be arrested again, because she had not formerly lived in Berlin, and the regulation is that only those may register and receive ration cards who were residents before 1945. The elder sister was in bad enough circumstances herself, but she would somehow or other have found room for both sisters, if only the United States authorities had permitted her to shelter them.

It was not only the poor and the victims of Communism who aroused one's pity in Berlin. The most overworked widows and wives of prisoners of war, if they had children, were perhaps less unhappy than such lonely girls as Elsa, the housekeeper of my billet in the Press Camp. She looked after an empty house reserved for visiting American women journalists, who were so few and far between that it was usually empty. No longer a girl, but still not old and quite good looking, she spent day after day alone. Her fiancé had been killed in the war and her only surviving relative was her mother who was not allowed to live with her in the house reserved for the conquerors and their servants. As one of the latter she had more to eat than most Berliners, but the hunger of the heart is perhaps worse than physical starvation. She was not the type for light love affairs and had no "boy friend" among the Americans; nor was it likely she would ever have the opportunity of social intercourse to meet a German who might marry her. The future offered her nothing but loneliness.

In contrast to the timid and gentle Elsa for whom there was no place in the harsh world of today, Annalena von Caprivi, editor of the

Women's Page of the British licensed *Telegraph*, had the spirit, intelligence, and adaptability to overcome the handicap of an aristocratic origin and an unhappy marriage. Her maiden name was Lindquist, and her family, originally of Swedish origin, had owned the island of Ruetgen in the Baltic for centuries past. Her grandfather had been one of Bismarck's ministers, and her father, Ambassador to South Africa before World War I. Annalena was therefore of real Junker origin, but many Prussian aristocrats, like her parents, had never been pro-Nazi, or taken office under Hitler. Her parents, who had for long been living retired lives on their island, had committed suicide when the Russians came. Annalena had found them dead when, after the war's end, she had made her way on foot from Western Germany to the Russian zone, carrying a bundle on her back and dressed like a peasant.

The Russians had, of course, confiscated the family property and Annalena now worked for the support of her two little girls as well as herself. She had divorced her husband, heir also to an ancient name and as incapable of adapting himself to conditions in defeated Germany as his wife was capable.

I came to know Annalena von Caprivi well and to have a great liking and respect for her character and keen and objective mind. She was not in the least sorry for herself and somehow managed always to look well groomed, and even elegant, although her clothes were made out of such relics as her grandfather's military uniform.

There are one hundred women to every 60 men in Germany and the tragedy of many of them is that they have no hope of marriage. But Annalena, who is both attractive and intelligent, wrote an article for her newspaper in which she said that many German women could not now "afford" a husband. German men, she said, still expected to be waited upon hand and foot by their wives, as if they were the breadwinners, even if their wives were earning the family's living. It was too much to expect, and unless German men would abandon their lordly ways they could not expect any capable women to marry them.

A young unmarried woman who had been a war correspondent, but had taken up a rifle and fought herself in the last desperate days of Berlin's defense against the Red Army, gave me another angle on the relation between the sexes in Germany. She said that German men not only cannot forget that they were once "brilliant and victorious" and are therefore incapable of adapting themselves to the lowly work and status which is all life now offers them. She also thought that they were too bitterly ashamed of their failure to defend their country and save its women from rape and rough treatment at Russian hands to be psychologically capable of loving.

They hate the girls who go around with Americans but are themselves unable to offer companionship or any possibility for happiness in marriage.

Of course not all German men have developed complexes which keep them in bitter isolation and drive German women either to have affairs with the "conquerors" or to live alone. But even in undefeated and prosperous countries men who have spent years soldiering find it difficult to settle down to civilian life. In Germany where many men have spent ten years of their life in the army, and the younger ones have known no other life since they left school; where most jobs offer a bare livelihood and where there are so many sick as well as crippled veterans, the problem is even more acute.

In these days of adversity it is the endurance of German women and their determination to keep their families alive that constitutes the strength of Germany even in defeat.

Having lived six years in Soviet Russia, I too had been a wife struggling for food and shelter for my family in a world not very different from theirs. Consequently, I felt a sense of identification with the people of Berlin. Today I was one of the privileged enjoying the same comforts, conveniences and luxuries as the rest of the American and British correspondents and occupying forces, but I did not feel that I belonged with them. The memory of my life in Moscow, when I lived as ordinary Russians do, was still too vivid.

Most Americans and even the British have no real conception of what hunger means, nor any repugnance to eating well and driving in automobiles or jeeps, while the "natives" starve and walk. It was not that I was better than the rest, or even that I had more imagination. It was simply my past experience and the close presence of the Soviet Power which so vividly recalled it to me.

When I saw German women carrying heavy loads in the streets, I remembered how I had once thought nothing of carrying home 44 pounds of potatoes, happy only to have obtained so much food. When I saw the thin, sad-eyed Berlin children, I remembered my own son, born in Moscow, who had never suffered actual hunger but would have become like these German children if I had not escaped with him from Russia after my husband's arrest. When I visited German homes consisting of one dilapidated room, I recalled similar crowded and damp places where I and my Russian friends and acquaintances had lived.

When I bought my cigarettes, chocolate, and soap ration at the PX store, I remembered how much in those distant days in Moscow a gift of coffee, soap, or toilet paper from some friend in England, had meant to me.

In Germany I felt ashamed to be like one of those foreign visitors to Moscow who had gorged themselves in the Intourist Hotels while the Russians starved. When I invited Germans to eat with me at the Press Club, I remembered what it had once meant to me to be invited to a good meal in a Moscow hotel by some visiting foreigner.

As I watched the German waiters at "our" clubs and hotels, I remembered those in the Moscow Intourist ones, who like these Germans served good food to others without ever partaking of it themselves. Tips had been forbidden in Communist Russia, where Russians still gave them but foreigners rarely did, because they had been told it was beneath the dignity of a waiter to accept them in the "Socialist fatherland." In Germany, one was not allowed to give tips either (since our occupation money could not legally be used by Germans) except in the form of a cigarette or two left on the table.

Worst of all, the attitude of the Military Government officials toward the Germans reminded me all too forcibly of the aloof disdain with which the Communist bureaucracy had treated the Russian "common man". Not, of course, that Americans had yet learned to behave with the same arrogance as Soviet Russia's ruling class. There was still a good bit left of the natural American tendency to be friendly and generous to everyone. But these Americans had been taught to treat the Germans as inferiors and many of them thought that to show sympathy or kindness, would be what the British call "bad form."

I could not feel superior to the Germans for I too had once been guilty. If the Germans deserved to suffer indefinitely for having followed the false and evil lead of the Nazis, so I also, and many other Britishers and Americans, should also be punished for once having been Communists or Communist fellow travelers and dupes. "There, but for the Grace of God, go I," was the thought which came to me continually in Berlin and the other bombed cities of Germany, where a people condemned by all the world, defenseless, hungry and without rights or liberties, continues to live only because of its indestructible vitality or the consolations offered by religion.

I knew that the impulses and illusions which led me to become a Communist in my youth were not fundamentally so different to those which led many young Germans to follow Hitler. Being English, having been brought up a socialist, and living in a rich country and in the capital of an Empire upon which, in those days, the sun never set, I had been concerned with the emancipation of the human race, not that of my own country. I had embraced communism because it promised equality of all men, irrespective of nation, race, or creed. The Communist ideal had seemed to me the fulfillment of the age-long struggle of mankind for freedom and justice.

The Nazis had not appealed to the same generous impulses and international ideals as the Communists had done. But to many a young German, Nazism must originally have seemed the only way to obtain freedom and equality for the German people, "shackled", as they saw it, by the Versailles Treaty. When Hitler promised them bread and work, an end to unemployment, and a proud and strong Germany in place of the weak and defenseless Weimar Republic, most of them could not have known that he would lead them to commit horrible atrocities and wage aggressive war; no more than I had known that communism meant the liquidation of millions of Russian peasants, starvation for the workers, and slave labor on a scale never seen before. In Russia I had seen how young men and women were induced by an appeal to "idealism" to carry out the operation of liquidating the so-called kulaks—a crime as great and horrible as the Nazi liquidation of the Jews. For to me it seems equally terrible to kill people or send them to concentration camps for their "class" as for their "race."

It is incomprehensible to me that the very same Americans who had glorified Stalin's bloody dictatorship during and after the war are now most insistent in demanding endless punishment for all Germans. If all the Germans are to be considered guilty of Hitler's crimes, and anyone who was ever a Nazi to be damned forever, then Communists in all countries, and also those who were their dupes and supported them, must be held accountable for the atrocities committed by Stalin.

I had escaped from Russia, and as a foreigner I had been able to get out of the Communist Party without being liquidated years before I left the Soviet Union. But I knew that if I had stayed, I might have been forced by the Soviet dictatorship to do horrible things myself, if the life of my husband or son were the penalty for disobedience. Having lived under the Communist dictatorship, and knowing what terror means, I cannot blame the Germans for not having "revolted against Hitler," as others do who are safe in America and have all their lives enjoyed inherited liberties.

Another reason, besides my Russian experiences, for my inability to regard the Germans as more wicked than other peoples, is no doubt the fact that I was born an Englishwoman. I recognize the fact that the Germans made the profound mistake of endeavoring to follow in the footsteps of Britain, France, Holland, and Belgium, in an age when empire building is no longer respectable except for Communists. But I cannot quite see why the Germans, who have no Asiatic and African colonies to exploit, should be considered as innately more aggressive than the Western European nations who derive revenues from their colonial empires.

My old anti-imperialist sentiments, and intense dislike for the sight of any one lot of people denying to another the rights and liberties it claims for itself, had made me both anti-Communist and anti-Nazi. But I could not, on account of my own past mistakes and lost illusions, consider the whole German people as guilty of Nazi crimes, any more than I considered myself responsible for the past evil doings of British imperialists, or past and present atrocities committed by Stalin and his followers. My punishment for my past foolishness, if nothing worse, had been the loss of my husband in Russia. But I had saved my son and escaped with him to the free Western world. The Germans, innocent and guilty alike, had suffered obliteration bombing attacks, starvation, the torture of husbands, sons and brothers in Russian prisons, and the opprobrium of the world. I could not but feel that their punishment was out of proportion to mine.

It was with a sense of shame that I heard the German driver of the automobile assigned to me in Berlin say: "I have worked for three years for the Americans and you are the first who has spoken to me as a human being."

I had asked him how much he earned, how many hours he worked, whether he had a wife and family, whether they got enough to eat, and how he got home at night after leaving me at my hotel. It was not, I think, the fact that I displayed some interest in his personal situation, or my gifts of chocolate, soap, and cigarettes, or my sharing with him the ample breakfast I received, which eventually broke down the barrier he had erected between us by his correct behavior as a servant, or as one of the conquered toward the new master race. It was after I remarked to him one day that we were treating the Germans like colonial subjects that he became communicative and friendly. My observation had been occasioned by my first sight of the half-naked, barefoot young German boys who pick up the balls on the Press Club tennis courts. It had seemed to me they should be playing games themselves instead of running around like little slaves.

It was from this chauffeur of mine that I got a view, from the other end of the telescope, so to speak, of how our original "treat the Germans rough" occupation policy affected the mass of the German people. "I suppose," he said, "that the rudeness and lack of consideration of the Americans is due to the great size of their country. Probably many Americans never go to school and learn good manners, and that is why they are so rough and tactless."

I told him that he was mistaken and tried to explain that Americans were not really either uneducated or heartless; that it was the hatred of Nazi brutality and the consequent belief that all Germans deserved punishment and rough treatment which had originally inspired our occupation policy. But he remained unconvinced. How, he asked me, could I explain the American attitude of friendliness and consideration toward the Russians if it was Nazi Germany's atrocities which had inspired the American lack of humanity toward the conquered Germans?

The word which he used, and which I have translated as "lack of humanity," was *Unmenschlichkeit*. *Menschlichkeit*, its opposite, was the word I heard most often on the lips of Germans. It is a word difficult to translate because it means so much: behavior worthy of a human being, decency, kindness, consideration for others, respect for the individual irrespective of nationality, class, religion, or power—everything which should distinguish a free *man* from a brute, a slave, or a robot.

It is the realization that the Rights of Man, in the good oldfashioned eighteenth-century sense which inspired the French and American revolutions, are primary, and that no economic and social system which denies them is bearable; it was this realization that had united the Socialist, Liberal, and Christian-Democratic parties of Berlin in face of the Communist threat to their liberty.

Here, in the front line of the conflict between Western democracy and Soviet totalitarian tyranny, there was a reborn faith in the ideals of the Renaissance, the Reformation and the Counter Reformation.

There was a unity to be found nowhere else in Europe, between agnostics and Christians, Protestants and Catholics, socialists, liberals, and conservatives, because they one and all realized that the struggle for the world is primarily one between the individual and the machine, or state, which seeks to reduce everyone to slavery; between the totalitarians who would drag us all down to the level of beasts by denying individual responsibility, conscience, and *Menschlichkeit*, and those who insist that "security" is only to be won by submission to tyranny.

Perhaps, I thought, it is the new content of socialism, as demonstrated in Berlin, where the Social Democrats are the largest party and the leaders in the anti-Communist resistance, which holds out most hope for Western civilization.

"The change in the inner content of German socialism is the most important development in Europe today," was the comment made to me by Frau Doctor Ulrich-Biel, a woman leader of Berlin's Liberal Party. A white-haired elderly lady whose former husband is a professor of philosophy at Harvard, and whose son had been miraculously restored to her through his daring escape from a Russian prison camp, she is today mainly occupied in trying to secure relief for the homeless, ragged, and starved German refugees from the East, many of whom are in the Russian zone of occupation.

In her little room in an apartment house in what was once a sector of Berlin with a large Jewish population, she said to me:

I could not in the past join the Socialists because of my fear of regimentation and because of the Socialist opposition to religion. Not that I was a churchgoer, but because I always had respect for the secret of the world and could not reduce everything to materialistic terms. Now after all I have seen and experienced, all the sorrow and fear and misery of our life in Berlin these past fifteen years, I look to having the church on my side. The life of man is too short and he is too frail for him to dispense with a home for the great truths of Christianity. Men are too weak to preserve the truth alone; they must have a tradition to preserve it: a church. Many German Socialists realize this today. They are more concerned with preserving the values men live by than with economic theories. All those who do not believe that liberty and human rights are the primary concern have gone over to the SED [Socialist Unity party].

Otto Stolz, a young man who had been expelled from the University of Berlin for his anti-Communist activities and had already made a name for himself as a writer, told me that he and many other German Socialists no longer believed that "nationalization of the means of production and distribution" would solve the problems of human society.

"We know now," he said, "that the end of capitalism may, as in Russia, lead only to tyranny."

Writing on the anniversary of the Revolution of 1848 which had failed, in Germany, to establish the liberal principles and democratic rights won in Western Europe, Otto Stolz, although he belongs to the Socialist party, reminded his countrymen that the struggle then and now is not for "an economic theory of production and distribution" but for the rights of man: equality before the law, individual responsibility and freedom, security of personal rights, government by consent, freedom of speech and opinion, freedom from arbitrary arrest and imprisonment without trial by due process of law.

From these premises he developed the thesis that in the twentieth century, in countries where representative government and free speech have already been secured, no violent revolution is required to establish greater social justice and a better economic system. Revolutions today, far from being progressive, lead to the establishment of authoritarian governments under "popular" dictators. Thus revolutions in democratically governed countries are in fact counterrevolutions led by reactionaries calling themselves progressives, but wanting to lead the world back to the predemocratic era when liberty of the individual and human rights were denied by autocratic monarchies, as they are today denied by Nazis and Communists.

"The real revolution of our time," said Otto Stolz, "is a spiritual one, not economic or social. And here in Europe it must be directed toward the establishment of a European family of nations, with equal rights for all in a democratic federation."

The unity displayed by the Socialist, Christian-Democratic, and Liberal-Democratic parties in resisting the Communist onslaught was made possible by the recognition by members of all three parties that no one has a monopoly of truth, and that tolerance, integrity and *Menschlichkeit* are the primary needs of a free society.

Lothar Wille, *Bürgermeister* of the Berlin borough of Steglitz, who is a Catholic and a Christian Democrat, said to me:

"Our party, the Christian-Democratic Union, should have leaders who are not specifically Catholic or Protestant but *Christian*. To defend the Christian culture and values of Europe the primary need is good men. The best religion is a good moral life and a man who never goes to church, even an agnostic, may be in fact a good Christian. The important thing is to recognize one's duty to society and perform it." "The Catholic church," he added with a smile, "has also got to change with the times and become more catholic."

Most people in Berlin have nothing to lose but their freedom. Perhaps it is this and the terrible trials and privations they have endured that gives them their clear view of essentials and their inner strength. They have become so inured to material hardships and have experienced such great sorrows that those who have not been broken have acquired a rare spiritual fortitude.

Nora Melle, a City Council representative of the Liberal-Democratic party who had been thrown into the street with her little girl when the Russians came, had seen her husband carried off by them, her sister raped, her father killed, and her mother die of shock, said to me: "We are no longer influenced by fear of losing our possessions, since we have none, and because we have lost so much more than material comforts. Germans in the Western zones may think that there could be nothing worse than the Anglo-American occupation, and the loss of their savings through the recent currency reform. But in Berlin we know that all that is nothing compared to the ultimate horror of the Communist domination."

Jeanette Wolff told me: "The Berliners, unlike other people, do not wear blinkers. They know what they are up against and are facing it. It is vital to the survival of Western civilization that this political center of resistance to totalitarian tyranny be preserved."

Jeanette Wolff herself is one of the finest persons I ever met. An old Socialist of Weimar Republic days, she spent six long and terrible years in Hitler's concentration camps and lost her whole family except for one daughter who was crippled by the Nazis. But, instead of hating the German people, like so many others who have never even seen them;

Jeanette has become one of the bestloved leaders of the Berlin population. An eloquent and moving speaker, elected member of the City Council in 1946, she is called the Trumpet of the Socialist party. A woman with a warm heart which has somehow failed to be corroded by the sufferings she has undergone, she is full of compassion for all the oppressed and miserable people of the world and also too good a socialist of the old international kind to consider any one nation or race as worse or better than another. Her understanding and human feeling are so great that she has been known to argue on denazification boards for the release of men who had belonged to the party which tortured her and killed her family, saying she knew that many young men had followed Hitler out of ignorance and should be forgiven if they would "go and sin no more."

I first met Jeanette Wolff, thanks to Hanna Bornovsky, a German girl engaged to George Silver, who worked in the manpower division of Military Government. George Silver was a former AFL trade unionist from Philadelphia. Although a young man, he had the same, prewar vintage, international socialist outlook as Jeanette. Hanna's Jewish mother had been killed in one of our air raids and her Aryan father was also dead. After having been treated as a second-class citizen by the Nazis because she was half-Jewish, Hanna had not been allowed to marry George because we considered her a German. But now that he was about to leave Germany after three years service there, they were getting married.

Many American visitors who might otherwise never have met any Germans socially got to know the leading democratic leaders of Berlin at the Silvers' house. Hanna had also managed to raise funds to reconstruct a part of Ribbentrop's bombed-out Berlin residence, which she had renamed Leuschner House and established as a meeting place for the Germans who were taking the lead in Berlin's anti-Communist struggle.

I owe a lot to the Silvers who put me in touch with many Germans, both prominent and unknown, and gave me the opportunity to meet men and women of all parties at their home.

Hanna and George were practicing socialists. She cooked a meal every other day, out of her husband's American rations and the vegetables she grew in the gardens of Leuschner House, for the students who came to her house, and who, like most German students today, are the poorest of the poor and always hungry. These Berlin students were extraordinarily mature in their thinking. I was impressed most of all by the fact that war, defeat, hunger, and the ever-present fear of ending up in a Soviet concentration camp had not broken their spirit or sapped their energies.

It seemed to me surprising that our original occupation policy had not succeeded in turning German youths into cynics, timeservers, or ruthless egotists. For in the first two years of our occupation we had made a mockery of our democratic professions and ideals, not only by treating all of the Germans, including the victims of Hitler's prisons, as pariahs, but also by condoning Soviet atrocities and treating Communists as democrats. We had even insisted upon the inclusion of Communists in the City and Länder administrations and put Communists on denazification boards.

In Berlin, for instance, although the October 1946 elections had given the Socialists, Liberals, and Christian Democrats 80 per cent of the votes, the allied *Kommandatura* had refused to allow majority rule, insisting instead on the inclusion of Communists in a "coalition," although their party (Socialist Unity party—SED) had polled only 19 per cent of the city's vote. And even today, I was told, the British and American Occupation authorities do not permit the Germans to oust the Communists who still hold some positions in the Food, Labor and Health offices of the Western sectors of Berlin unless they are proved to be incompetent, or sending "open" reports to the Russians!

"Yet you still place your trust in us?" I enquired.

"Yes," replied a pretty girl with red hair and an impudent smile, "we know we must have patience and wait until Americans stop being political babies."

"All the same," said a young man studying Slavonic languages, "it's funny to hear you Americans now saying the same things about the Soviet Union which you used to forbid us to say and regarded as a proof of our being pro-Nazi."

I am aware, of course, that not only is Berlin not Prague; it is also not all of Germany. The important fact, it seemed to me in Berlin, is that there is a movement there which could lead Germany to become a real democracy, and which might also reinvigorate and unite by its example the divided and confused antitotalitarian forces of Europe and America.

There was a sinister reverse side of the hopeful Berlin picture. Some of the die-hard Nazis have made common cause with the Communists, and there was the threat of a recrudescence of aggressive German nationalism under a Red instead of a Black flag.

Former National Socialist theoreticians today hold leading positions in the University of Berlin and other universities under Russian control. The head of the disciplinary Court of the University of Berlin, Fritz Moglich, who now gives lectures on the social and political situation, which all Berlin students must attend, was formerly a leading Nazi anti-Semite and anti-Catholic writer. In a famous book on Ludendorff he had once urged a union of German and Russian National Bolshevism against the West.

Many other examples could be cited. Perhaps even more important is the fact that the Russians are using the full force of economic pressure to suppress the democratic opposition. Only "reliable" students can get grants to study, and special privileges in money and kind are given to those who support the Communist dictatorship. All Germans who can and will be useful to Russia are offered "Stalin parcels" of food and fuel. Those who join the Socialist Unity party for the material advantages this gives them can perhaps not be counted upon by the Russians. Their most reliable allies, and the most dangerous to us, are the former Nazis who hope that by submitting to the Soviets now, and working with them against the West, Hitler's "Thousand-Year Reich" will eventually be restored.

The political weakness of the Communists, evident in Berlin, proves that there are as yet too few Nazi or other collaborators of the Communists to bolster up their dictatorship.

Nevertheless, it is a mistake to assume that the Germans must inevitably remain on our side, even if we continue to refuse them the rights of free men.

3

THE MATERIAL COST OF VENGEANCE

L EAVING BERLIN ON THE AIRLIFT EARLY IN SEPTEMBER AND ARRIVING in the United States zone, I felt I had traveled farther in time than in space. In Berlin, in spite of the gross inequalities between the Germans and ourselves in sacrifice, privation, and danger, we were standing shoulder to shoulder in resisting Soviet aggression. But in Bizonia we still seemed to be fighting the last war. Here we were acting as if Germany, not Soviet Russia, now menaces the peace of the world and the freedom of Europe. We were still dismantling German industry, and in general carrying out the Yalta and Potsdam agreements as if Soviet Russia had never broken them, and with an almost total disregard of the Marshall Plan and the Truman Doctrine which Americans at home imagined were now the basis of United States policy.

Large shipments of "reparations and restitutions" were still going to Russia, Czechoslovakia, Poland, Yugoslavia, and other countries behind the Iron Curtain, not only from the British and French zones but also from the American.

Following the start, in June, of Soviet Russia's blockade of Berlin, such shipments from Bizonia and the French zone to the countries behind the Iron Curtain, instead of being stopped, had been doubled in quantity. The bulk of the shipments to the Soviet Union in July 1948 and subsequent months went from the British zone, and deliveries from the United States zone direct to Russia had been stopped. But the United States had continued to give aid and comfort to the Communists by supplying the Czechs, Poles, and Yugoslavs with 5,790 tons of German machinery and other assets in that one month. At the end of October, when bad weather was endangering the lives of American pilots on the air lift and the Berlin population was already shivering in its unheated homes, the total reparations and restitutions shipments to the countries behind the Iron Curtain from Bizonia and the French zone combined, had been stepped up to nearly nine thousand tons, from the six and a half thousand sent before Stalin started the blockade of Berlin.

Factories were being dismantled in Western Germany to the detriment of the whole European economy, and with a cynical disregard of the needs of the German people and the danger of losing Western Germany to the Communists while attempting to save Berlin from them.

The cost to the United States taxpayer of subsidizing a pauperized Germany, and a Europe deprived of the products of German industry, was apparently also being disregarded not only by our Western allies, but by the American authorities responsible for our German policy.

In spite of the fact that it had been announced that Germany was to participate in the rebuilding of Europe under the Marshall Plan, the United States and Britain were implementing the 1947 "Revised Level of Industry Plan," which severely limits Germany's capacity to produce in most major industries and was drawn up with no provision for German exports of steel, machinery, and other goods most urgently required for European reconstruction.

From the British point of view dismantlement makes sense, since it helps to reduce Germany's competitive power on the world market. Originally the British authorities had held out for a higher level of industry than the United States was willing to allow. They understood that Western Germany could not be self-sustaining if the reparations program were carried through; and so long as they were themselves financially responsible for feeding the industrial population of their zone, they pursued a more enlightened policy than the United States. But since the merging of the British and American zones and the United States' commitment to meet the deficits of Bizonia, Britain's competitive motive has had free rein, and the British now oppose revision of the dismantlement program. In their frantic efforts to free themselves from dependence on dollar subsidies, they have abandoned the policy of wisdom and restraint toward defeated enemies which formerly made Britain great and strong.

Today the British are sacrificing their long-term interests by themselves exporting airplanes and capital goods to Soviet Russia, and by alienating the Germans and weakening Continental Europe by shipments of large quantities of dismantled German machines to Stalin's empire. According to figures given in a British Military Government communique, published in *"Die Tat,"* on February 6, 1949, out of a total of 598,000 tons of machinery and other materials taken from German factories, 163,896 tons had been delivered to Russia, 18,618 tons to Czechoslovakia, 1,789 to Albania, and 45,135 to Yugoslavia. The British have had no scruples even in delivering armament factories to Russia. On December 20, 1948, the London *Times* reported that the Borbeck-Krupps Armaments Works was in process of being shipped to the Soviet Union.

In the French zone one could hardly have imagined that there is such a thing as a Communist danger, a Marshall Plan or any such question as the defense of Western Europe. The blindness of the French, their obsession with a past danger, and seeming unawareness of the lively present danger of Soviet aggression, their squeezing of their German zone to subsidize their own mismanaged economy, and their futile parade of the trappings of a nonexistent military might before the cowed but secretly mocking German population, require a separate chapter. Here I shall be concerned only with Bizonia, as the partially merged British and American zones are called.

Whereas both the British and French treatment of the Germans is easy to understand, if not to condone, American policy is incomprehensible. America has nothing to gain, and everything to lose economically, politically, and militarily by dismantlement. Yet the United States has exerted no strong pressure to bring it to an end in the British and French zones, and has continued to carry it out even in the American zone.

The comfortable assumption in America that the Marshall Plan has replaced the Morgenthau Plan is, I quickly perceived, a delusion. The spirit of Morgenthau, although it no longer dominates our German policy, still inspires it. The fact that there is now a Marshall Plan looking toward the integration of a revived and democratic Germany in a reconstructed and self-supporting Europe means that we are busy repairing with our right hand the damage done by our left hand. It is as if one team of Americans were rebuilding a bombed dwelling while another team is destroying the foundations.

It would have been funny, were it not so tragic, to witness the unending struggle between those Americans who had been sent to Germany to revive industry and trade, and those whose orders were to destroy the German economy. The conflict between the destroyers and the rebuilders was even more acrimonious and bitter than that between competitive Washington departments.

In Frankfurt, Essen, and Stuttgart, I have smiled to hear American coal, steel, and railway experts plotting, or pleading, to stop dismantlement of the factories producing the mining, railway, and other equipment without which coal production could not be increased or the railways restored. I heard revealing conversations between American and German authorities in which the former warned the latter about which Americans were on the constructive side and which on the destructive.

If there were some sort of collaboration between the Germans and those Americans who are engaged in restoring the German economy and furthering the Marshall Plan, there was naturally a far closer relationship between the American "destroyers" and the British Military Government. The United States experts endeavoring to increase coal and steel production and to reconstruct transportation facilities were dependent on the British, since not only the mines and iron and steel works are in the British zone, but also most of the factories producing mining equipment and railroad supplies. The predicament of the American experts can be understood if one notes the fact that the dismantlement list includes forty-seven factories making mining equipment and thirty-two specializing in the production of supplies for the German railways.

Fortunately there were some enlightened British officials also, who were anxious to revive the German economy, so the conflict between the constructors and the destroyers was not as unequal as it might otherwise have been. The British official in charge of the Bizonal Iron and Steel office in Düsseldorf, for instance, worked in complete harmony with his American counterpart, and in 1948 they succeeded in bringing about an astonishing increase in steel production. On the other hand, while $24,000,000 worth of American mining equipment had been earmarked for Germany by ECA, the British insisted on continuing to dismantle the German factories which could have supplied this machinery. Among others they were dismantling the plants producing 90 per cent of the pneumatic mining tools produced in the Western zone.

Obviously the British, in view of their dependence on American subsidies, could have been induced to stop the dismantlement of German factories, the loss of whose production had to be made good by ECA allocations. The trouble was that some United States Military Government and Washington officials were still pursuing a camouflaged Morgenthau line of policy.

Whether or not the contradictory and self-defeating nature of American activities in Germany was due more to individual sentiments or to Washington's desire to win votes by being all things to all men, both the American destroyers of the German economy and its rebuilders could claim they were only doing their duty. Both were carrying out the orders they had received.

The situation was aptly summarized by one United States official who told me:

"We are caught between opposing policies and are unable to move forward. The forces of destruction, born of war hysteria, and set in motion by the Morgenthau Plan, are still in operation; while the constructive forces which the Marshall Plan was intended to release are stymied for lack of new directives from Washington." "The American people," he continued, "are only now beginning to realize that unconditional surrender and total victory force them to assume the same responsibilities in Germany as the inheritor of a property. Although the bills are rolling in, and America has to pay them; we still fail to understand fully that we must stop the destruction of Germany's assets if the United States is not to go bankrupt. At present the old destructive policy is merely overlaid by the new constructive one."

Some American officials were in the awkward position of holding positions with the destroyers and the reconstructors at the same time. Major Holbrook, for instance, whom I met in Stuttgart, was both Reparations Officer for Württemberg and Governor LaFollette's Chief of Industry and Commerce. While he had to fulfill the dismantlement orders which came to him from the Reparations Division of Military Government in Berlin, he also had to endeavor to increase production in his province. This he had managed to do with considerable ingenuity.

In the United States zone machinery is classified as already dismantled when the bolts attaching it to the floor have been unscrewed and it has been placed on wooden blocks. By allowing the Germans to continue using it in this condition, Major Holbrook had not only lightened the load of the American taxpayer by enabling more Germans to earn their own living than would otherwise have been possible; he had also kept the "dismantled" machinery in good working order for use in other countries when the time came to ship it. Elsewhere, particularly in the British zone, I saw piles of rusty factory equipment long since dismantled which was gradually becoming unusable as it lay in the open air or in unheated damp depots. For it is the British practice to dismantle machinery even when no country entitled to receive reparations wants it. Hence the tremendous waste entailed by the Revised Level of Industry program, which is implemented with the primary objective of depriving the Germans of the capacity to produce, rather than helping other countries to reconstruct their economies with German reparations. Were the latter the real aim, new and better machinery could be supplied to them in far less time by stopping dismantlement and allowing the Germans to work to produce reparations.

Major Holbrook had also restored production in many of the factories from which reparations had been taken, by scouring Württemberg for unused machines which could have been taken in the first place, had the Berlin Military Government authorities not preferred to interrupt production and waste German labor by taking reparations from factories actually working instead of from those closed down.

Before I visited Stuttgart toward the end of October, I had believed that the various statements made by General Marshall and other representatives of the State Department in Washington, and by General Clay and his subordinates in Germany, meant that dismantlement had been completed or stopped in the United States zone. I was as bewildered as the Germans when I found that the expected arrival of the ECA's "Humphrey Committee" experts— sent to Germany in accordance with the 1948 Foreign Aid Act to ascertain which plants on the dismantlement list could better contribute to European recovery by being left in Germany—far from stopping reparations deliveries had led to a speed-up in shipments of machinery out of the United States zone. Evidently it was not only the British and French who were anxious to confront Paul Hoffman's Committee with a *fait accompli*. The United States Reparations Office at Military Government headquarters in Berlin had issued orders to crate and ship out immediately the machinery which had hitherto been permitted to continue operating in its "dismantled" condition on account of the great need of its products in Germany or for export.

The Germans had been led to assume that the arrival of the ECA revision committee meant a halt in reparations deliveries. The Württemberg-Baden Ministry of Economics had been informed, in a letter written by the United States chief of the Commerce and Industry Group of the Bipartite Control Office in Frankfurt on October 11, that removal of equipment from five plants in that area would be held in abeyance until completion of the ECA review. But a week or two later orders had come to crate and rush shipment of this same equipment out of Germany in record time. I was told that the United States official in Berlin who had given these orders had said on the telephone that the European Recovery Program might or might not be a good thing, but that in any case it had nothing to do with him. Nor had he any interest in the contrary orders given by the United States Commerce and Industry authorities in Frankfurt.

The Germans, in addition to their impotent resentment at being deprived of their means of livelihood, could not but reflect that this democracy, which we told them was such a good and just thing, could not be trusted, since the official promises made by one set of United States authorities were not honored by others.

One of the factories which came under the hammer as a result of the determination of the Berlin Reparations Office of Military Government to forestall the ECA, was the Kiefer Works. In Stuttgart I visited this plant which produces ventilation and heating equipment for factories and hospitals. Although the only factory in Bizonia producing air-conditioning equipment for hospitals, it was to be shipped to Greece. The Greek mission which had visited the factory had told the Germans that they had neither the market, nor the raw materials, nor the technical experts to make use of it. The machinery would, no doubt, end up on the scrap heap but it was "on the list." Its main equipment had been shipped and the Germans were trying to carry on production by cutting sheets by hand and nailing instead of soldering the parts.

I also saw the Zaiser Works in Stuttgart, now stopped from producing elevators and electric cranes, although the dismantlement by the Russians of the Flohr Works in Berlin and Vienna had left Germany with only five plants of this type, one of which was also being dismantled; and although British dismantlement of a multitude of cranes in the Ruhr had led to a large demand for new cranes which could not be met. Nor was there any hope of Zaiser's being able to acquire new machines: most of those they required are produced only in the Russian zone. I visited several other factories in Stuttgart, none of which could be classified either as potential armament factories or as "surplus" to Bizonia's needs, but all of which were having their machinery taken away, presumably to forestall any action to save them by the ECA authorities.

All over the United States zone the same thing was happening. One case brought to my notice was that of the Frank factory in Birkenau in Hesse, which produced artificial eyes for the blind, measuring instruments for the textile industry, and fine optical instruments. It should presumably never have been put on the dismantlement list. After representations to the Military Government by the owners, they had been informed that dismantlement would be halted pending review by the Humphrey Committee. But in the second week of October, orders came from Berlin to start crating and shipping the machinery at once. By October 22, before the ECA experts could arrive, the whole plant had been stripped and carried off.

Another example is that of the Gendorf factory in Bavaria which produced chlornatrium, a chemical required by the artificial fiber industry, which the Germans have been told is to be built up into one of their major export industries. The other major producer of chlornatrium in Western Germany, at Rheinfelden in the French zone, was long ago stopped from working. In September the United States Military Government ordered the Gendorf plant dismantled and shipped to Czechoslovakia.

The outstanding example of the determination of someone, somewhere, to sabotage the Marshall Plan, and strengthen the Communists, was the order given on October 4 to dismantle the power plant of the Norddeutsche Hütte at Bremen and ship it to Czechoslovakia.

Bremen is America's only large port in Germany and the gate of entry of all United States Army and ERP supplies. The hasty shipment to a Soviet satellite country of its main power plant at a time when Berlin was being blockaded and after an announcement that shipments of reparations from the Western zones would be halted pending the ECA review of the dismantlement list, could, it seemed, have no other explanation than the influence of the "Morgenthau boys" in Berlin or in Washington.

Dismantlement of the Bremen power plant caused an immediate drastic cut in the supply of current to the town and port, and one of the ECA experts informed me that it might be necessary to use United States Navy vessels operating off shore to supply the deficiency. While the United States Air Force had to be used to supply blockaded Berlin, the United States Navy might have to be called in to make good our voluntary curtailment of Bremen's power supply for the benefit of Communist Europe.

Under military government it is always difficult to fix responsibility. It is therefore impossible to say whether Washington or General Clay's economic advisors were responsible for the curious decision to ship as much machinery as possible out of the United States zone before the ECA could stop it. To the Germans it seemed that it was impossible to trust any American promises. The hopes raised by various official pronouncements that the dismantlement program was to be reviewed and shipments halted pending the ECA investigation were dashed. The assurances given that

Germany was to participate in the Marshall Plan for European reconstruction could no longer be believed, since the Military Government had given orders to rush shipments even of the machinery recognized as vital to the minimum requirements of the economy of Bizonia.

When the German Economic Administration ventured to protest, it was forbidden by both British and United States military governments to approach the ECA authorities directly. In a letter sent on September 21, 1948, to Dr. Pünder, head of Bizonia's Economic Administration, and signed jointly by Mr. Wilkinson, economic advisor to General Clay, and Sir Cecil Weir, who holds the same position in the British Military Government, it was written:

"It is not appropriate for you to communicate directly with ECA, since the Military Governors, as the supreme authorities, are responsible for the relations of the Bizonal areas with the ECA."

ECA's representatives in Germany never admitted that they were precluded from any direct contact with the Germans. Unfortunately, however, Paul Hoffman, when he paid a flying visit to Germany in November, spent only twenty minutes with the German Economic Administration representatives who had come to meet him at Frankfurt. The latter were able to hand him the printed report they had drawn up on *"The Effect of Envisaged Dismantling on Germany's Economic Situation and Her Role in European Reconstruction,"* but they were given no opportunity to discuss their case. Hoffman spent weeks in Paris, but either never had time to study the German situation, or was unwilling to challenge the Military Government's claim to exclusive power by a conference with the German representatives of Bizonia, or with German industrialists and labor leaders.

The Germans hate waste. These economical, hard-working and practical people simply cannot understand why, in the British zone, huge quantities of dismantled machinery lie rusting in the open or in unheated warehouses; why so much unallocated machinery is dismantled and converted into scrap; why the Germans are not allowed to work to repair the damage done by the Nazis in the countries they occupied instead of being converted into paupers supported by an American dole.

"We can understand the justice of demanding that we make reparations to the countries which suffered from German aggression," I was told over and over again in the British zone by German officials, workers, executives, and factory owners. "But we cannot understand the decision to *destroy* factory equipment taken from peacetime industries. This is not reparation; it is just waste."

Of course, not all the machinery taken from German factories in the British zone is thrown on the scrap heap. But even in the case of machinery shipped abroad the huge gap between its economic value in Germany, and its "residual value" after dismantlement, as listed on the reparations account, is a measure of the waste entailed. If the cost of labor involved in the dismantlement and re-erection process is also taken into account the whole reparations program appears ridiculous.

The far-reaching effects of dismantlement on the German economy are obscured by the method adopted in valuing the machinery. This is done by first establishing its value in 1938 and then deducting not only war damage but a fixed yearly rate of depreciation which takes no account of repairs and improvements. This frequently results in machinery being valued at nothing, although prior to dismantlement it was working full time. From the German point of view it seems wholly unjust that a good proportion of the machinery they lose through dismantlement is not even booked to their credit on the reparations account.

This method of reckoning the value of the machinery taken as reparations is of no help in determining the effect of dismantlement on the German economy. The replacement cost of the machinery, or its "economic value"—capitalization according to the net profits obtained before dismantlement—would be much fairer methods of calculating the loss.

According to figures furnished by the United States Military Government in October 1948, the value of the factory equipment already dismantled was as follows in 1938 value Reichsmarks:

U. S. zone 187 factories—212 million marks
British zone 496 factories—600-700 million marks
French zone[7] 84 factories—150-200 million marks

This makes a total of only about a billion prewar Reichsmarks, equivalent to $400,000,000. According to German calculations, however, the 1938 value of the plants already dismantled in the Western zones was about $1,800,000,000 and would cost far more to replace today.

According to an estimate made by Senator Harmssen of Bremen, the 1938 value of the machinery and equipment already taken from rump Germany is as follows:

Russian zone	1.6 billion Reichsmarks
French zone	1.2 billion Reichsmarks
Bizonia	3.5 billion Reichsmarks
Berlin	1.5 billion Reichsmarks

This calculation, although it may be exaggerated, gives a truer picture of the losses the Germans have suffered, than the "residual value" figures of the Military Government which obscure the effect of dismantlement on the German economy.

The value of the 335 plants still to be dismantled in the Western zones is about two billion dollars, according to German estimates, but appears as only a fraction of this sum on the reparations account which gives its residual value. The cost of replacement of the dismantled machinery is reckoned by the Germans as ten times its residual value.

Since correct total estimates cannot be obtained, the best method of ascertaining the loss to the European economy through dismantlement is to consider individual cases of dismantled factories, concerning which precise details can be obtained.

In the great G.H.H. (Good Hope) Works in the Ruhr, which I visited after their dismantlement, the cost of moving the machinery and of

---

[7] Exclusive of the machinery taken by the French for their own use without reference to the Inter-Allied Reparations Authority.

shipping it to the eleven nations to whom it had been allocated, amounted to between 800 and 1,000 marks a ton.

The cost of producing and installing new machinery for delivery as reparations would have been only 400. This plant could have "reproduced itself," that is to say, manufactured new machinery for delivery as reparations, in less time than it took to dismantle it. It had had a big export trade but its products had been lost for years, perhaps forever, since it was unlikely that the various nations to whom its equipment had been sent would ever be able to make use of the "bits and pieces" they received.

Nowhere was the waste entailed by dismantlement better illustrated than here. The Yugoslavs, who had received the lion's share, had got the press and hammer works and other shipbuilding machinery, and had insisted on shipment also of the bricks and girders and wharves. The Greeks had received the boiler house, including its roof which had been built in 1871. The Australians had been awarded a five-thousand-ton press for pressing steel ingots which they had no place to house—it was lying on some railway siding. England had taken an old freight wagon and some molds as scrap. Pakistan had received a crane capable of lifting 125 tons which it probably had no use for; India received the equipment which should have gone with the crane. A press, a pump, and an accumulator taken out of one department of the works had each been sent to a different nation.

Prior to the dismantlement the G.H.H. Works had export orders on their books for a million D marks of oil-burning machinery, and the Germans believed it had been torn down by the British to eliminate its competition with their less efficient industry.

Fifteen thousand workers had lost their jobs through the dismantlement of this one plant.

In the case of the Hörde Iron and Steel Works at Dortmund the estimated cost of dismantling its 16.5-foot rolling mill was 1,000,000 D marks and the minimum cost of re-erecting it, including the building, foundations, and the furnaces that served it, was 13,000,000. But the residual value as stated on the reparations account was only 2,200,000.

In the case of the famous Thyssen Works in the Ruhr, dismantlement costs were calculated at 65,000,000 marks, while the residual value came to only 40,000,000. The cost of "putting Humpty Dumpty together again" abroad was estimated to be 263,000,000 marks. Thus, if allowed to retain the plants, the Germans could easily have supplied new machinery in less time and worth far more than the equipment removed.

Rubble and steel scrap represent the end result of dismantling blast and open-hearth furnaces. Huge rolling mills and presses cannot be moved because their weight or size are too great for bridges or for rail clearances. Hydraulic piping, steam lines, electric conduits, automatic controls, and some other equipment cannot be economically dismantled and are a complete loss.

The State Department, in November 1947, said that the cost in labor and materials involved in the dismantling process is "relatively negligible." But the ECA experts I talked to in Germany estimated that the dismantlement program would cost about ninety thousand man-years of labor in Germany, and that at least the same amount of labor would be needed in the recipient countries to get the machines set up and working. In sum, their view was that the dismantlement program is wasteful, inefficient, and impractical. They said that if the high cost of moving the equipment, the time losses, and the production losses due to the separation of the tools and dies from machinery as well as the cost of replacing them, are all counted in, the value actually realized by the European economy through the recipient nations is negligible, when measured against either the cost of European recovery or the cost to the United States of meeting the deficit in Germany's balance of payments.

Whatever the exact cost, a telling argument was made in a *New York Times* editorial of November 13, 1947, which said:

Having poured out billions to aid Europe in place of the reparations that Germany did not pay [the United States] is entitled to ask that these billions be counted against German reparations at least to the extent of preventing an increase in American expenditures through economic strangulation and destruction in Germany. *Let the plants stand and get to work. The United States has more than paid for them.* (Italics added.)

Although every American taxpayer is bearing a share of the burden of supplying food and other essential imports to a semipauperized Germany, the connection between our German policy and high taxes is recognized by few. The cost of the vengeance wreaked on Germany in the first years of the occupation is not a subject which most politicians and journalists care to dwell upon. It is nevertheless essential to realize it, if Americans are not to pay as heavily in the future as up to date for the Morgenthau concepts which shaped our original occupation policies, and still color them in spite of assurances to the contrary.

The ignorance of the American public concerning the huge waste entailed by dismantlement is to be ascribed to a variety of reasons. In the first place, the Germans have neither a government, nor a free press, nor representatives abroad to present their case. In the second place, most American journalists, Congressmen and Senatorial committees take their information entirely from Military Government sources. Lastly, there is the fact that every one of the reports written by the experts sent out by the War and State departments and ECA have been suppressed. The Wolf Report, the Keenan Report, and most recently, the report of the ECA's Humphrey Committee, have all been kept secret. They are withheld both from the press and from most members of Congress.[8]

The Germans had imagined that, since the United States is a democracy, all these visits and investigations would result in the American voters' learning the facts of the situation. Over and over again I was asked what had been the reaction in America to the reports of the United States experts who had carefully surveyed the situation, and had to inform them that no one knew what these reports contained nor what had been recommended.

My own method of investigation in Germany was first to go to the German authorities for information and then to see for myself on the spot

---

[8] The Humphrey Committee report was not made public until April 1949, after Congress had already voted the ECA appropriations demanded, without knowledge of the extent to which dismantlement is responsible for high taxes in America.

whether or not what they said seemed to be true. After this I asked the Military Government for its answer to the German contentions and its explanation for what I had seen. This was apparently a novel method of procedure, and I found myself regarded, if not with suspicion, at least as unorthodox in my method of investigation, since it was unusual for journalists to listen first, if at all, to what the Germans had to say. There was a goodly number of United States officials, however, who were as anxious as I was to have the true facts concerning the effects of dismantlement presented to the American public. This was particularly true of the ECA authorities who told me their door was open to any German who had facts to give them or representations to make which concerned the European Recovery Program. So it was with the knowledge that I was not alone in my desire to stop what former President Hoover has called "Destruction at our Expense," that I advised the Germans in the British, United States, and French zones to visit the ECA officials in Frankfurt and lay before them the facts relating to the retarding of European recovery through dismantlement.

Herr Nolting, the Minister of Economics for North-Rhine Westphalia, which comprises the Ruhr, told me in Düsseldorf that when the dismantlement list was handed to the Germans in October 1947, they had said to the British: "Look, you can have all the machines you ask for; only let us decide where they are to be taken from. If you will let us select the machines, present production need not be interrupted and our whole economy disorganized; if you will leave it to us to deliver what you ask for, we will also be able to ensure that the burden of reparations is equally distributed. Surely you can see the injustice of mining some employers and workers while letting others go scot free."

The British had refused, although acceptance of the German plea would have saved much time and labor as well as creating confidence in democratic justice.

The fact that the British, instead of taking general-purpose machinery, insisted on dismantling specialized factories whose production could not be compensated for by others, strengthened the impression that the objective was not reparations but the elimination of German competition.

The High Cost of Vengeance

In September 1948, after the announcement of the Marshall Plan had given hope to the Germans that the program of destruction of Germany's industrial capacity would be stopped, Nolting had had an interview with Brigadier Noel, the top British reparations official in the Ruhr. The German minister had informed Noel that, since representations to the British for changes in the dismantlement program had proved useless, he had referred the German plea to Mr. Hoffman. Brigadier Noel was very angry and said: "Mr. Hoffman is only a private individual in so far as His Majesty's Government is concerned, and the British Foreign Office will not consider any proposals brought forward by a private person." Brigadier Noel had gone on to advise Nolting not to rely on any "interference" by Mr. Hoffman.

According to what I was told by one of Minister Nolting's subordinates, Nolting had been summoned to London a few days later, and urged not to demand a general stoppage of dismantlement in the Ruhr, because this would not only embarrass the British Labour Government but would cause such a furor in France that De Gaulle might come to power. He had also been assured that if he would cooperate with the British, they would "discuss" with the Germans the elimination from the dismantlement list of certain plants.

This slightly more conciliatory attitude of the British was ascribed by my informant as due to ECA pressure and the British desire to prevent direct contact between the Germans and the ECA authorities of the United States.

As I shall relate in a subsequent chapter, the British have taken advantage all along of the German Social Democrats' tendency to regard the British Labour party as an ally, and to trust it more than "capitalist" America. But the touching faith of the German Socialists in the British Labour Government was now being sorely tried by the fact that the British, in the summer and fall of 1948, were rushing dismantlement in order to present the United States ECA investigators with a *fait accompli*. Like Nolting, other Social Democratic ministers in North-Rhine Westphalia, were not yet prepared to reveal to correspondents the secret of their negotiations with the British Labour Government, but some of their subordinates were too outraged by the contrast between British Labour's statements and practices to be discreet.[9]

It would be unfair to the British to hold them mainly responsible for the dismantlement program, although today, like the French, they are opposing its discontinuance. Originally it was the United States, under Roosevelt's directives, which joined hands with the Russians to implement the Morgenthau Plan for transforming Germany into a "goat pasture." The British in 1945 and 1946 were the only Allied Power which opposed this program. They understood then that the destruction of German industries and mass unemployment and destitution in Germany was hardly conducive to the "democratization" of the German people and would, in any case, prove impossible to carry out once the British and American people came to realize the mass starvation it would entail.

Even if all occupied Germany had been administered as an economic unit, as promised by the Soviet Government at Potsdam, millions of Germans would have been condemned to die of hunger under the original occupation directives. For the Polish and Russian seizure of Germany's bread basket east of the Oder and Neisse rivers not only deprived Germany of a quarter of its arable land, it also drove the millions of Germans who had lived in these territories for hundreds of years into the truncated Reich.

If the Soviet Government had not at once proceeded to cut the British, United States, and French zones off from the food supplies of Soviet-occupied Germany, there would still have been no possibility for the Western Germans to obtain enough food to keep alive under the Morgenthau Plan, which incidentally also advocated detaching the Saar, the Ruhr, and some slices of German territory next to Holland and Belgium. It is, therefore, no exaggeration to say that in comparison with the Morgenthau Plan even the Nazis would have appeared as comparatively humane conquerors. Its recommendation that the Germans

---

[9] According to the October 1948 report of the British Control Commission for Germany reports "continued progress" in dismantlement, with 25 plants completely dismantled that month. This made a total of 216 for the year with a further 208 plants in process of being dismantled. The volume of machinery already torn out of German factories was given as 528,000 tons, of which only 270,000 had been shipped to recipient nations.

should become self-subsistent farmers on the already overpopulated German soil is shown to be only a disguised program for genocide by the fact that the average yield per acre in Western Germany is already 50 per cent higher than that in the United States. There is obviously no room for a larger agricultural population in Germany than already exists.

American soldiers were too humane to be capable of watching masses of the defeated enemy people dying before their eyes. Moreover, it was recognized even in Washington that the health and safety of Americans would be endangered by widespread "disease and unrest." So almost from the beginning the United States started importing food into Germany to provide a minimum ration, just sufficient to maintain life and prevent people from dropping dead of hunger in the streets.

Nevertheless, in 1946, a "Level of Industry Plan" was worked out with the Russians which, if carried into effect, would have precluded any possibility of the Germans ever being able to produce enough for their own support, and converted millions of them into paupers.

This result was in fact recognized by General Draper and his experts in the economics division of the United States Military Government. The Potsdam agreement with Soviet Russia had stipulated that the German standard of living was to be no higher than the average in Continental Europe, excluding England and the U.S.S.R. The Draper memorandum stated that "the data indicates that the German standard in 1932 was near the average for the remainder of the Continent for the years 1930 to 1938. For this reason figures for 1932 consumption in Germany can be used as a secondary basis of comparison or guide."

In Germany the worst year of the Great Depression was 1932, when there were some six million unemployed. Thus, it was the declared aim of the United States in 1946 to reproduce in Germany the conditions which had brought Hitler to power. Since the Level of Industry Plan then drawn up would actually have reduced millions of Germans to far worse destitution than in 1932, the logical result could have been expected to be a bigger and worse Hitler in the future—in a word a German Stalin.

It is not necessary to go into the details of this plan, since it was based on the fictitious assumption that the four zones of Germany would be administered as an economic unit, and since the program for the huge destruction and removals of German industrial equipment it envisaged, was modified after it became obvious that the Russian zone would continue to be treated as a purely Russian preserve.

In 1947 a "Revised Level of Industry Plan" was worked out by the American and British Occupation authorities on the assumption that Western Germany would have to exist without the resources of the Soviet zone, as well as without those of the former German territories east of the Oder. A list of plants to be dismantled as "surplus" to German needs at the level of existence to be permitted by their conquerors was drawn up on the basis of this plan and published in October 1947.

A cursory examination of the Revised Plan shows unmistakably that it fails to allow Western Germany to retain sufficient productive capacity to pay its own way, even on the assumption that the Germans are to continue indefinitely on their present diet, described by the ECA's chief representative in Germany as "subnormal both in calories and proteins."

Western Germany with forty-two millions has more than half of the original Reich's population, less than half of its arable land, three-quarters of its hard-coal, and about a third of its brown-coal production. According to the evidence given to Congress in February 1949 by Mr. N. H. Collisson, Deputy Chief of the ECA mission to Bizonia, Western Germany can never produce more than 50 per cent of the food it needs to feed its non-self-suppliers within reasonable dietary levels. The remaining 50 per cent must therefore be imported, and this can only be done if Germany can "so revive its industries that it may produce cheaply and efficiently and compete on world markets."[10]

---

[10] In a pamphlet entitled *Is There Still a Chance for Germany?* (Hinsdale, Ill., Henry Regnery Company, 1948), Karl Brandt, Professor of Agricultural Economics, Food Research Institute, Stanford University, and an internationally recognized authority in this field, maintains that "doubt is warranted that Western Germany, as presently constituted, will ever be able to attain the degree of productivity that will permit her to pay her food bill" (p. 14). Brandt is not alone in this opinion; it is shared by other competent experts.

Mr. Collisson pointed out that production per acre in Germany is already 50 per cent higher than in the United States, so that there is little or no possibility of increasing the yield. He further stated that even the bountiful harvest of 1948 had only increased the average daily diet of the nonfarming population to about 2,400 calories; that the 1949-50 program plans for a still lower ration, and that the goal of the long-term recovery program is only 2,700 calories. By 1952-53 the Germans are expected to be still existing on a diet consisting mainly of potatoes and other carbohydrates, and insufficient for productive efficiency.

Mr. Collisson stated that even the maintenance of the "sub-normal" diet in Western Germany and the continued denial to the Germans of "desperately needed essential commodities" and adequate housing, would require imports of $2,800,000,000 worth of food and raw materials and a correspondingly high level of exports of German manufacturers and coal.

As against these ECA estimates, the 1947 Level of Industry Plan envisages exports amounting to only two billion dollars to pay for Western Germany's essential imports of food, fertilizer, and raw materials. This figure of two billion dollars, although well below the ECA estimate, requires a 15 per cent increase over the 1936 figure of German exports.

The authors of the plan themselves recognized that this estimate is probably too low, difficult as it is to imagine where in the world such a volume of consumer goods is to be sold. They say that "at least" two billion dollars is the minimum import requirement, but they add: "Since trade between the Bizonal area and the rest of Germany is subject to greater uncertainty than former internal trade, the result may be to increase still further the need for trade with other countries."

In other words, as late as 1947, American authorities, in deciding how much machinery to tear out of the German economy, still refused to recognize as the basis of their calculations the fact that the Eastern zone under the Russians is completely severed from the rest of Germany.

But it is studiously ignored in public discussion, whether unofficial or official, because, if the thesis is true, it takes away all ground from under Allied policies since Potsdam.

Even assuming that two billion dollars is a correct figure for the volume of exports required to meet Western Germany's minimum needs, the Revised Level of Industry Plan makes it impossible for her ever to export this much, for it drastically limits her production of steel, and thus precludes large exports of the machinery and construction materials in greatest demand on the world market, which made up the bulk of Germany's prewar exports. Instead, Germany is envisaged as having the possibility of exporting unlimited quantities of textiles, ceramics, and other products of light industry. The difficulty of finding outlets for the planned huge increase in consumer-goods exports is recognized, but not taken into account. The preamble to the plan states:

Before the war, the broad fields of metals, machinery and chemicals accounted for two-thirds of the total exports. Production of textiles, ceramics, and consumer goods can be raised, but the extent to which additional sales above prewar levels can be sold on the export markets is difficult to predict. Exports from the unrestricted industries would need to be increased approximately 90 per cent if the higher export requirements were provided entirely from the unrestricted industries, which is obviously impracticable. Therefore the level of exports from the restricted industries will need to be greater than prewar.

Having cut the ground from under their own feet by this statement, the authors of the plan proceed to outline the cuts to be made in the productive capacity of the German steel industry, mechanical and electrical industries, chemicals and other vital branches of a modern economy. It also expressly states that no provision is made in the plan for repayment of the advances made by the occupying powers for imports of food, seed and fertilizer. Reparations are thus given priority over Germany's debt to the United States.

The plan limits Western Germany's steel production to 10.7 million tons a year, as against her 1936 production of 17.5 million tons, and the United States estimate of 19.2 million tons as her end of the war capacity. According to the Germans this latter figure takes insufficient account of air-raid damage. They claim therefore that the 6.5 million tons of steel capacity being dismantled will actually reduce Germany's capacity below the 10.7 million tons allowed in the Revised Level of Industry Plan.

Whichever figures are accepted as correct, there is no doubt that the planned dismantlement must deprive Western Germany of any possibility of becoming self-supporting. It envisages a Germany producing far less, and exporting more, than before the war. It makes no provision for the rebuilding of Germany's bombed cities and bridges, the repair of railroads and rolling stock, and the replacement of the engines and freight cars looted by the Russians, Poles, and French; nor for the housing of the millions of expellees from the East; nor for the support of the uncounted numbers of disabled men, women, and children; nor for the hospitalization of the many prisoners of war sent home from Russia, France, and Yugoslavia only after they have become too ill and weak to be of any use as slave laborers.

Like the old Level of Industry Plan it provides, even theoretically, for a German income at the lowest level of the Depression years, when Germany had six million unemployed. It is specifically stated that per capita productive capacity is to be reduced to 75 per cent of the 1936 level, which is precisely the 1932 level. In practice, Germany's per capita income would be reduced even lower than this, for the plan gravely underestimates the present and expected population increase of the Western zones.

The number of expellees from Silesia, the Sudetenland, and other parts of Eastern Europe was about twelve million. Some three million are estimated to have died of starvation and exposure, and some are in the Soviet zone. But against this reduction of the total figure of those who have to be provided for in Western Germany, there is the constant and increasingly large influx of refugees fleeing to Germany both from the Eastern zone and from all the countries under Communist dictatorship. These refugees include many nationalities, even Russians, but are not, for the most part, admitted into the DP camps, and have to be provided for by the German economy (see Chapter 7.)

If all these factors are taken into consideration the envisaged reduction in the standard of living of the population of Western Germany is almost 50 per cent below prewar. Without American subsidies it is bound to be even more miserably inadequate than at present.

Since it provides only for minimum German needs, the Revised Level of Industry Plan is also incompatible with the Marshall Plan, which envisages German industries and skills contributing to the rehabilitation of Western Europe. The ceiling placed on German steel production is alone sufficient to preclude any possibility of Germany's contributing to the reconstruction and defense of Western Europe.

As the London *Economist* pointed out on August 6, 1946, Germany used five million tons of steel before the war for the output only of such necessary peacetime requirements as nails, sheet iron, cutlery, stoves, furnaces, pipes, tools, and household utensils. Even in the last year of World War II 40 per cent of Greater Germany's steel output (8 or 9 million tons out of 22 to 24 million, according to the *Economist* figures) was used for civilian purposes.

According to the calculations of German economists, Western Germany needs, not 10.7, but at least 14 million tons of ingot steel a year for the next five years for domestic use, even if a very low standard of living is maintained. No one who has seen the havoc wrought by bombing and battle all over the Western zone will quarrel with this estimate. With rare exceptions every town, large or small, is in ruins. British and French removal of vast quantities of timber from German forests has increased the need of metal in place of wood for rebuilding. Yet Germany's structural-steel production is being reduced by 40 per cent.

Steel allocations for highway maintenance and repair of the Rhine bridges alone came to 8,000 tons in the first half of 1948. The future need is calculated at 40,000 tons a year for the next seven years. Rail repair requires a minimum of 150,000 tons a year for several years to come.

To anyone not blinded by the desire for revenge, it is obvious that Western Germany can never support itself unless permitted to produce at least as much steel for its own requirements, and to export even larger quantities of machinery, than before the war. As Mr. Collisson told Congress:

The industries of Western Germany need steel for the processing and manufacturing of the machinery, apparatus and precision goods *which constitute the bulk of its export trade.* Into these finished goods go the skills and craftsmanship which represent the ingredient contributing the most to the value of the finished article.

Germany is a country with practically no raw materials except coal; her "riches" consist in the skills and industry of her working population. Unless allowed to use them for her own benefit and that of Europe she cannot support her people. At the same time Europe desperately needs German machinery. Nevertheless ninetyfour iron and steel plants were placed on the dismantlement list handed to the Germans in October 1947. The list included Germany's most up-to-date and efficient plants.

As every American iron and steel man will tell you, a blast furnace, or melting or annealing furnace, can not be transplanted. It can only be destroyed. Thus a "dismantled" iron and steel works yields as reparations, at most, 20 to 25 per cent of its former production facilities. Germany's loss of her capacity to produce steel constitutes a lasting loss to the whole European economy.

The American public has not been permitted to see the Wolf Report on the German iron and steel industry. It is, however, no secret that Mr. Wolf reported that even the 10.7 million tons of steel ingots permitted under the Revised Level of Industry Plan would be useless if the machinery necessary to roll it at low cost in labor and materials is not retained in Germany; and that scheduled dismantlements of rolling mills would make this impossible.

Some 80 per cent of German steel production consists of rolled products. According to the German Bizonal Economic Administration the dismantlement of rolling mills being carried out will reduce productive capacity far below the 10.7 million tons steel level prescribed, and nearer to the 6 million tons level insisted upon by the Russians in 1946.

Since the capacity of the United States to meet even the home demand for sheets and strips is estimated to be insufficient, where is Europe to obtain its basic requirements if the British insist on carrying through the scheduled dismantlements in the Ruhr? As Mr. Collisson said in his evidence before the Senate Foreign Relations Committee, "The critical shortage of steel in the world today demands maximum use of facilities permitted to remain in Germany."

According to the Herter Committee report, the United States, up to 1951, will not be in a position to supply either the home market or the European and Near Eastern demand for rolled pipes of large diameter. Yet 46 per cent of Germany's welded-pipe producing capacity is being dismantled, and her large-diameter pipe production entirely destroyed.

Ten per cent of Germany's rolled milled products consists of steel wire. Thus she should have been left the capacity to produce 800,000 tons, but scheduled dismantlements are reducing it to only 530,000.

In visiting the Ruhr I was made aware of the fact that the manner in which dismantlement is carried out also greatly increases German costs of production, coal consumption, and transport charges. With an eye mainly to the elimination of German competition, the British are crippling a large number of plants instead of completely dismantling only a few. By this method they raise German costs of production to noncompetitive levels, while making it appear that the total reparations removals are comparatively small.

In a modern iron and steel works the whole process of extracting iron from the ore in a blast furnace, making steel ingots from pig iron or scrap in a furnace, and shaping the red-hot steel into bars, plates, wire, or tubes is carried out in the same plant. This economizes fuel, power, and transport. The British in the Ruhr disrupt the process by removing a part of the equipment.

In one plant they remove the rolling mill, in another the presses, and in others they destroy the furnaces. Thus, in one iron and steel works the steel used can no longer be produced on the premises, while in others it can no longer be rolled or pressed and has to be sent elsewhere for processing.

At the Hörde Works in Dortmund, for instance, I saw the giant 16.5-foot rolling mill, which is the only one of its kind in Europe and has a production capacity of 200,000 tons of rolled steel a year, standing idle by British order. It had been producing some 7,000 tons a month before the British ordered it dismantled in the fall of 1948. The greater part of the steel produced at Hörde's and formerly immediately processed, now had to be cooled and sent elsewhere for use, with consequently greatly increased coal consumption and transport costs. The latter charges were high since there was no water transport and no other rolling mill in the vicinity to make use of the steel produced at Hörde's.

Not only would the Hörde Works no longer be able to operate profitably. The Dutch, Swedes, and Norwegians had placed orders in the Ruhr for 200,000 tons of wide metal plates for shipbuilding, which England and France could not supply, and which dismantlement of the Hörde 16.5-foot rolling mill prevented Germany from producing. There was no other rolling mill in Europe making such large plates. The two German plants in existence producing 14.7and 13.5-foot plates had insufficient capacity to fulfill the whole foreign shipbuilding order in addition to their existing commitments, since the demand in Germany for wide steel plates was also very great. The Hörde Works had, for instance, produced the plates for rebuilding the bridge over the Rhine at Cologne, reopened in the fall of 1948, and there were many other destroyed German bridges waiting to be rebuilt.

In February 1949, following the visit of the Norwegian Foreign Minister to Washington to discuss Norway's adherence to the Atlantic Pact, it was reported in the press that the United States had promised to deliver American steel plates for the reconstruction of Norway's mercantile marine, in place, presumably, of the German deliveries which had been cut off.

The Germans had offered to deliver a new rolling mill in place of Hörde's. This new equipment was already half finished and could have been completed in nine months, whereas three and a half years would be required to dismantle, pack, and ship the Hörde mill, if it could ever be accomplished, and this was most unlikely in view of its huge size and weight. Nevertheless the offer was refused by the British Reparations Office in Düsseldorf.

The Hörde workers, at the time of my visit, had succeeded in preventing dismantlement by forming a picket line and preventing the wrecking crew from entering the plant. The giant mill stood idle, since use of it was forbidden, and no one knew whether the British would use troops to force the workers to give way, and use DP's to destroy the mill should German workers refuse the task.

The workers had put up notices on blackboards which read:

"Hands off! You are taking away the livelihood of 8.000 workers and their families."
"Marshall Plan: Reconstruction or Destruction?"
"Let us work! We want to help in the rebuilding of Europe!"

I spent several hours at the Hörde Works where thin and undernourished German workers left their arduous labors in the smelting works to ask me if there was any hope that America would intervene to prevent the destruction of their livelihood. I gave them all the encouragement I could, saying that I was sure that in time the American people would stop the senseless and cruel destruction of Germany's industrial capacity. But not wishing to raise false hopes I admitted that America's awakening might not come in time to save their jobs.

Early in 1949, while writing this book, I received a letter from Herr Wilms, the engineer in charge of the 16.5-foot rolling mill. He wrote to tell me that after stopping dismantlement according to their promises to the ECA the British had removed and shipped to England the turning lathe and grinding machine without which the mill cannot operate. He added:

On November 1, 1948, in "honor of the visit" of Mr. King, the Wolf Commission expert, the first of these machines was removed; and now, on Christmas Eve, the second one has been torn out and both essential machines shipped to England via Hamburg. Yet there is no one in England who wants them. The Thomson Houston Company in Rugby has refused to take them, and Messrs. Francis Shaw in Manchester have accepted delivery with reluctance.

At the end of his letter Herr Wilms remarks:

The belief in Germany that the American view concerning European rehabilitation would prevail and bring an end to dismantlement, is fading. I myself still hope for the best while preparing for the worst. Can you give us some good advice? Perhaps now that masculine reason is in eclipse, feminine feeling will achieve better results!

Unfortunately for the Hörde workers, the ECA Commission deferred to the British, who presumably wish to prevent reconstruction of the Norwegian and Dutch merchant marine. So the giant rolling mill is now being torn down.

In Dortmund I also visited the Dortmund Union Works which after the decartelization operation had been cut off from its coal mines, subsuppliers, and markets. Here again I found that the whole works was not being dismantled, but measures had been taken to ensure that the steel produced in its foundry could no longer be used on the premises in its molten state. A gigantic press, far too big to be moved but nevertheless placed on the reparations list, was being destroyed. The ovens which served it had already been torn down, and the press itself being irremovable would presumably be broken up and converted into scrap. It had originally been constructed on the premises and was the largest press in Europe. Two other presses and four steam hammers had already been dismantled and 29 ovens destroyed; one crane able to lift a weight of 250 tons had been torn down, and five smaller cranes removed.

This plant had formerly manufactured equipment for the mining and electrical industries, and gears for large sea-going ships, all of which production depended on the presses which were being destroyed or dismantled.

The value of the annual output of the Dortmund Union Works prior to dismantlement had been 25,000,000 marks a year. Its residual value on reparations account was only a fraction of this sum. The plant could not be reconstituted because its former affiliated works, the Wagner Company which made presses, had already been dismantled and its equipment shipped to India.

The Germans had offered to supply new machinery to India instead, and India would have preferred to receive machinery made to its specifications, but the British had insisted that Wagner's be dismantled. It could only be presumed that from the British point of view it was better that the Indians should receive factory equipment they could make no use of, than machinery with which to compete with the British. Dismantlement both eliminated German competition and prevented the creation of effective new competitors.

Following its dismantlement, the Wagner Company in Dortmund had made a contract with the British to use its labor force to dismantle other factories. But, faced with the rising tide of German resentment at the destruction of their country's assets, the reluctance of all German workers to dismantle the machinery which their fellow trade-unionists depended upon for their livelihood, and the general opprobrium attached to all Germans who collaborated with the British in destroying Germany's productive capacity, Wagner's in October 1948 had refused to renew their contract. As punishment the British, at the time of my visit to Dortmund, had announced their intention of tearing down the empty Wagner buildings which had hitherto been spared and used as a storage depot for the machinery torn out of other factories in the town.

The "captains of industry" I met in Dortmund considered the Revised Level of Industry Plan limiting future German production worse than dismantlement, costly as the latter is. This was also the view of the trade-union representatives with whom I talked in the Ruhr. Executives and workers, indignant as they all were at the senseless destruction of machinery going on, had faith in German capacity to repair the damage if only they were allowed to work.

The most terrible thing about Allied occupation policies was the setting of limits to man's endeavor, inventiveness, and willingness to work.

Germany's coal, iron, and steel industry was formerly the most closely and economically integrated in Europe. Combines used their own locally mined coal to produce steel and roll it immediately into plates or strips or press it into shape while still red hot. In many plants production from blasting to finished products, such as pipes and wire, was all carried out on the same premises, with a minimum cost for handling and transport.

Dismantlement, coupled with so-called "decartelization" is wiping out these economies and reducing Germany's coal, iron, and steel industry to a nineteenth century level of efficiency.

"Decartelization" was originally sold to the American people under a false label. It was represented as a method of eliminating "monopoly," and clearing the ground for free private enterprise. In fact, however, under the influence of Communist fellow travelers in key positions in the economic division of the United States Military Government, decartelization became an instrument for undermining the capitalist system. "Operation Severance," as it was called, first set 1,000 employees as the maximum for any German enterprise. Later the figure was raised to 10,000, but even this number of permitted workers destroyed the former economic and efficient vertical integration of the German coal, iron, and steel industry.

Communist sympathizers, in combination with the disciples of Morgenthau, no longer enjoy predominant influence in the United States Military Government. Many of them have been sent home. Those who remain are careful to camouflage their real objectives. Nevertheless they are by no means eliminated and still exert considerable undercover influence. They can still work through the British, who, although they never subscribed to the absurdities of the Morgenthau Plan or let Communist sympathizers direct their policy, took advantage of the decartelization program to decrease Germany's productive capacity and raise her costs of production to the advantage of her British competitors on the world market.

The outstanding example of dismantlement of a model enterprise is the August Thyssen works in the Ruhr. This was the most efficient smelting works in Europe. It formerly produced 1,250,000 tons of crude steel, all used on the spot to turn out high quality dynamo and transformer sheets, materials for bridge building, and heat resistant and acid-proof steels. Situated on the river, it had its own wharves for the landing of coal and iron ore and for shipping of finished products. The Thyssen works formerly accounted for half of Germany's total production of the transformer sheets now so desperately needed. Ever since the end of the war the British have prohibited its operation, and it is now being dismantled.

Repeated testimony before Congressional committees, and statements by ECA and United States Military Government spokesmen, confirm the fact that the basic limiting factor in the German recovery program is the power shortage. This is caused by the result of our air raids, long-neglected repairs, dismantlement of power plants, and shortage of coal supplies. Without new supplies of electrical sheets for transformers and dynamos the power shortage cannot be remedied. Fifty per cent of Bizonia's capacity for the production of electrical sheets was located in the August Thyssen Works.

Yet the State Department, in its memorandum of March 1, 1948, asserted that "no plants producing electric generating equipment are scheduled for dismantlement in the British Zone."

How is this statement to be explained? Are the experts of the State Department even more ignorant of technology and the requirements of modern industry than the author of this book? Or is someone interested in misleading the Secretary of State, Congress, and the American public? Or is it worth nearly a billion dollars a year to preserve the reputations of the incompetents who made the past mistakes?

Technical progress in all countries is leading to increased use of electric and fine steels, and the Level of Industry Plan requires that Germany produce more, not less, of the high-grade machine tools and fine optical and electrotechnical instruments which require such steel. But Germany's capacity to produce electric steel is being reduced to a mere 300,000 tons a year. One hundred and eighteen electric furnaces out of a total of 209 are being dismantled.

Thus, while promising that the Germans would be allowed to increase their production and export of machine tools and optical instruments, we are busy depriving them of the capacity to procure the specialized steels these industries require.

This crippling of Germany's capacity to produce the fine steels increasingly in demand on the world market is of particular importance to the American taxpayer, since it drastically reduces Germany's capacity to export high quality tools, and perpetuates the unfavorable balance of trade now met by American food subsidies.

It also cripples the chemical industry because Germany will henceforth be unable to produce sufficient quantities of heatand acidproof stainless steel.

It was promised in the Revised Level of Industry Plan that the fine machine-tool mechanics and optical-instrument industry would not be touched, but even in this field factories have been dismantled in the United States zone, sometimes with the excuse that they had been "substantially modified" for war use. There has also been dismantlement of factories producing fine precision tools essential to the permitted export industries.

It was also stated that the production of agricultural machinery and road tractors in the Bizone was insufficient, and none should be taken for reparations. But here again a promise to the Germans was broken. In 1948 the section of Krupps producing agricultural machinery was dismantled in spite of bitter protests by the workers employed there.

In spite of the admitted necessity to increase German exports of machinery, the 1947 plan provides for the following removals of productive capacity:

Thirty-five per cent of the production facilities of the heavy mechanical engineering industry.

Twenty-three per cent of the capacity of the light machinery industry.

Thirty-five per cent of the present productive capacity of the machine-tool industry.

Removal of "only" three electrical engineering plants, because "the pre-war requirements of the Bizonal area were in large part met from capacities in Berlin, which have been almost totally dismantled."

Regarding automobiles and trucks, the plan states that capacity to produce 160.000 passenger cars and 61,500 commercial vehicles will be left in Western Germany. Prewar production was far above this level. It should be noted that up to 1948 practically the whole production of *Volkswagen* and trucks was taken by the British and French occupation authorities for their own use or for sale for their own profit. Moreover, a large number of German automobiles and trucks were confiscated at the beginning of the occupation. Thus very few Germans still have automobiles and those still in their possession are usually very old. Most business enterprises lack essential transport. The backlog demand is accordingly huge.

As for chemicals, 40 to 50 per cent of existing capacity is to be removed or destroyed. All explosive plants are to be removed or destroyed. A quarter of the capacity of the plastics industry is made available for reparations. Less than the prewar capacity of dyestuffs is to be retained. The production of atabrine is to be reduced below prewar by removal of a pharmaceutical plant. Fifteen per cent of the capacity of the "miscellaneous chemicals" group is to be removed, and 17 per cent of the capacity of the "basic, organic and inorganic" chemical industries.

The prohibited list of industries still includes ships, aluminum, beryllium, vanadium, magnesium, ball bearings, synthetic ammonia, rubber, gasoline, and oil.

Under a temporary provision Germany has been allowed to continue producing some ball bearings until such time as her exports shall enable her to buy them abroad. Both the British and Americans now agree this is impracticable, but in the meantime half the equipment at the large ball-bearing factory at Schweinfurt in Bavaria has been sent to the Soviet Union.

The British, obviously because they want no German competition in this sphere, have as yet refused to agree to remove the ban on shipbuilding except for small and slow vessels.

The British in their implementation of the plan have included the light-metal industries in the category of "light machine industry" scheduled for a 23 per cent reduction in productive capacity. In spite of German protests the British have dismantled factories making coffee pots, skillets, kettles, and other household goods made of sheet metal. Some 40 plants producing such peacetime necessities were included on the British dismantlement list.

The State Department has contended that the task of selecting the plants to be dismantled was performed with great care, that none of them could be used in Germany if retained there, and that their removal facilitates the economic recovery of the recipient nations.

This statement must be based on inadequate information. For nothing is more obvious in Germany than the fact that many of the plants being dismantled are precisely those working to full capacity, having been given priority in the allocation of coal and raw materials, precisely because their products were essential to the working of the civilian economy. Telling the Germans that the machinery being dismantled is "surplus" to their requirements is a heartless joke.

The State Department's contention that the plants dismantled were those which could not be used in Germany if retained there is contradicted by information given by the Military Government, as well as by the evidence presented by the Germans. I was told by Military Government authorities in Berlin in November 1948 that the plants dismantled in the United States zone were now once again producing half as much as before they were dismantled. They had been put back into production by providing them with equipment formerly unused in plants which were not dismantled. In other words, reparations were *not* taken from "surplus" capacity in idle factories, but from those working to capacity.

In any case the contention that German reparations have not impeded recovery because capacities are not fully utilized, begs the question. It should, instead, be asked why potential capacities have not been fully utilized in view of Europe's needs. The answer reveals the vicious cycle for which the Allied wrecking policy in Germany is responsible.

The inadequate food supplied to the German miners and their families, and their miserable housing conditions, combined with the dismantlement of the factories producing mining equipment, has held down coal production.

The obligation to export 20 per cent of the Ruhr's coal production (mainly to France) and the loss of the Saar and of the brown coal of Eastern Germany, has further drastically curtailed the amount of coal available for German consumption.

This in turn limits steel production and has led some iron and steel works to be represented as "surplus," only because Germany is not permitted to obtain the coal and iron ore she requires to make a major contribution to European recovery.

The real reason for dismantlement is that given by the head of the Steel Production Board in Düsseldorf, who in August 1948, said to my friend Mrs. John Crane, who was representing Senator George W. Malone: "There is no intention that Germany will be left with enough steel-making capacity ever again to be able to export steel or steel products in significant quantities."

The Revised Plan would be unrealistic in view of the necessity for increased German exports, even if based on a correct estimate of existing capacities. There is, however, evidence that the list of plants to be dismantled was drawn up without a proper survey of what equipment remained in Germany.

The Germans contend that the basis of United States-British calculations of productive capacity was the maximum output reached temporarily during the war and impossible to sustain. Normal utilization is only 80 to 90 per cent, and the many years during which no repairs were carried out have reduced the capacity by a greater degree than normal depreciation. These facts too were not taken into consideration. They also contend that the use of gross capacities in Allied calculations results in an overestimation of production facilities, since some subsuppliers are counted twice over.

Secondly, the Germans say, since the most efficient plants were chosen for dismantlement, and since the destruction of one branch of an industry deprives others of the material they use, the net reduction in productive capacity is far greater than indicated by the total figures of dismantlement. Insuperable bottlenecks result from reparations deliveries which affect the whole German economy, and in some cases the whole of Europe, since some plants can never be reconstructed in other countries, and even those which are re-erected take months or years before they can produce again.

Thirdly, the basis on which Germany's productive capacity was calculated was not, as the State Department has asserted, any "careful" investigation of existing capacity. The basis was apparently the so called "Mecit" reports of the winter of 1945-46 when the German factory owners were instructed to fill in forms stating the productive capacity of their plants. The object of these questionnaires was not stated at the time and the Germans thought they were to be the basis for fuel and raw-material allocations. Human nature being what it is, they almost all overestimated their productive capacities at a time when no one expected to be supplied with anything but a small proportion of their needs. It was certainly the Germans' fault that productive capacities were accordingly overestimated, but the fact remains that these "Mecit" reports are not reliable, and should not have been taken as the basis for the calculation of which plants are surplus under the Revised Level of Industry Plan.

There are numerous established cases in which data on plants have been so inaccurate that they were not even listed in the right industry.

Even if the original Anglo-American estimates of Germany's productive capacity are accepted as correct, British "multilateral deliveries," French *"prélèvements,"* and "restitutions" from all three zones have destroyed their validity. No one, not even the Germans, now knows exactly what is left of Germany's productive capacity.

"Multilateral deliveries" is the British term for the removal of specially valuable, or special-purpose and frequently irreplaceable, machinery from German factories to England. "*Prélèvements*" is the French term for their seizure of whole plants and of individual machines in their zone without reference to the Inter-Allied Reparations Authority (IARA) in Brussels. Both terms are a "legalized" synonym for what would be described as looting if practiced by an enemy country.

In the British zone a commission would come to a German factory not on the dismantlement list, pick out certain machines, and order them dismantled "to meet United Kingdom requirements." Although on October 18, 1947, General Robertson made an official promise that no further multilateral deliveries would be demanded, in the fall of 1948 they were resumed in some places. In Düsseldorf, for instance, in September 1948, the British demanded seventy-two machines, this time however from factories on the dismantlement list. The point, of course, was that these machines had to be delivered earlier than the dates set for general dismantlement, and the Germans were convinced that the British hoped thus to forestall the ECA commission's recommendations.

The machines taken as multilateral deliveries were for British use, since they were not being allocated by the IARA at Brussels. Some of the machinery thus torn out of German factories and not taken into consideration in drawing up the Level of Industry Plan is irreplaceable, because it is made only in the Russian zone. Many factories have been permanently crippled although they do not figure on the dismantlement list.

"Restitutions" have further invalidated the original estimate of Germany's productive assets. Originally the term "restitutions" was taken to mean only the restoration of property stolen by the Germans in occupied countries, or transferred to German ownership "under duress." Confined to this interpretation restitutions are entirely justified on both moral and economic grounds. But, in July 1948, the United States Military Government began to give an interpretation to the term "restitutions" which has no basis in law or equity. The 1946 ruling by General Clay, according to which "duress" had to be proved, was canceled, and it was decreed that no transfers of property under German occupation were to be considered as "normal commercial transactions." According to this ruling machinery and other goods, bought and paid for by German merchants or manufacturers, must be returned to the country of origin as restitutions without any need to prove they were sold under duress.

Even if the German buyer can produce documentary evidence that the seller considers that he was properly paid and does not now claim return of the property, the German purchaser has to give it up without compensation, because, "restitution claims are government claims and not those of individuals." As a result of this United States Military Government ruling, property for restitution is not delivered to those who originally sold it to the Germans, but to foreign governments. Most of the foreign governments who thus obtain restitution of the machinery and other goods originally sold by their nationals are Soviet satellites today, and they often dispose of the "restored" property by sale to foreign countries for dollars. In a considerable number of cases they have offered to sell these restitutions to their dispossessed German owners for foreign currency—to be used presumably for strengthening themselves against the "menace of American imperialism."

The only exception to this American ruling concerning the restoration to former occupied countries of the machinery and other goods bought by the Germans, is the proviso that if a German can produce "figures and dates" to prove that he bought the same kind of machinery or other goods in the same quantities before the war, he may perhaps be allowed to retain his property.

Commerce between Germany and France, Belgium, Holland, Czechoslovakia, and other East European countries, always large, naturally increased greatly during the war and blockade, especially since the Nazis concentrated as much production as possible in Czechoslovakia and France because of our air raids on Germany. The demand that all goods delivered to Germany during the war should be now returned to the country of origin, even if paid for, therefore opens up limitless demands on the economy of Bizonia.

A country like Czechoslovakia, which probably received more equipment from Germany than it sold to Germany, is in a particularly happy situation under the United States interpretation of restitutions, although it must be noted that in the case of Czechoslovakia the United States does not accept claims for the restitution of property sold to the Germans prior to the Allied London declaration of January 5, 1943, which warned Germany that we would set aside all forcible transfers of property in occupied countries. Nevertheless, Czechoslovakia, whose country was not bombed and never became a battlefield, and whose manufacturers made profits working for Germany during the war, is in far better position today in claiming "restitutions" than the Poles who suffered so much more under the German occupation and whose country never became a Nazi arsenal. The destruction of Warsaw caused the Poles to lose many of the records necessary to claim restitutions of the machinery taken from them by the Germans without compensation, whereas the Czechs and the French find little difficulty in specifying, finding, and claiming the machines they sold to Germany.

Perhaps it makes little difference in the end since Poland and Czechoslovakia are both under Stalin's domination, but I found myself sympathizing with the Polish officer who represented his country at the United States Restitutions Office in Karlsruhe, when he told me how great a handicap it was to the Poles not to be allowed to visit German factories, unless authorized to do so by the United States authorities, and unless they could give a description of the Polish machinery they expected to find and the date on which the Germans had taken it. Clearly Poland was at a great disadvantage as compared with Czechoslovakia and France which had collaborated with the Germans and knew to whom they had sold their manufactures, or as compared with Germany's former allies, Italy, Hungary, and Rumania, whose representatives in the United States zone also found it easy to claim restitutions.

The British, said my Polish informant, were far more co-operative than the Americans in enabling Poland to receive the machinery looted by the Germans. In the British zone the Poles could inspect all German factories at will, and had received hundreds of loaded railway cars of restitutions.

If the Poles were dissatisfied at the small number of restitutions they had been able to obtain in the United States zone, the sum total of which the Soviet satellite countries was getting was not inconsiderable.

When I arrived in Karlsruhe, where the Restitutions branch of the United States Military Government is located, I first ran into a group of Yugoslav officers whom at first sight I took to be Russians, on account of the similarity of their uniforms and gold and scarlet epaulettes. Then I met Poles, Czechs, Hungarians, Italians, and Rumanians and learnt that almost every nation in Europe (including Germany's former allies) is busy claiming something or other from Germany at our expense.

No accounts are kept concerning such "restitutions" to show the effect on the German economy. The head of the United States Restitutions Office, a German born American citizen, who has changed his name from *von*, to *de*, Kaiserlinck, told me that he "had not the least idea nor any interest in the quantity and volume of machinery" taken out of Germany in the form of restitutions. The only figures he could give me were the over-all values of restitution deliveries which amounted to 287,000,000 Reichsmarks of 1938 value.

I told Herr von, or Monsieur de, Kaiserlinck that, although my main interest was the economic effect of restitutions, I was also interested in ascertaining the legal justification for the wide interpretation given the term by his office, since in the future we might, like the Germans, be arraigned as "war criminals" for our failure to observe the Hague rules of land warfare concerning enemy property. His indignation at my statement was, at first, unbounded. But after a while he started telling me that if I would visit the Poles, the French, and other Allied representatives in Karlsruhe, I would revise my estimate of the attitude of the United States Restitutions Office. After talking to the Poles I understood what he meant. Nevertheless I continued to have my doubts about the legality of the orders issued by the United States Restitutions Office.

Just how broad the distinction of "restitutions" can he made is illustrated by a French demand in the summer of 1948 that certain purebred horses in Germany should be returned to France. None of the horses was more than three or four years old, and could not therefore have been stolen during the Nazi occupation. The French, however, contended that the horses in question had been sired by French stallions. It was assumed that a good and patriotic French horse could only have acted "under duress" when confronted by a German mare.

Other and less humorous examples of what restitutions can be held to cover are the following:

A tailor called Hans Schweighofer of Regen, having been bombed out, bought an old second-hand sewing machine of Czech make and got it repaired. He was ordered to "restitute" it to Czechoslovakia, and thus deprived of the possibility of earning his living and supporting his five children.

Frau Leni Kraus, whose husband was killed in action, lost all her property in Berlin by bombing. She bought some second-hand furniture at Mülhausen in Alsace and took it with her when she was evacuated to Bavaria. Now the French are claiming the bed she shares with her son as restitution.

The list of such cases could be continued indefinitely.

The French have given the term restitutions so wide a meaning that they have confiscated automobiles of French make bought by the Germans *before* the war.

The Americans are now confiscating the automobiles they sold to the Germans in the first years of the occupation from confiscated Wehrmacht supplies. Several thousands of automobiles paid for by the Germans are now being taken from them without compensation in the combined British and American zones, and "restituted" to the French and others who originally sold them to the Germans. American and British military governments, having first derived a profit from selling confiscated *Wehrmacht* property to the Germans, are now annulling the contract, and restoring it to the original seller at no cost to the Military Government.

The British with the respect for law which they display whenever it does not conflict with their vital interests, originally refused to accept restitution claims unless duress could be proved. Only such items were restituted from the British zone which had been illegally acquired from occupied territories. Since September 1948, however, the British have adopted the "more comprehensive" American interpretation of restitutions, and have been declaring property brought to Germany by legal business transactions as liable to be returned to the countries from which it was bought.

A confidential instruction issued by the British Foreign Office on August 18th, 1948, Reference No. 45 Basic (Saving), a copy of which was obtained by the Germans, reads as follows:

I also believe it to be in the economic and security interests of Europe that some of Germany's surplus industrial equipment should be removed and put to productive use elsewhere, *and a liberal restitution policy would be consonant with this aim* (italics added).

There is little doubt that the change in British practice last fall was due to the expected halt in the dismantlement of German factories to be shipped abroad as reparations. When I left Germany, restitutions from both the British and United States zones were already threatening to supplant reparations as the means to reduce Germany's industrial capacity and increase her need of American ECA aid.

On February 28, 1949, Dr. Kutscher, of the German Economic Administration for Bizonia, wrote to me that since I left Germany "the situation in the field of restitutions, especially in the British zone, has gone from bad to worse." According to the information he sent me, the productive assets being withdrawn from Western Germany under the heading of restitutions now almost equal reparations, and in the United States zone they are even greater.

According to the official statistics of the United States Military Government the value of restitutions from the United States zone, up to September 1948, amounted to 287,075,915 marks, as against a figure of 235,000,000 marks given as the residual value of the plants dismantled on reparation account.

In Hamburg, in the British zone, the Allied Missions compute restitutions already delivered as totalling 36,000,000 marks, as against the 32,000,000 marks residual value of the plants dismantled on the reparation account.

My German informant also wrote concerning the fresh blow delivered to the German economy by the decision to hand over to the Netherlands as restitutions five of the few surviving modernly equipped trawlers of the German fishing fleet, thereby reducing Germany's present small catch by 30 per cent. This is being done at a time when the United States is considering appropriating ECA funds for the purpose of enlarging the German fishing fleet, in order to reduce Germany's dependence on American food imports.

The Netherlands are also claiming restitution of nineteen tankers, the withdrawal of which from Germany will mean that Bizonia's crude oil supply will require the gift of American tankers. The fact that Holland is using her resources to impose the same kind of servitude on the Indonesians as the Dutch suffered under the Nazis, makes such restitutions at America's expense seem not only absurd but an outrage.

Restitutions are also now affecting the supply of essential machinery to the Ruhr mines. A number of coal mines are threatened with the necessity to close down or curtail operations, because the new equipment they need will not be delivered on account of restitutions.

According to a compilation made at the instigation of the AngloAmerican Bipartite Steel Production Office, restitution claims affecting the iron and steel industry amount to a total of more than 40,000,000 marks (1938 value). Losses through the disruption of production entailed by the removal of bottleneck machinery as restitutions, are calculated to amount to a far larger sum.

The Germans, having earlier been led to believe that the Marshall Plan meant an end to the wrecking of their economy, are becoming thoroughly disillusioned, now that restitutions are held to cover machinery legally acquired and fully paid for, and are taking the place of reparations as the means to deprive them of any possibility of earning a living.

They can see no end to the various methods adopted by their conquerors to reduce them to a pauper status. They can no longer place any trust even in the 1947 Revised Level of Industry Plan, which, harsh and unrealistic as it was, at least promised to allow them to retain the industrial capacity to produce to the limit in certain purely peacetime industries. The factories already dismantled, or now being dismantled, include many which are outside the categories scheduled to be delivered as reparations according to the Revised Level of Industry Plan.

Factories making soap, toys, furniture, pots and pans, fine optical instruments, agricultural machinery, hospital equipment, and a multitude of other peacetime needs and exports have been dismantled not only in the British and French zones, but also in the American. There were bad enough examples in the United States zone, but there seemed no limit to the injustice caused by the British desire to eliminate competition, or to the hypocritical excuses made by the British to obtain German assets for the purpose of decreasing their own dollar deficit.

There was, for instance, the case of the Diana Toy Factory in the French zone, making air guns, which the British had induced the French to classify as an "armaments factory" in order that they might obtain its equipment.

On the way out of Germany in December 1948 I happened to share a compartment on the train to Ostende with a British toy manufacturer on his way home from Nuremberg. He showed me samples of toy motor cars with three gears, and other examples of German inventiveness and ingenuity, saying that no other toy manufacturers could compete with the Germans. Then he told me how, immediately following the war's end, he and other British manufacturers had been told by the Board of Trade that they would be furnished suitable army or navy uniforms to go to Germany and pick out as "reparations officials" any machinery they wanted or thought they could make use of. He himself was friendly to the Germans and had no desire to deprive them of their livelihood, so he had not accepted the offer. In any case, he said, it paid him better to buy German toys than to make them in England. Because British workers were less efficient and refused to work as hard as the Germans it was cheaper to import German toys than to take German machinery to compete against them.

The outstanding example of the failure of the Western Powers to allow the Germans to retain even those industries which are not supposed to be on the dismantlement list, is the watch and clock industry. Centered in the Black Forest and consisting mainly of very small enterprises, this is one of the oldest of German industries and in no way related to armaments production. But the French at the beginning of the occupation started to destroy it and remove its equipment to France. The British were equally interested in stopping the Germans from making watches and clocks, and thanks to the efforts made by some liberal Englishmen, who have endeavored to stop dismantlement, the following excerpt from the trade journal, *British Jeweler and Metal Worker* received wide publicity in 1948.

Lengthy negotiations and discussions have been conducted by Mr. Barrett (Chairman of the Export Group) over the past three years with a view to fixing the future level of the German horological industry below the 72 per cent of the 1938 level which had been agreed by the Allied Control Commission. *It is pleasing to be able to record that the final result has been to reach agreement that the German industry is to be reduced to 50 per cent of the 1938 level.* This result is what we wanted to achieve; and although there can be no doubt that the Germans will ultimately redevelop their horological industry on a strong basis the present position means that the British industry has been given a certain amount of breathing space in order to become organized on a sound basis. The thanks of the Association have already been conveyed to Mr. Barrett for his patient and untiring work in achieving this result. Following upon this, the contents of a number of German factories are to be thrown up for reparations, and Mr.

W. W. Cope has recently made an inspection of these factories, as also of certain other machines which are available to this country.

The scandal occasioned in England by this exposure of the commercial motive which inspires dismantlement led to the appointment by the Foreign Office of a commission, headed by the former Soviet-friendly Labour M.P. Crossman, to investigate what was happening to the

German watch and clock industry. In Frankfurt I happened to meet the wife of an old English friend of mine, H. N. Brailsford, who is among the small number of liberals who have always fought for justice. Mrs. Brailsford had accompanied Crossman on his tour of the French zone, and had been horrified at what she had seen. She was full of sympathy for the German workers deprived of their livelihood by dismantlement, but, she said to me, "After all, America is to blame for it."

I couldn't quite get my bearings. America's sins might be great and her stupidities even greater, but I could not see how the United States could be held responsible for France's and England's destruction of the German watch and clock industry. Mrs. Brailsford enlightened me: "Don't you see," she said, "it's all due to America's failure to give enough dollars to Britain and France. They have to do these mean things in order to get enough dollars."

Although Mrs. Brailsford's remarks must strike any American as not only ungrateful but absurd, they revealed the basic problem which no Marshall Plan can resolve. Whether or not one believes that it was commercial competition which was the root cause of both world wars, the fact remains that Germany and Britain are the two European countries which must "Export or Die." True as this was before America's wartime President agreed to let Russia have most of Eastern Europe and its agricultural resources, it is even truer today. It would now seem that America has only the choice between subsidizing a Western Germany deprived of the possibility of sustaining itself because of British and French destruction of her assets, or of continuing to supply dollars to Britain under an everlasting European Reconstruction Program.

According to a report from the Ruhr, published in the *New York Herald Tribune* on February 27, 1949, Britons here do not deny that the West Germans with increased population and greatly decreased resources will have good arguments for raising production even beyond that of prewar. But they foresee that the production drive designed to end the billion-dollar-a-year subsidy being poured into Germany, mainly by the United States, will probably bring a bitter struggle for world markets.

Is America to side with the defeated enemy country which has become her ward, or with her British ally? The British, of course, have no doubts as to what American policy should be. "The British view as explained by a high official in Düsseldorf," continued Miss Marguerite Higgins' dispatch in the *Herald Tribune*, is as follows:

It is true that the slogan "Export or Die" holds good for both Britain and Germany. But from our point of view, if anybody has to die in the ensuing struggle for world markets, it is going to be the Germans. We feel entitled to demand the fruits of victory. Britain will demand sufficient priority on world markets to insure the success of its own great battle to become self-sustaining.

Miss Higgins further reports that the British view is that German production must be allowed to expand, but not to a point where it would interfere with efforts of Britain and France to sell enough abroad to pay for imports on which they must live.

I am not presuming to pronounce judgment, but it seems high time that Americans understood that, having twice intervened in Europe's "interminable wars" to prevent a settlement by the verdict of arms without benefit of American aid of the conflict between Germany and England for industrial and political supremacy, the United States cannot now refuse to arbitrate, unless all Europe is to succumb to Soviet Russia by reason of its internal conflicts.

The British, having lost a large part of their colonial Empire and foreign investments, are now in a situation comparable to that of the Germans between the two World Wars; but the Germans, by reason of their defeat and lost territories, are in a far worse situation. The old commercial rivalry between England and Germany, therefore leads inevitably to cutthroat competition, in which Britain's advantage as a victor is counterbalanced by Germany's greater capacity for hard work, and America's interest in preventing her remaining an economic dead weight around the American taxpayer's neck.

On the other hand, the bitter competition for markets among the nations of Europe seems an absurdity today since the whole world is short of the manufactures they can supply. Moreover, Germany and England, however difficult it is for them to be reconciled, have an equal interest in preventing further encroachments on European territory by Soviet Russia. Some way must be found to stop the internecine struggle, if Western European and American civilization are to be saved. The issue and the desperate need for a solution are only obscured by the passionate appeal to hatred and the desire for vengeance on the Germans as an aggressor nation.

When I returned to Berlin at the end of November, I endeavored to ascertain not only the cause of our self-defeating reparations policy, but also how it was that the Military Government's official statements on dismantlement failed to correspond to the facts as I had seen them.

After interviewing various Military Government officials, it seemed to me that the explanation of both phenomena was partly political and partly ignorance. The camouflaged influence of Morgenthau's remaining disciples, some of whom are still ensconced in the economic and financial divisions of the United States Military Government, had, it seemed to me, given the highest authorities an incomplete, if not actually false, account of the dismantlement operation.

Either because of their preoccupation with the Cold War in Berlin and consequent reliance on civilian subordinates for economic information, or because of sentiment at home and Washington's directives, or because of the reluctance of the British and French to back up the United States against the Soviet Union, I found that the highest United States Military Government authorities in Berlin refused to consider dismantlement as a matter of urgent importance.

General Hays, who is General Clay's deputy, and is far from being an apostle of vengeance, was clearly misinformed on the question of the cost and effect of dismantlement. He quoted a figure of only sixty or eighty million dollars as the value of the equipment of the 215 German factories in the American Zone on the dismantlement list. This he considered negligible in comparison with the need to reach an agreement with the French on the Ruhr and the formation of a West German state.

Besides having accepted the fictitiously low value placed on the machinery delivered as reparations, General Hays, like so many other Americans, thinking in American terms of large natural resources and industrial capacity, considered German losses through dismantlement as easily remediable by ECA aid. In the summer, when I had interviewed General Clay, I had found him similarly inclined to dismiss German complaints and to consider Germany's loss through dismantlement as insignificant and easily remediable.

The assumption that a few more million dollars of ECA aid can make good the loss ignores the social and political effects of dismantlement. As Carlo Schmidt, the Social-Democratic leader from the French zone, said to me in Bonn:

"Men are losing hope and the spirit of enterprise. Denied the right to work and be independent by Western occupation policies, they are beginning to view foreigners in the light of who can give them something. You are destroying morality and self-respect and pauperizing us by your dismantlement and other economic policies. Those who only hope for charity will never be able to resist Communism."

I understood the obstacles to clear judgment better after I heard the views expressed to me by Mr. Wilkinson, General Clay's chief economic adviser.

Mr. Wilkinson, who had served in Germany since the beginning of the occupation and was appointed while Mr. Morgenthau and his friends ran the Treasury Department, told me that he "couldn't care less" about what the Germans felt about dismantlement. He had, he said, very vivid memories of what the Germans had done in occupied countries when they were the conquerors. He "neither liked nor trusted any Germans."

Having thus proclaimed his readiness to indict the whole German nation, Mr. Wilkinson proceeded to tell me that the Germans, in his view, "did not deserve any consideration" from their conquerors. He was, however, intelligent enough to realize that Europe could not recover unless the Germans were allowed and encouraged to work. "Just as you can't get a horse to work unless you give it enough to eat," he said to me in his

Berlin office, "so also the German people must be made contented enough to labor."

The inverted Nazi sentiments expressed to me by General Clay's chief economic adviser went far to explain the otherwise incomprehensible policies I had seen being implemented in the United States zone. Racial antipathies, or the blind desire for retribution on a defeated people, preclude wise statesmanship. By playing upon such feelings the Communists are able to induce us to follow policies detrimental to our own interests. I was therefore not greatly surprised when Mr. Wilkinson handed me a copy of the latest issue of the journal of the "Society for the Prevention of World War III," with the suggestion that I read the article it contained on dismantlement and reparations. He was, I presume, completely unaware of the manner in which this notorious organization's propaganda of hatred and vengeance helps the Communists.

After talking to Mr. Wilkinson in Berlin I have been better able to comprehend why dismantled equipment from the United States zone is still being shipped to the Communist countries of Eastern Europe. One example is that of the firm of Martin Beilhack at Rosenheim, from which 115 tons of machinery were shipped to Czechoslovakia and 190 tons to Yugoslavia as late as February 1949. A horizontal forging press of 900 tons pressure capacity is also, I learned in a letter received from Germany, to be handed over to the Czech Communists. The fact that this Beilhack firm is listed in the ERP program to be aided with new machinery for the construction of freight cars shows the cost to America of dismantlement for the benefit of Soviet Russia and her satellites.

Sir Cecil Weir, the British Chief of Reparations whom I interviewed next day, could not be accused of hatred for the Germans like his American counterpart. He is a mild little man who, far from desiring to treat the Germans as work horses, was full of humane and decent sentiments. Unfortunately, he obviously had no idea of what was going on in the Ruhr. He assured me over and over again that no machinery was being removed as reparations which was not surplus to the needs of the German economy. I felt convinced that he believed his assertion that reparations were not being taken from factories serving the essential needs of Germany's peacetime economy and that "never had a victor treated a vanquished nation so well" as the Western Powers were treating the Germans. It was no use telling him that he was misinformed. He simply would not believe that I had seen machinery being dismantled which was anything but surplus, and that much of it was being thrown on the scrap heap.

Mr. Wilkinson had appalled me by his cold-blooded hatred of the German people. Sir Cecil Weir made me wonder whether the ignorance of highly placed members of the Military Government was not even more destructive of the democratic cause in Europe than the race hatred of Morgenthau's disciples. Since leaving Germany I have wondered if he knew that his subordinates were shipping the Borbeck Krupps Armaments Works to the Soviet Union. The London *Times* reported this on December 20, 1948, but it is possible that Sr. Cecil Weir does not know it.

My interview with Mr. McJunkins, chief of the reparations division of the United States Military Government and a subordinate of Mr. Wilkinson, was far less revealing. According to McJunkins, the United States Military Government had no choice but to deliver the reparations promised to Czechoslovakia, Yugoslavia, and other Communist countries. He was the model civil servant carrying out his orders without prejudice or favor. I was unable to judge how far he himself was responsible for the orders to dismantle and ship from the American zone the machinery which would otherwise have been able to contribute to both German and European recovery. He never once displayed his personal antipathies as Mr. Wilkinson had done. Yet he is held mainly responsible for the sabotage of the ECA program by local United States authorities in the American zone.

One thing I learned in Berlin in November gave cause for hope of a future intelligent United States policy. The United States Military Government had begun to take the line that the Revised Level of Industry Plan was not intended to tie the German economy down permanently to the low levels prescribed, but was merely an estimate of how much machinery could be removed as reparations. In practice, in the United States zone, no obstacles have been placed in the way of German installation of new machines to replace the dismantled ones, when the factory owners are able to do so. The British and French have, however, not accepted this view, nor, in fact, does it seem that this was the original American attitude. It is rather that the United States authorities, without admitting that the Level of Industry Plan was a mistake from the beginning, have adapted themselves to the changed international situation. They have not stopped dismantlement and reparations shipments, to which they consider themselves committed by earlier agreements, but they see the necessity for letting the Germans produce all they can if Europe is to resist the Communist threat and America be relieved of permanent annual contributions of billions of dollars to Europe.

In regard to steel, however, the 10.7 million tons of steel capacity envisaged in the plan is still accepted by the United States as a permanent ceiling in spite of the tremendous need for steel in Europe and the strain on the United States economy of supplying even a part of the present European deficit. According to the Herter Committee's report, fulfilling the most urgent requirements of the sixteen nations receiving ECA assistance will increase the steel deficit in America from 1.6 to 5 million tons.

The whole futility, stupidity, and expense of the dismantlement program is best illustrated by the long-term report of the Bizonal representatives to the Organization for European Economic Cooperation (OEEC) in October 1948. This report recommends a 10 per cent *increase* over the 1936 level in Germany's productive capacity, to be realized by 1952 through Marshall Plan assistance. Washington ECA authorities consider that, if Western Germany is to be able to support itself, an even greater increase is required— 15 or 20 per cent instead of 10 per cent.

Thus, while busy *reducing* Western Germany's capacity to threequarters of the 1936 figure by dismantlement, the United States is planning to *increase* it by 10 or 15 per cent out of funds supplied by the American taxpayer.

Dismantlement today no longer even pretends to remove only surplus equipment. The 1947 Revised Level of Industry Plan has become an absurdity now that we plan to replace the machinery being torn out of German factories. As the ECA representative in Germany has said: "We find in Western Germany today the paradox of outside aid for recovery, and on the other hand, restrictions as to the extent to which such recovery is permitted. The current dismantlement program is one under which a percentage of industries will be removed or scrapped."

There is no validity left in the State Department argument that shortage of labor and materials precludes the use of Germany's existing productive capacity, and that reparations removals are therefore economically as well as morally justified. For the OEEC rates Germany as a country where there will be unemployment in the future even if the Marshall recovery plan, as now drawn, is carried out. As regards shortages of raw materials, it is surely one of the main objectives of ECA to enable the countries of Europe to obtain the raw materials necessary to make them self-supporting instead of living on an American dole.

Digging holes in the ground and paying the unemployed to fill them up again in the United States in depression years was an economic operation as compared with present United States policy.

The cost of vengeance is even higher than the cost of economic crisis and unemployment. The State Department may, or may not be justified in its insistence as late as February 2, 1948, that: "The obligation of the aggressor to pay the maximum reparations compatible with economic political realities is incontestable." The important point is that the economic and political realities of the world situation require an end to reparations and the reconstruction of Germany as an integral part of a self-supporting Europe, able to resist Communist propaganda and Soviet aggression without making impossible demands on American resources.

In the present world situation our endeavor should not be to make restrictive plans on the basis of incomplete information, but to encourage the highest possible amount of production. Only by reviving the profit motive and encouraging initiative, self-help, and hard work can Germany and Europe be rendered self-supporting and cease to be a millstone around the neck of the American people.

In 1949-50 the American taxpayer contributed close to a billion dollars to Germany ($987,000,000), consisting of $573.400.000 of Army appropriations for the "prevention of disease and unrest," and $414.000,000 under the European Reconstruction Program which consisted mainly of raw material supplies. The total for 1949-50 is estimated at $881,600,000, but the ECA authorities consider that the capital investment figure included is too small to contribute appreciably to the recovery essential to make Germany self-supporting.

The strain on the American economy resulting from the European Recovery Program as a whole could be appreciably diminished if dismantlement were stopped, the Revised Level of Industry Plan scrapped, and Germany permitted to supply the countries of Western Europe with the steel, machinery, and other industrial products which America now has to give to them.

To quote Mr. Collisson once again:

I have stated my firm conviction that recovery in Western Europe is not possible without the important contribution which Western Germany can and must make. Every foreign trade delegation coming to Western Germany has pleaded for more goods of the kind Germany once supplied, in fact in amounts far beyond Germany's present ability to produce. To satisfy these requirements for a peaceful rehabilitation of Europe, recovery in Western Germany must be brought about. It is in this light that we have made our recommendations; not a pattern of what is good for Germany alone, but of what is best for Europe as a whole.

There is little doubt that if the American public were made aware of the facts of the situation, the postwar policy, described by the London *Economist* as one of "keeping Germany in chains and Europe in rags," would be completely abandoned, instead of modified as at present by American subsidies.

Unfortunately most Americans are unaware of the degree to which the ECA and the State Department have deferred to Britain's desire to eliminate German competition and the blind fears of France. When on April 13, 1949, the State Department announced the final intergovernmental agreement on dismantlement, reached with Britain and

France, the American press as a whole failed to point out that destruction at our expense is to be continued.

The Humphrey Committee, whose report was made public at the same time, had considered 381 of the original 900-odd factories on the 1947 dismantlement list, and had recommended the retention of only 148 in whole and of another 19 in part. And the State Department gave way to France and Britain concerning the most important plants recommended for retention in Germany by the ECA; for example, the August Thyssen and the Bochum iron and steel works and the Oppau fertilizer plant (see Chapter 10). The ECA Committee had proposed retaining only 21 of the 84 steel plants it surveyed, and allowing 47 to be removed, with another 16 to be partially allocated as reparations. The State Department went further and agreed to sacrifice the five largest and most efficient of the steel plants recommended for retention by the ECA. In spite of the grave shortage of power in Germany which now prevents further recovery the State Department agreed that two power plants are to be torn down. Similarly in regard to the chemical industry: 43 plants are "released" for reparations and only 32 retained out of a total of 75 surveyed. Thus the final agreement on dismantlement has only slightly modified the original program, and therefore not substantially altered the picture given in this chapter.

4

TRAGEDY IN SIEGERLAND

BILLION-DOLLAR CALCULATIONS AND OVER-ALL STATISTICS ARE LESS easy for the human mind to grasp than individual tragedies. My visit to Siegerland in the southeast corner of the British zone enabled me to appraise in human terms the effect of the blueprint for dismantlement drawn up in Berlin without regard for the social and political consequences, or the ruin it brings to innocent people.

Siegerland takes its name from a river which flows into the Rhine below Bonn, winding first through a beautiful valley at the edge of the Westerwald—the western forest which extends southward into Hesse in the United States zone.

The town of Siegen, which like Rome is built on seven hills, is seven hundred years old and the center of an ancient industry based on the iron ores of the surrounding hills. These ore deposits, although not abundant according to modern standards, are of good quality and have been mined since the fourth century B.C. A century ago, before Prussia had forged the modern German state, the ironmasters of Siegen had begun to develop a modern, highly specialized industry. Even today nearly all of the Siegen factories are small and individually owned, and have always depended on skill, enterprise, and hard work, not on large capital assets or government favors, for their existence.

The Siegen workers, who usually spend their whole lives in one factory, and apprentice their sons there, feel themselves part of the enterprise in which they work. Many of the factory owners started as workers and class divisions are almost nonexistent. Some of the workers own small tracts of poor land cleared on the forest hillsides, or garden plots, and graze a cow on the common land.

Some come to work in Siegen from little villages ten or twenty miles away in the forest, depending on industry for a part, but not all, of their income.

Neither Nazis nor Communists had ever been able to make headway in the town and villages of Siegerland where almost everyone has a stake in free private enterprise, and almost all the people are devout Protestants.

Here in a word was the Germany of pre-Hitler and pre-Prussian days. The peaceful Germany which gave America some of her best citizens: a deeply religious, industrious, and hardworking people among whom skillful farmers, artisans, and engineers predominate. Yet, Siegerland had been marked out for destruction. Twenty-eight factories had been or were to be dismantled, and a third of the working population deprived of its main income. The Russians could hardly have done a better job in destroying private property, free enterprise and the free institutions built upon it, and in preparing the way for Communism, than the British were doing in Siegerland.

Driving to Siegen from Frankfurt for the first time, on a lovely September morning, I first crossed the Taunus Range which once formed the limits of the Roman Empire. I stopped at Saalburg to see the Roman fort there, which had been one of a chain of fortified posts stretching between the Rhine and the Danube. The Saalburg fort was restored by Kaiser Wilhelm, and was never bombed, so it looks much the same as it did nearly two thousand years ago when Roman legions guarded the gates of the Empire from the Teutonic tribes to the north.

There is a museum at Saalburg stocked with spears, swords and armor, pottery, old shoes, and other relics of the days before the Franks, who were to give their name to the future kingdom of France, burst the barriers of the Empire and entered Gaul. The Romans are long since forgotten, but the wars between Teutons and Latins seem to go on forever, although the people of South Germany and Northern France are of similar mixed ancestry.

From Saalburg the road winds downward and passes through picturesque Old World cities and villages before entering the green Westerwald. As we drew near to Siegen the glorious woods of pine, fir, and beech were broken by small villages close to ancient iron works, and green meadows where the cattle owned by the peasants grazed on the common land as in centuries past.

As in Roman times, as in the Middle Ages, as in the terrible days when the Thirty Years' War between Protestants and Catholics drenched these lands in blood, and as in early modern times when Siegen formed part of the domain of the Princes of Orange, the people are part farmers, part miners, ironworkers and leatherworkers. There has also always been hunting in the forest but the soil is too poor for the little farms to support the people. Today they produce only enough food to feed Siegerland forty days in the year. Part of the living of the population always had to be gained in the forges of Siegen and its surrounding villages.

Before the war, in spite of its belching factory chimneys, Siegen still had a medieval appearance with narrow streets of Hans Christian Andersen houses, a fine old Rathaus and the strong walled castle of the Princes of Orange-Nassau dominating the town.

Two bombing attacks completely destroyed more than half of the town altogether, and partially destroyed another quarter of it. The old Evangelical Church of St. Nicholas was reduced to a shell, and many other beautiful buildings wiped out. But war could not impair the beauty of the wooded hills and meadows which surround the Siegen Valley.

Many factories had been bombed and many people killed and maimed in the air raids, while others had died in the fierce fighting which occurred before the Nazis blew up the bridges and died or retreated northward. Those who survived had started to work again, expecting they could at long last live in peace in the fruits of their labor, however hard the task of reconstruction. But in the fall of 1948, they had to fear something worse even than bombing: the ruin of their land by the conquerors who were busy removing the machinery without which they could no longer earn their bread. One of the oldest industrial centers in Europe was being destroyed by dismantlement.

Although never a center of war industries, nor a Nazi stronghold, Siegerland had been marked down for relatively heavier losses of productive capacity than any other area I visited, or heard of, in Germany. It only covered 43 square miles and had some 35,000 inhabitants, but was losing 25 factories. Several neighboring villages were also having their factories dismantled, bringing the total figure to 28. Originally there had been 29 on the list, but one, belonging to a Catholic, a rarity in Siegen, had been saved by the intervention of a Catholic Cardinal.

The ruin of one enterprise affected many others dependent on it for supplies or as customers. At least a quarter of the population was losing its income, and even before dismantlement there were already fifteen hundred unemployed.

Siegen not only had its own population to take care of, including sixteen hundred disabled people, and widows and orphans of the fallen and of those still held in Russia as prisoners of war. It also had a large number of expellees from the East of Germany to house and feed. A large transient camp had been established in its damaged barracks, through which nearly a quarter of a million of these destitute victims of racial persecution had already passed, and kept on coming. Three thousand German refugees were permanently quartered on the town and had to be provided with food, clothing, and furniture, as well as precious space in the bombed houses and cellars where most of the population lived.

It was in Siegen that I learned that in Germany as a whole only one of every four or five children has a bed of its own, and that five million children are orphans, half of whom come from the lost Eastern territories.

Siegen's hinterland, from which it had formerly derived food, was now in the French zone where all agricultural produce which could be wrung out of the peasants is taken for French consumption. So in 1946 the Siegen population had starved and even in 1947 it had had to exist on less than 1,000 calories a day. Tuberculosis had increased alarmingly.

Children of fourteen and fifteen who were already working looked no more than ten or eleven years old, so stunted was their growth.

The local British reparations officer hated his job and told me he felt like a criminal, especially because Siegen reminded him of his own North Country England. "A miniature Sheffield," he called it. He told me that all his life until now he had been engaged in constructing, having been apprenticed in a Lancashire engineering works at the age of twelve and having worked his way up to an executive position. "I just can't feel it's right to destroy machinery." he said, "but if I didn't keep this job someone else would take it; and at least I try to carry out the dismantlement program with as little damage as possible."

As against this kind and decent Englishman I was told about the local *Gauleiter*, the British military governor of the area who had left-wing sympathies and had carried through many highhanded acts, and took a malicious joy in ruining the Germans under a "socialist" cover. His personal reputation was also unsavory, for he had sent a man to prison on a false charge to clear the way for his seduction of a German woman. The victim, whose name was Zezulak, spoke good English and acted as interpreter for the Germans. He had a wife and child whom he was obviously devoted to, and he had had no interest in the woman the governor coveted, but had protected her from the English major's rude advances. This all sounds like a grade C movie, but such things do happen, and the truth of the story was attested to by the doctor who had subsequently performed an abortion for the lady at the British major's expense.

The factories being dismantled in Siegen were producing mining and railway equipment, pipes and flanges, welding torches and cutting machinery, rolling-mill equipment, food-processing machinery, steel containers for the transport of gas, fittings for the automobile industry, kitchen utensils, garbage containers, and other necessary articles for a peacetime economy. The one really big plant dismantled was the Waldrich Iron and Steel Works, shipped to Czechoslovakia. One smaller plant which had manufactured munitions, the Inko Works which had made flame throwers, and whose owner was a Nazi, was not to be dismantled and was producing typewriters.

Many Siegen factories had already lost their most valuable machinery through the "multilateral deliveries" demanded by the British for their own use. In other factories also the most necessary machinery was now being removed even when they were not "on the list" for total destruction.

There was, for instance, the case of Herr Steinmetz, whom I found up a tree picking apples in the garden behind his small factory on a Saturday afternoon. In addition to losing half his sheet scrubbing and shearing machines, his crane was to be removed the following Monday. He had offered to supply a new crane instead of the old one, so that his factory would not be put out of commission for months by his inability to get a motor to work the new one he had managed to buy. The offer had been refused although the old crane would have to be cut in two to get it down. The old crane must be delivered to the scrap heap although Herr Steinmetz had a hundred thousand dollars worth of orders to fulfill. Unable now to fill his orders from Holland and Belgium for sheet-metal-working machinery, such foreign exchange would be lost to the German economy and American taxpayers.

The decisions of the British authorities in Düsseldorf were quite incalculable. In another case they accepted a new crane instead of the old one scheduled for dismantlement, but decreed that the new one should at once be converted into scrap!

Most of the machinery I saw being dismantled in Siegen would never be set up and utilized in other countries. Having been built for a special purpose, and much of it being too old to be used by any other workers than the skilled men of Siegen who had worked on it for decades, it was of no use to anyone else. Yet many machines could not be replaced because they were made only in the Russian zone.

In every one of the nine Siegen factories I personally visited, the representatives of the countries entitled to reparations had expressed no interest in acquiring the dismantled machines. It was all taken away to rust at the depot. The same was true of most of the others scheduled for dismantlement. The British were taking away the livelihood of thousands of people for no rhyme or reason — except vengeance, or, in some cases, for the advantage of Germany's British competitors in European markets.

Saddest of all was my sight of Herr Fuchs, an old man of sixtyeight who had lost his only son in the war, who had never taken a holiday in his life, and whose whole being was wrapped up in his factory which had produced nothing but stowing pipes for the Ruhr mines—the pipes of highly resistant steel which are used to blow rubble by air pressure into the empty spaces left after the coal has been mined, to prevent collapse of the walls.

Every bit of machinery had already been taken out of Herr Fuchs' plant and his life's work wrecked. And to what purpose, I thought, as we stood in the empty building, and he told me, with tears in his eyes, that after his son had fallen in the war, and his factory had been bombed and left with only walls standing, he and his faithful workers had just managed to rebuild it and repair the machines, when the British ordered it to be dismantled.

Although the Bizonal coal commission had placed Herr Fuchs' factory on the list of essential factories, and although no foreign country wanted his machinery and it was now rotting away at the storage depot, he had been ruined and his 130 workers and their families deprived of their livelihood. I was close to tears myself as I said good-bye to poor old Herr Fuchs as the sun went down behind the mountains in sad Siegerland.

Herr Fuchs was too old to start again.

Others, like Herr Hensch, whose factory I visited the same day, made me think that all the cruelty and stupidity of Allied occupation policies could not permanently down the German people. However hard we tried to turn them into paupers, they would insist on trying to go on working.

Faced with utter ruin, for the British had already torn down his furnaces and dismantled almost all his machines, Fritz Hensch was going somehow or other to start over again. His factory, the Siegerthaler Works in the village of Eisenfeld, made vacuum equipment (giant pressure cookers) for the food industry, and flanges for large pipes. He had been allowed to keep a few machines for a few weeks longer to complete an order for the Iraq Petroleum Company because no British factory could supply the large diameter flanges required. But as soon as this order was fulfilled dismantlement was to be completed. His ten cranes and all his buttwelding machinery, specially built for his factory and useless to anyone else, was to be put on the scrap heap.

Hensch had started life as an apprentice without a cent, since he was one of ten children of a tailor. Through the years he had built up his own factory, adding machine after machine through his own efforts, each built to his specifications for a special purpose. Production was so efficiently arranged that each worker could help himself by means of the many small cranes built into the roof.

Here was a man who loved his machines, knew every detail of every process in his factory, and had a craftman's pride in his products. Middle-aged, thin and wiry, with keen intelligent eyes, Hensch was a living embodiment of the spirit of free enterprise which will not be killed however hard we try to extinguish it in Germany.

The 300 tons of machinery being dismantled was valued at half a million marks in 1938 and would cost one and a half million D marks to replace today, but the British had put it down on the reparations list as worth only 160,000. Hensch had no money to replace the machinery scheduled for destruction, but he was building a new furnace out of the bricks torn out of the dismantled one and left lying around; and he had managed to borrow one new ringbending machine from a friend in another town. He was starting again. He was the living embodiment of the German people who, knocked out and kicked while down, refusing to die, stagger to their feet and start struggling again.

The Bender brothers, whose factory I also visited, were like Tweedledum and Tweedledee, fat and short with faces so alike that I could not tell one from the other. They were old and seemed resigned to the fate which was stripping their factory bare, although, like Herr Fuchs', it manufactured stowing pipes for the Ruhr mines, and 90 per cent of

Bizonia's production of this essential product would be wiped out when the Benders' machinery followed Fuchs' to the scrap heap.

One of the Bender brothers had a son who was as eloquent as his father and uncle were dumb. This young Bender had been a prisoner of war in the States, spoke slangy colloquial American with great fluency and hoped eventually to be able to emigrate to America where he has relatives. He was certain that the Bender factory was being dismantled by mistake, but owing to British competition. The dismantlement list referred to "boilers, tanks and oil pipes" and did not mention stowing pipes. Young Bender suggested that some ignorant British official did not know the difference between one kind of pipe and another, but knew that the British wanted to wipe out German competition in oil pipe lines and had therefore put Benders on the dismantlement list.

It was this young Bender who also first drew my attention to the fact that dismantlement on a big scale had begun following the currency reform of June 1948 which had wiped out all savings. If it had been carried out sooner the factory owners might still have been able to get new machinery, and German competition would still have been dangerous to the British.

Dismantlement, like bombing, or the rain, takes no account of the just and the unjust. The factories to be torn down had evidently been selected by rule of thumb, not by any idea of punishing the guilty any more than of preserving the elements most likely to contribute to the conversion of Germany into a democracy. The case of the Weber family, with whom I stayed in Siegen and whom I came to know well, is an illustration.

While her four sons were away fighting on the Russian front, the widow Weber and her teen-age daughter Margarita, had got into trouble with the Nazi authorities on account of their kindness to the French and Russian prisoners assigned to work in the Weber factory. Frau Weber could not forbear from occasionally giving a good warm meal to the poor wretches who worked in the factory by day and slept in a little house at the bottom of her garden. One of the prisoners was a young Frenchman who used to talk to Margarita from the barred window of his prison as she worked in the evenings in the Weber vegetable patch. René was frail and unaccustomed to hard physical labor, so kind-hearted Frau Weber, seeing him one day staggering under a heavy load, had assigned him to clerical work. Soon he was being invited into the Weber house and started giving French lessons to Margarita. The young couple fell in love. Unfortunately, a Nazi workman in the factory heard of this "fraternization" with the enemy and reported it to the authorities. Frau Weber was severely reprimanded and René was removed to another factory in Siegen where he was so brutally treated that he ran away, and, after being caught, was assigned to a punishment camp in Poland. Here he developed tuberculosis and was sent to a prison hospital in Cologne. On Christmas Eve of 1944 Margarita traveled there with a cake and a few apples which she tried to smuggle in to her lover. She was caught and sent to prison for six months by the Nazis, and a Nazi manager was installed in the Weber factory.

One of Frau Weber's sons, Otto, on leave from the Russian front at the time, tried to commit suicide but survived with the loss of one eye. Later the Weber factory was bombed to the ground. Their house, also bombed, was saved from complete destruction by Russian prisoners who, remembering Frau Weber's kindness, rushed to put out the flames. At the war's end these former prisoners also saved Frau Weber from being robbed by the many other ex-prisoners who now became displaced persons.

The second of Frau Weber's sons, Günther, died of starvation in April 1946, after working for two years as a Russian prisoner in the stone quarries near Kuibyshev. One of his comrades, who later returned to Siegen, told the Webers that Günther, who had been a big man weighing 260 pounds, had been reduced to a living skeleton weighing 48 pounds before he died. A Russian doctor had tried to save his life after he collapsed and was sent to a hospital, but it was too late. Frau Weber had loved Günther best of all her sons. He was, she told me often, the boy with the sweetest disposition, the strongest and most loving. All the rest of her days she would live with the thought of the agonies he had suffered before dying of hunger, and remembering him, she would weep even when the rest of the family was happy.

The youngest Weber boy, Helmuth, is today slowly dying in hospital from the injuries he sustained during and after the war. His kidneys having been injured while a soldier, the disease was rendered incurable by the treatment he received after the war's end. As an American prisoner of war, although ill, he was kept for months sleeping on the cold wet ground without even a tent to cover him. His shrunken kidneys now no longer function to clear the bloodstream of poisonous matter, and the doctors expect he will go mad or blind before he dies.

Erhardt came home after three years at the Russian front as a private, and a year and a half of slave labor. He had first worked in a coal mine at Karaganda in Siberia, 800 miles from the Chinese frontier. After he had been discovered throwing dirt instead of coal into the tubs, he was beaten and threatened with death. This had meant little to him. "Many of us," he said, "had reached the point at which one no longer cares whether one lives or dies."

After it was found that he was a qualified engineer, Erhardt had been taken out of the mines but he had already developed water swelling in his feet through starvation and was sent to a hospital on the Volga. The patients here were all Germans and they were as badly starved as before. Sometimes they received no bread for a month and existed entirely on spoonfuls of gruel given them morning and evening and a midday bowl of watery soup. When they complained to the woman doctor in charge she told them to go to Hitler for food. Finally, in November 1945, when his weight had sunk to 92 pounds and he could not stand upright Erhardt had been sent home to die. But he had gradually recovered under his mother's care. When I met him he was still terribly emaciated, with deep sunken eyes, still a young man but one who smiled rarely and talked very little. When I asked him what had sustained him through his terrible experiences, he said simply that it was the hope of coming home. He had fought through the whole war, been at Dunkirk and in occupied France, marched thousands of miles and refused a commission because he hated the army, but he had done his duty as a man and a German and felt the ruin of his country as deeply as his family's personal losses.

Margarita had meanwhile married her René, who had been sent home by the Germans after he became useless as a slave laborer, but had rushed back to Siegen from France to find his love, immediately the war ended.

René Devilliers was slim and elegant, witty, intellectual, and sophisticated. Margarita was like a little girl in a fairy tale, simply dressed, without make-up, gay and sweet, with her heart on her sleeve. I have rarely seen two young people so much in love and so devoted to one another. Margarita had a kidney ailment as the legacy of her ill treatment in prison, and René was tubercular, but they were both radiantly happy, and when they visited the Weber house the sad atmosphere gave way to gaiety.

Erhardt and René, so different in temperament, one so very French and the other so very German, were good friends—better friends than Erhardt and his brother Otto who was the black sheep of the family, and earned his living by his wits rather than by hard work. René and Erhardt had both fought and suffered and endured the horrors of forced labor and hunger as prisoners of war, and although they had been on opposite sides they understood and respected each other while Margarita adored them both. Each represented in his own way the best qualities of their two nations. Erhardt complained that René, being a Frenchman, did not know how to work hard, while René said Erhardt was married to his factory and had never learned to enjoy life.

I used to think, while staying with the Webers, that I had the whole picture of Germany and France in that household. If only the two nations could get together and combine their virtues and their talents, the Germans putting diligence and endurance into the French, and the French teaching the Germans the graces of life, Europe could be made peaceful and strong. In fact, there is not really so wide a gap between the South Germans and the Northern French. René came from the Vosges district on the other side of the Rhine and in ages past his ancestors and Erhardt's were one people.

As soon as he was able to walk and work, Erhardt had started to dig out the machinery from under the debris of the Weber Works, and repair it with the aid of the skilled workers who from generation to generation had worked for the Weber family. By 1947 the factory was working again producing welding torches, gas cutting machines, and other badly needed reconstruction machinery, and employing a hundred workers. Frau Weber now had German refugees from the East to feed and care for instead of Russian and French prisoners. Otto was married and had a child. The vegetable and flower gardens which were Frau Weber's pride were both blooming. New red brick walls were rising where the original bombed-out buildings had stood. For a few months it had seemed that the Webers' troubles were ended, although Frau Weber's dearest son, Günther, would never come home and Helmuth was slowly dying.

Then the British ordered the Weber works dismantled. All Erhardt's gallant labors had gone for nothing. He and his family were to be ruined. Margarita and René would also be destitute, for René having married a German had to give up the career of an officer in the French Army, which his father had followed before him, and was also working for Webers.

The residual value of the Weber Works was calculated at only 36,000 marks, but the cost of replacing the machinery to be sent to the scrap heap was 750,000, a sum way beyond the reach of the family, for they had not hoarded before currency reform, but sold all the product of their factory. The annual production of their works, according to the orders on their books, was five times its dismantled value.

The planned destruction of the Weber Works could affect many other firms, since Webers supplied the welding and cutting equipment and sheet-metal-working machinery required to start up production again after dismantlement. This was proved by the fact that the Webers had received orders from other countries for their machine tools but had been refused permission to export by the Allied authorities because of the need for their products in Germany. Czechs, Yugoslavs, Belgians, Indians, and representatives of other countries entitled to reparations had inspected the Weber Works, but none had desired to acquire the machinery, much of which was old and all of which required skilled labor to operate. The whole equipment to be dismantled was destined for the scrap heap.

I spent hours watching the Weber workers, who were working night and day in two long shifts to earn as much as possible before being deprived of their livelihood. One of them said to me: "We thought that after Hitler's overthrow the German workers would be helped. Now we must assume the contrary. England and America evidently want to destroy us. Why else would they be taking away our jobs?"

In an appeal which Erhardt Weber subsequently sent to the ECA authorities in Frankfurt he wrote:

This is a last hour appeal to the victors of this war not to create new wounds, and by senseless destruction create more misery. At this hour when reconstruction of Europe is required and can be carried out only by substantial sacrifices, lend a helping hand to the peaceful will to work for it.

Dismantlement of the Weber Works was to begin on October 2, a few days ahead of my first visit to Siegen. I was so disturbed by this injustice, and had by then already come to feel such sympathy for the Weber family and their workers, that I decided to go to Detmold and appeal to Mr. Whitham, the British official responsible for reparations shipments.

Erhardt drove me there in his ancient Mercedes which was liable to break down occasionally but was the only one of their automobiles which had not been confiscated by the British. On the way north he told me what the men of Hitler's armies had gone through in Russia, both during and after the war. A reserved and embittered young man whose best years had been spent in fighting, and whose experiences in Russia as a prisoner had been too terrible to talk about even to his family, he slowly relaxed and unburdened himself to me, after I had convinced him that I, too, knew the bitterness of existence in Soviet Russia. He had served three years on the Russian front before being wounded and taken prisoner. He had been starved and frozen and had suffered about as much as a human being can bear, both physically and mentally. I began to understand that his absorption in the Weber factory was his defense against memories which would otherwise make life unendurable.

We passed out of Siegerland into Sauerland and thence through the flat plains of Hanoverian territory. Every now and again in Sauerland Erhardt would point to the ugly naked hills where forests had once flourished, but which had been stripped bare by the British, who had not spared even the young trees and had left nothing but raw stumps.

We spent the night at Bad Oyenhausen, headquarters of the British Army of the Rhine, where I had a friend whom I had not seen since 1938 in Singapore, and who was now a brigadier in charge of all British Army automobile transport.

British quarters at Bad Oyenhausen were surrounded by barbed wire to keep out "the natives." Erhardt was probably the first German whom Joss and his wife had received in their house. But one had to admit that the British were better than the Americans in at least one respect. They allowed their soldiers to marry German girls and live with them in camp, whereas the United States did not permit such marriages unless an officer or GI was about to return home. It was also true that although the British army of occupation was enjoying far better material conditions than the British at home, their allowances of food were far below the United States standard. In respect to housing and personnel services they were, however, exacting a higher toll from the Germans than the American occupation forces.

Erhardt spoke little the whole evening while I argued with Joss and his wife, who nice as they were, often resorted to the stock British argument when confronted by examples of our treatment of the Germans: "We won the war, didn't we?" But next morning, on our way to see Mr. Whitham at Detmold, Erhardt remarked that it was kind of funny that the British used this phrase so often since, whoever had won the war, it certainly wasn't England.

Joss had warned me that Mr. Whitham was a tough nut to crack; that he even insisted on dismantling factories needed by the British Army for repairs and equipment. "Be very American," he had said to me, "but don't lose your temper. Try to appeal to him as a gentleman and maybe, though I doubt it, you will save Herr Weber's factory."

I succeeded with Mr. Whitham, though only after more than an hour's argument and only temporarily. He finally agreed to suspend the dismantlement order, but would not say for how many weeks. In the course of our discussion during which Erhardt waited outside because Whitham did not wish to see him, this British official who wielded such great power waved his hand toward the window and said, "These Germans still have more resources than we have."

Arriving back at Siegen at midnight we found that dismantlement, which had started that morning, had been stopped in the afternoon. Knowing that I had secured only a suspension of sentence, I determined to see what could be done with the Industry and Commerce Division of the Bizone administration in Frankfurt. But first I spent a few days more in Siegen seeing other factories, and also visiting the barracks where thousands of German expellees were being cared for in Siegen. Other *flüchtlinge*, as the Germans call the millions of poor wretches expelled from their homes in Silesia, the Sudetenland and other Eastern territories, were housed in private homes. A considerable number of them were working in the factories marked down for destruction.

The other family I came to know well in Siegen were the Bartens who owned the ancient firm of Achenbach Söhne. This modern iron and steel works had grown out of a forge which began working the iron ores of the Westerwald in 1452. It had begun its development as a modern factory in 1846, before Bismarck had been heard of, and while Siegen was still part of a principality of the house of Orange which today rules Holland. Achenbach produced high quality rolling-mill equipment which used to be exported all over Europe and which is so well known that a British Birmingham firm today advertises the quality of its products by showing a picture with the Achenbach name on its machinery. This part of the plant had already been dismantled and shipped to England. Now Achenbach was also to lose the special purpose machine tools used exclusively for the production of spare locomotive parts. Achenbach was producing 90 per cent of the piston ring requirements of Bizonia's railways, but dismantlement was scheduled to begin in December. The absurdity of the proceeding was apparent since this department of Achenbach had been placed on the list of "absolutely essential plants" to be immediately reconstructed following dismantlement. Allied officials concerned with the reconstruction of the German transport system had recently visited Achenbach's to find out how quickly it could get production going again. But, as old Dr. Barten pointed out, the British were not only removing his machinery; they were also going to tear down and destroy the three cranes which were built into the roof of his railway plant, and this damage was irreparable at the present time. (As I learned later in Stuttgart, the reparations branch of the United States Military Government was busy there dismantling one of the few factories in Western Germany which makes cranes.)

Repeated protests to the British authorities had been unavailing, although several British officers had admitted that an error had almost certainly been made in the first place. There is hardly ever any way of getting errors on the dismantlement list corrected. One office refers the matter to another, and no one can or will take the responsibility of canceling an order once given.

Achenbach's was a larger enterprise than the Weber Works and had employed three hundred workers. The residual value of its equipment was set at only 17,000 Reichsmarks, but its replacement value at 1948 prices was 3,000,000 D marks. Before the war its monthly output was 250,000 marks a month—a larger figure than the total value of its dismantled machinery as calculated by the reparations authorities. Thus Achenbach's could have produced in a single month new equipment worth more than the total being destroyed. Dismantlement in this and many other cases could have been aptly described as "Operation Killing the Goose."

When I visited the Achenbach factory I was struck by the number of young women working there. When I spoke to them I found they were all refugees from the East, whom the Bartens were housing as well as training. They were quick and able workers and some were already earning 1.20 marks an hour turning out piston rings. A large proportion of the expellees are women, since the Poles and Czechs and Yugoslavs kept many German men as slave laborers while throwing out the women and children. These women, shortly to lose their jobs through dismantlement just after having acquired the means to support themselves and their children, would have to return to the crowded refugee camps again to become paupers.

Even the machines on which boy apprentices were being taught to be engineers were to be taken away. Thirty youngsters whom I saw as immersed in their work as if they were constructing toy airplanes, were to be deprived of the opportunity to learn a trade. The Achenbach foreman, having a brother in Milwaukee who sends him food parcels, feels very friendly to America. But, he said to me, how can we or the British hope to save Europe from communism if we drive the German workers to despair by our policies, and deprive their sons of technical training?

Later in the day I visited some of the refugee workers in the temporary homes constructed for them close to the factory. Here I talked to an old gaunt worker from Silesia called Winter. He had been a blacksmith with his own small forge in a village near Glatz where the population was part German and part Polish. He had been on friendly terms with the Polish peasants of his district, and they had tried to save him from expropriation. But the Polish Communist government had thrown him out of his house together with his wife and his grandchildren, and they had all walked hundreds of miles before they got to Berlin. There he had managed to find work, but the Russians soon came and dismantled the factory where he had a job. So they had started again on their travels and ended up at Siegen. Now for the third time the old blacksmith faced destitution just when he had expected to live out the rest of his life in peace.

The Bartens were better off than the Webers in some respects. There was a better chance of saving their factory, as I found out later in Frankfurt. The only Barten son, a tall handsome young man with a gay temperament, had come home safe from the wars, and was newly married to a charming girl from the Saar. Young Barten had endured the hardships of the Russian front like so many others of the men I talked to in Siegen, but he had not been a Russian prisoner of war like Erhardt Weber, and there were no such shadows of death and horror at the Bartens as those which darkened the Weber home. On one occasion I asked young Barten and his wife how they managed to be so happy in spite of the ruin which threatened them, and he said: "We younger Germans who have survived the war have learned to live in danger; we know how good it is to be alive, whatever the future may bring."

Barten senior was stout, red faced and kindly; the type of German who is represented in caricatures as swilling beer in some summer cafe on the Rhine, but was energetic and intelligent and kindhearted. His wife is a Berliner and looked almost young enough to be his daughter. Fair, elegant and witty, with a lovely singing voice, she had the same happy temperament as her son. She did not mind so much that the British had requisitioned the Barten home and were keeping its twelve rooms for the use of two bachelors, but she longed to get her piano back. When I happened to be invited in for a drink by the two British officials who occupied the Barten house, I asked them whether they did not think they might let Frau Barten have the use of the piano which meant so much to her. They protested that although they could not play themselves, it was used when they entertained, and I should remember that the British in Siegen had precious little to amuse them. This was of course quite true. If the pattern of occupation had followed normal lines, with the conquerors billeted in the houses of the conquered instead of throwing them out of their homes for an indefinite period, whether or not the whole space requisitioned was needed, the British Tommies and American GI's, officers, and civilians, as well as the Germans, would have been far happier. The race discrimination policy adopted by both the British and Americans was almost as hard on the occupying forces as the occupied. True, the original "nonfraternization" rules had been modified, but a great gulf still separated the conquerors from the conquered in both zones.

In Siegen the racial bar meant that the handful of Britishers there had nothing much to do in their leisure hours, if they were married men unwilling to seek the only companionship possible: association with ladies of easy virtue. In a small community like Siegen, where almost everyone knows everyone else, and where puritanical Protestant morality was little undermined by the Nazis and has not been destroyed even by defeat and hunger, "*fräuleins*," in the accepted occupation meaning of the term, are few and hard to come by. On the other hand the British reparations people were naturally not *persona grata* with the Germans, while the resident British "governor," as I have already mentioned, was extremely unpopular both on account of his reputed seductions by pressure, and his suspected Communist sympathies. So it was seldom that the lonely British occupation officials entered a German home.

There were no British military forces in Siegerland, which was part of the area occupied by Belgian troops. The latter, while occupying a great deal of precious housing space, were doing a profitable black-market business. Like the French they are unhampered by the regulations and customs controls which rendered the import and sale of cigarettes, cognac, coffee, and other luxuries, and the export of German manufactures or currency, hazardous for the Americans and the British. The Belgians were on better personal terms with the Germans than the British or Americans, since there was less of a language barrier as well as no regulation "master race" behavior. The Germans regarded them as a minor pest, since although they complained of their dirtiness and drunkenness, they were not concerned with dismantlement, and their cigarette and coffee black-marketing brought prices down. Compared with the Belgians even the French soldiers in Germany looked smart— which is saying a lot. Frenchmen, whatever their other vices, rarely drink too much, but the Belgians I saw in Siegen were as drunk as they were dirty and unmilitary in appearance. Nor did they make any pretense of ever intending to fight. They frankly told the Germans that if war came they would at once run away.

I spent a few more days in Siegerland after my return with Erhardt Weber from Detmold. I visited many factories, talked to the workers and visited their homes; spent a few hours in the museum in the castle where there was also an exhibition of striking paintings of Russia done by returned prisoners of war; visited René and Margarita in their home a few miles away in the French zone, and spent another day in the French zone with Otto and Helmuth. I now felt as if I had known these people all my life; I was admitted to the intimacy of their family quarrels, and came to appreciate the good and bad qualities of each member of the family. The differences in their characters and outlook were as great as their solidarity as a family. Poor Frau Weber used to sigh for her husband who had known how to reconcile these differences among her sons, while she could only bewail them and mourn the death of Günther who had had the virtues of each and the vices of none. The curious thing in the Weber family was that only the men quarreled. Otto's wife, Margarita, and Frau Weber lived on the most amicable terms.

I returned to Frankfurt, determined to see what could be done to save the people of the town and forest villages, whose troubles I had come to feel were my concern. Surely, I thought, either the Anglo-American officials engaged in restoring the railways and increasing coal production, or the ECA authorities, would be interested in stopping the destruction of some of the Siegen factories.

The first morning in Frankfurt I left the Press Center bright and early to visit the Commerce and Industry Division of Bicom, the joint Anglo-American administration of the combined British and American zones. Frankfurt is the *de facto* capital of Bizonia and the Bipartite offices are situated in the huge I. G. Farben building which we refrained from bombing during the war. It is not much smaller than the Pentagon and, since the various departments are continually playing General Post, you have to be employed there to know where to find what any day in the week. However, there is always the fun of traveling up and down in the moving boxes accommodating two persons, which take the place of elevators or escalators in the most modern German buildings.

Finally, I located the brigadier supposed to be at the head of the British section of the Bipartite Commerce and Industry Division. I could accomplish this feat because I was an American correspondent and could wander about the corridors at will. But few Germans, permitted to enter the buildings only if they got a pass, and able to get a pass only if they knew exactly whom they needed to see, could succeed in putting their grievance or appeal before the proper authorities. To make it just so much more difficult for them, the Information desk is situated inside, so that they cannot find out whom they want to see and where they are to be found, until after they get the permit which allows them to pass the sentries at the door. Not that the girls at the Information desk usually know anything, but at least you can consult the book giving the names and locations of the many and varied departments; although the rooms given are rarely the right ones, you can start out and eventually find what you want.

The British brigadier was amiable and quite decent as well he might be since he didn't seem to be doing anything, and his room and anteroom were empty of visitors. He told me he had just been appointed to his job, and as yet didn't know the faintest thing about it. "Go and see Mr. Radford, further along the corridor," he suggested. "He's the fellow who knows all about German industry."

So I walked along the corridor and found Mr. Radford. Unfortunately, Mr. Radford hadn't the slightest interest in my story. He made it clear at once that he was a Vansittartist—the British equivalent of one of the Morgenthau Boys. He smiled coldly when I started to tell him about Siegen, and said: "I have fought twice against Germany and lost my brothers in the war. *This time*, I assure you, we are going to make the Germans pay."

It was obviously useless to argue with a man like Radford, even about the outstanding case of Achenbach, although as deputy head of the British Section of the Bipartite Commerce and Industry Division, he was *supposed* to be concerned with reconstruction rather than vengeance.

So I left him and sought out his American counterpart, Mr. Messler. Here I had a totally different reception. Mr. Messler was very much interested, although he told me that the decisions of the Military Government reparations authorities in Berlin were "outside the terms of reference" of the Frankfurt authorities. Here for the first time I was up against the disastrous duality of American occupation policies. The officials concerned with reconstruction of the German economy had nothing to do with the reparations authorities whose mandate was to destroy Germany's capacity for self-support.

Messler sent for a Mr. Yule who was in charge, among other things, of the reconstruction of the German railways. Mr. Yule proved to be one of the most active, well-informed and unprejudiced United States officials I met in Germany. He said that he knew Achenbach's production was absolutely essential to the railways; that it was quite true that it produced almost the whole of the Bizonia railways' piston rings, and that its dismantlement would be disastrous. Mr. Yule took me off to see the two United States technical experts concerned with Reichsbahn supplies, Mr. Pumphrey and Mr. Hartlaub, on leave of absence from the Pennsylvania and New York Central railways to help the German railways overcome the difficulties which threatened to block European recovery.

Unlike the offices of the big shots with military titles, the room and anteroom occupied by Mr. Pumphrey and Mr. Hartlaub were full of Germans, and wonder of wonders, both these Americans spoke German themselves. They were actually dealing directly with the Germans and helping them solve their problems and ours. It was a refreshing experience, for most United States officials in Germany seemed only to deal with the Germans through their secretaries, and it was almost as hard for a German to get to see an American official as for the proverbial camel to pass through the needle's eye.

I told these Americans that I was a *Readers' Digest* correspondent, but that I had come to see them, not as a writer seeking information, but in order to tell them some facts I had learned of immediate concern to them, and indeed to all Americans. Since I am not an engineer and could not therefore give them all the details, I suggested they should talk to Dr. Barten.

All three immediately agreed and asked me to try and get Barten to come over from Siegen the following day. They warned me, as Mr. Messler had done, that reparations deliveries were outside their sphere, but they nevertheless made it clear that they were prepared to fight to prevent the Morgenthau boys in Berlin from dismantling, or permitting the British to dismantle, the factories most essential to the reconstruction of the railways.

Dr. Barten will never forget his meeting with these American technical experts. They were the first Americans he had met, and he was overwhelmed; not only by the contrast between the way they received him and the manner in which he was accustomed to be treated by the British, but also by the difference between American and German officials.

Beaming with joy as we left the I. G. Farben building after the interview, he said:

"Really, we Germans have something to learn from America. It's almost incredible! Those American gentlemen didn't even keep me waiting a half hour or so to show their importance, as a German bureaucrat would certainly have done. And they talked to me so kindly, as if I were a friend, without any pompousness or formality. Perhaps this American democracy really means something. Ach, its unbelievable how I was treated. I want to get back home to tell everyone about it."

Dr. Barten wanted to take me off to have dinner at a German restaurant with him and Zezulak, who had accompanied him from Siegen as interpreter, but whose services had hardly been necessary since Hartlaub spoke German fluently, and both Pumphrey and Yule were sufficiently conversant with the language. I insisted that they should both, instead, come with me to Schuman Hall, the Post Exchange cafeteria where there are no race or class distinctions, and GI's and officers can both bring their German guests. Here again Dr. Barten waxed enthusiastic over American ways. "How sensible it was to take a tray and wait on yourself." "How extraordinary to see American officers standing in line behind GI's." "How friendly everyone seemed." "How unexpected to see Germans and Americans sitting down together. One could not imagine such a thing happening in the British zone where no Germans are admitted to British restaurants and clubs."

"Wirklich, wir könnten von den Amerikanern viel gutes lernen," he repeated again, too busy observing the noisy crowded cafeteria, to eat his sandwiches. He had received a practical lesson in democracy worth more than a thousand lectures, or any amount of radio and newspaper propaganda. He had seen the reality of American democracy, usually obscured by Military Government, and had met Americans who behaved as if they were at home, instead of as conquerors ruling over a beaten people.

I was not, of course, satisfied by the prospect that Achenbach's would in all probability be saved. Dr. Barten's plant was only one of the most obviously indefensible examples of dismantlement in Siegerland, but the United States railways experts whom I had found to be so keen on their reconstruction job, could not help the Webers, or Hensch, or others, the destruction of whose factories constituted sabotage of the Marshall Plan, but was not of direct concern to the railways.

My next appeal, accordingly, was to the ECA authorities. Thanks to Mr. Haroldson, the State Department representative in Frankfurt and one of the real liberals I met in Germany, I met Mr. Collisson, the ECA representative in Germany, and Commander Paul F. Griffin, USNR, who had just arrived from Washington with the experts of the Humphrey Committee charged by Congress to find out which plants on the dismantlement list could better contribute to European reconstruction by being left in Germany.

I first asked the ECA representatives whether they intended to get information direct from the Germans, or would deal with them only through Military Government. I was assured that "the door is open here to anyone who has information to give us which bears upon the European Recovery Program."

I welcomed this statement and subsequently passed it on to the Germans in the Ruhr and the French zone, with the result that the ECA offices in Frankfurt received quite a stream of letters and visits from the German industrialists and labor leaders I met in my travels. I made it quite clear, of course, that Mr. Collisson and his colleagues could not be approached by just anyone who had a grievance; that their competence extended only to such cases where the question of European recovery was involved.

For the moment, however, I was still concerned mainly with enlisting ECA's interest in the Siegerland tragedy. After hearing my story with great patience and interest, Mr. Collisson agreed to receive a deputation from Siegen.

A week or two later, after I had left Frankfurt for the Ruhr, five representatives of Siegerland industries were received by Mr. Collisson, who, after hearing them state their case, promised that Siegen would soon be visited by the ECA technical experts.

Actually the ECA experts visited Siegen twice. The first time, the British refused to allow the Siegen people to have their own interpreter and the factory owners who could speak no English were at a serious disadvantage. Those, like Erhardt Weber, who understands English moderately well, heard the British interpreter giving false information to the delegation, but did not know whether his protest, in halting English, was understood or not. However, Mr. Lewis, the ECA expert, made a great impression in Siegen, for he arrived early in the morning and worked without let-up all day, noting everything and refusing British offers of hospitality. He was, it seemed, a man with a big and difficult job to do, working ten to twelve hours a day, showing favor to none, an impartial highly qualified expert making the detailed survey assigned to him and caring nothing for anything but his job.

After my return to the United States I received a letter from Hans Zezulak, informing me that members of the Humphrey Committee had visited Siegen on December 3 and 4 and inspected fourteen of the plants on the dismantlement list. Mr. Lewis came again, but this time he was accompanied by Frederick V. Geier of the Cincinnati Milling Machine Company, who was said to be a brother-in-law of Albert Einstein. Mr. Geier, Zezulak wrote, seemed to be very well informed in every detail and when a British Military Government interpreter was offered him, declined on the ground that he spoke German fluently. This turned the tables on the British who had refused to let the Germans have an interpreter on the occasion of Mr. Lewis' first visit. As Zezulak reported to me: "So the British left their interpreter behind and all the firms spoke German to him, and the British could not follow the conversation and the people could speak what they liked freely. It was a great day indeed.".

Whether or not Paul Hoffman or Washington would make proper use of it, there seemed no doubt from the example of Siegen that Mr. Geier and Mr. Lewis and their colleagues must have provided Washington with the material to make an intelligent and realistic decision about dismantlement.

I visited Siegen again after visiting the Ruhr in October, and was detained there for a week, having developed an inflammation of the lungs—no doubt on account of my too strenuous investigation of dismantlement in Düsseldorf, Dortmund, and Essen. During my stay in bed at the Weber house I got to know this family better than many old friends, and also had frequent visits from the Bartens, Senior and Junior. Even Mr. Paisley, the British reparations officer, came to visit me and became distantly friendly with the Webers, once he realized that they did not account him personally responsible for dismantlement. He said I was probably depriving him of his job by my activities on behalf of Siegen, but he did not resent this and was himself longing for the day when he would be working to create instead of to destroy. One evening, in his presence, the Webers told me that many Siegen people were asking if there was not something they could do for me in gratitude for my attempts to save the town. I said, laughing, that I thought they ought to erect a gold statue to me in the market place, if it proved that I really had saved Siegerland from destruction. Paisley thereupon remarked that if so the statue should represent me standing with my foot on his dead body.

This joke had a sequel which touched me very much. Just before I left Germany the Bartens, Senior and Junior, Erhardt Weber, and Zezulak arrived in Frankfurt with a small bronze replica of the huge old medieval statue of an ironworker which used to stand beside the bridge over the river Sieg. On it they had had inscribed: "In friendly remembrance of the visit of Mrs. Freda Utley to Siegerland, and her successful efforts in saving the existence of the industries of the district."

They told me it was not a gift only from themselves, but was intended to express the gratitude of many others. The statue weighed at least a hundred pounds and, as I was flying back to the United States, I had to leave it to be sent on to me. I only hoped that I had really helped to save the livelihood of the people of Siegerland, and not merely postponed the day of their ruin.

Erhardt Weber now looked more gaunt than ever. His brother was in the hospital and had been given up for lost by the doctors.

Otto, the unstable though charming and gay member of the Weber family, had taken to drink and no longer did any work. He saw no sense in working, since Germans were apparently doomed to become paupers. Why struggle? He would gather such few rosebuds as might come his way and forget his own and others' sorrows in alcohol.

Erhardt was of stiffer fiber. Whether or not the Weber factory would finally be dismantled, he was continuing to rebuild it. Another red brick wall had gone up. Three buildings would soon be restored. In spite of Otto's protests that it was senseless to reconstruct if all the machinery was to be taken away; in spite of Helmuth's contention that the only way to make money in Germany today is by buying and selling on or off the black market, Erhardt, head of the family (or its dictator as his brothers said) insisted on work, and yet more work. If the British took away all the fruits of his and his workers' labors, *he* for one, was not going to give up hope. Grimly and silently, insisting that work must go on, and sparing himself least of anyone, Erhardt refused to say die. He epitomized the best of the German spirit, which seems indomitable, perhaps because it has never been softened by facile conquests and easy living. Erhardt had never been a Nazi and had refused a commission in the German Army, but he was a patriot in the best sense. No one I met in Germany made me realize as vividly as Erhardt the bitter sorrow which the destruction and virtual enslavement of their country means to the Germans.

Old beyond his years, unmarried and with no time for the women attracted by his aloofness and lean good looks, he was a lover of music and poetry, with a gentle sense of humor under his reserve; loved less by his mother than her weaker sons, given to few words or expressions of affection, but sensitive and intelligent, Erhardt had an unconquerable spirit. He might die of overwork but he would never surrender to Giant Despair.

Germans like Erhardt Weber and other Siegerlanders, given the chance to utilize their energies and talents for peace instead of the wars they fight but never want, are capable of rebuilding Germany and teaching Western Europe how to live by its own labors, instead of depending upon the revenues from vanishing colonial empires or the American subsidies which have taken their place.

5

GERMAN DEMOCRACY BETWEEN SCYLLA AND CHARYBDIS

THE MARSHALL PLAN IS BASED ON THE ASSUMPTION THAT POVERTY and despair lead people to reject democracy and follow the Communist lead; and that, in order to save the Western world from totalitarian tyranny, America must give the European nations on our side of the Iron Curtain enough dollars to reconstruct their economies and afford their people the opportunity to earn a decent living.

This theory is not, however, applied to Germany. We refuse to admit that it was poverty, unemployment, and despair which brought the Nazis to power, and may once again drive the German people to reject the political concepts and moral values of the West. Instead, we regard the Germans as a naturally aggressive people with a predilection for authoritarian rule, and treat them as if they were possessed of a devil which must be driven out by chastising them.

It is today forgotten that the Nazis did not win power by advocating war. They appealed in the first place to the German people's longing for delivery from intolerable disorders and economic chaos. Their main slogan was "bread and work." Hitler did not start to talk about the need to obtain *Lebensraum* by force until after he came to power, and while many a German joined the Nazi party because it was anti-Communist, others supported it because of the failure of the democratic parties to solve the unemployment problem or to induce the democracies to make the concessions necessary for the German people to exist.

At the First Assembly of the Nazi Reichstag on May 17, 1933, Hitler specifically abjured war, saying:

> The outcome of war would be greater insecurity, increased economic misery and yet more wars. To start such utterly senseless action would lead to the collapse of the present order of society. A Europe sinking into Communist chaos would produce a period of crisis the duration of which cannot he estimated. The three principles which are the mainspring of our revolution do not menace the interests of other nations at all. On the contrary they can prevent the threatening Communist upheaval and lead to the construction of a people's state based on the principle of private property as the basis of culture. The re-establishment of a stable and authoritative state leadership.[11]

Since many foreigners believed Hitler's lies, it is hardly surprising that so many Germans did. To account them all guilty of Hitler's crimes, after it was too late for them to escape from his tyranny, is to be unaware of the nature of totalitarian rule. It is doubtful whether any other nation, placed as Germany was, would have resisted the lure of Nazi propaganda. It should have been our objective after the second World War to convince the German people that Hitler had not only failed but had been wrong, and that democracy offers life and hope.

Instead, for the second time in thirty years, democracy has become synonymous in Germany with submission to intolerable conditions, and the denial of freedom, security and self-respect to the German people.

It is one of the paradoxes of modern times that in an age in which psychology is studied even in the schoolroom, and psychological warfare has become a branch of military science, we should conduct our foreign policy with less understanding of other peoples than our ancestors whose knowledge was confined to history and philosophy.

The lessons of psychology are apparently considered as having no application to the Germans. For although most Americans have been sold on the idea that criminal tendencies are the result of environment and that

---

[11] Quoted by Gunther Reimann in *Germany: World Power or World Revolution?*

juvenile delinquency can be cured by psychological treatment, they believe that the way to reform the Germans is to treat them as hardened criminals, and punish them all, including the children who were unborn when Hitler came to power.

"If you call a child a thief often enough," a German said to me, "he eventually becomes one. Similarly by treating all Germans as Nazi criminals, you have made more Nazis than Hitler ever did."

The same idea was expressed in a variety show called "Mousetrap" which my friend Joan Crane saw in Stuttgart. In one scene a dog who had done something naughty was shown as very ashamed of himself. But after a succession of people had screamed "Guilty, guilty," and punished him, the dog became very fierce and completely untamable.

People cannot be bludgeoned into repentance. They must retain their self-respect if they are to admit their guilt. Many Germans never realized what they were doing, or abetting, under Nazi rule, but might have been shocked into repentance after Nazi atrocities in occupied countries were revealed to them following Germany's defeat, had not they themselves become the victims of similar "crimes against humanity." All we have done is to convince them that everyone is bad and cruel.

How can we expect to bring home to the Germans a consciousness of their "guilt", if we ourselves or our allies treat them as the Nazis treated the conquered? Today the Germans, far from being repentant, consider themselves to be the most oppressed of all peoples, and see no difference between Nazi rule and that of Western military government.

As Dr. Helmuth Becker, son of the internationally known educator who was Minister of Education in Prussia before 1933, said to me at Nuremberg: "If the Military Government's conception of democracy continues much longer, there will be no chance for democracy in Germany for a hundred years."

"Few Americans," he continued, "realize that Germany followed Hitler because the democratic parties were bankrupt. Nor do they see that Military Government is very similar to Nazi rule. The Nazis and the

Military Government would have got on very well together. They have the same belief in authoritarian rule, and they are regarded by the Germans in much the same light.

"We don't believe your propaganda any more than we believed Nazi propaganda after the first year or two. We judge you by what you do, not by what you say, and what you do is much the same as what the Nazis did."

There is an inescapable contradiction between democracy, which means government by consent of the governed, and military government based on force and the power of the conquerors to impose their will on the conquered. This contradiction has been accentuated by the attitude and behavior prescribed for the occupation forces in Germany; but it would in any case preclude the growth of a vigorous democratic movement in Germany.

Inevitably the German democrats in the Western zones appear in the eyes of most of their compatriots as quislings carrying out the orders of the conquerors. Since those orders have kept the Germans starving in the bombed-out remnants of their cities without allowing them to rebuild them, deprived the workers of their livelihood by dismantlement, and the whole population of freedom, democracy has once again become synonymous with defeat, misery, injustice, and servitude.

Once again, as in the days of the Weimar Republic, and to a far greater degree, we are denying the German democrats any possibility of proving to their countrymen that justice, the right to work and earn a living wage, and equality among the nations can be obtained except by force.

The predicament of the German Social Democrats outside of Berlin illustrates the sad consequences of our undemocratic attitude toward the Germans.

Talking to German labor leaders in the Ruhr, I could have imagined myself back in the days of the Weimar Republic when I had often visited Germany. The old Socialists who had survived both Nazi persecution and the war were back where they had been twenty years ago, but more gravely handicapped in their efforts to "sell democracy" to the German people. Yet they still had faith in peaceful methods and rational argument. They eschewed "direct action" or revolutionary methods to obtain just demands. They still believed in the possibility of uniting the "workers of the world"; they still placed their trust in British and French Socialists; they are as law abiding under British Military Government as under former German governments; they are not lacking in courage, but they seem incapable of bold and decisive action in a crisis.

They are in the tragic position of not being able to learn from past experience because to do so would be a denial of the democratic basis of their beliefs. And since the situation they face today is similar to the one they faced following the first World War, they are once again in danger of losing the support of the German workers, and giving the right of way to the demagogues and apostles of violence and tyranny: to the extreme nationalists on the right and the Communists on the left who once before destroyed German democracy.

The Germans always seem to "go the whole hog." Either they are extreme nationalists and violently aggressive, or they are more pacific, rational, and internationally minded than the socialists and liberals of any other country.

As one young German trade-union official said to me in Düsseldorf: "Placed as we are in the center of Europe, influences from all sides meet and clash most violently in Germany. Here issues are more sharply defined than in any other country. Germans are inclined to make every issue a question of basic philosophy. The religious wars were more destructive in Germany than anywhere else because we embrace our beliefs so wholeheartedly and see no virtue in compromise. So today in politics we go to the same extremes: from ultranationalism to the repudiation of all nationalist sentiment. We adopt our politics with religious conviction and see an enemy in everyone who thinks differently. Like the power generated by positive and negative in electricity, the strongest incentives for good or ill are present in the German character."

When nationalism is in the ascendant, the Germans are among the most violent and unscrupulous peoples; when they turn to pacifism, internationalism, and reasonableness, they turn the other cheek with a restraint in face of provocation, injustice, and suffering which few other nations ever exhibit. This tendency to go to extremes and eschew compromise also accounts for the violent party strife which helped destroy the Weimar Republic. Unlike the English, who instinctively put the national interest above party interests, the Germans carry political antagonisms to such lengths that, except when united for war under authoritarian rule, internal conflicts split the nation into warring factions. This is no doubt the reason why even liberal Germans will tell you today that Germany needs a monarchy, because only an established authority recognized by all parties can overcome the schisms which tear Germany apart.

Germany is not, perhaps, peculiar in this respect. The French are displaying a similar incapacity in making democracy work, and the British had their civil wars in the past. It is the comparative youthfulness of the German state which has caused the swing from overemphasis on nationalism, to internecine strife regardless of the national interest, and back again to extreme nationalism.

The renunciation of nationalist sentiment and aims by the German Social Democrats plays into the hands of both the extreme nationalists, and the Communists, who use German national sentiment to further Russian aims: Many German Socialists in the Western zones strengthen the impression that they are puppets by seeming to echo the views of the conquerors who demand that the Germans, unlike other nations, should have no national feelings.

Patriotism, regarded as a virtue by the victors, is considered to be a sign of perverse tendencies when displayed by Germans. Every sign of "reviving German nationalism" is made the excuse for the revival of repressive measures. We treat the Germans like sexual delinquents who must be castrated or kept in prison and deprived of normal sexual intercourse, while their jailers are permitted to indulge their natural human instincts to the full.

Yesterday it was the Nazis; today it is their erstwhile allies and spiritual brothers, the Communists, who are taking advantage of Germany's treatment at the hands of the Allies and of the weakness of German democracy. The Communists are appealing to the same passions and hatreds and aggressive nationalistic sentiments as the Nazis. They are leading the struggle against dismantlement and the so-called internationalization of the Ruhr, and in general showing up the incapacity of the German democrats to obtain, and the unwillingness of the democratic powers to grant, elementary justice to the German people.

Although German experience of Communist terror in the Eastern zone and Berlin, and the German Army's first-hand view of Soviet Russia as soldiers and prisoners of war, have so far prevented the revival of a strong German Communist movement, there is a substantial minority of Communists in the Ruhr held in check only by the Socialists and Christian Democrats who still hope the Western Powers will come to their senses in face of the Soviet danger and permit the German people to live and work.

About a third of the German trade-union members in the coal and steel industries of the Ruhr are reputed to be Communists or to follow the Communist lead. This substantial minority is bound to increase if only the Communists seem to be fighting against dismantlement. It must also grow if the occupation authorities, desirous of re-establishing free enterprise in Germany but refusing to release the German economy from the burden of reparations payments and the tight controls established in the interests of Germany's British and French competitors on the world market, continue to promote the scarcity and inflation which keep the German workers without the necessities of life.

If the German Socialists who control the trade unions in the Ruhr fail to see that they will never obtain a fair deal from the British by collaborating with them; if they continue to hold back the rank and file from organized strikes against dismantlement; if they fail in every possible way to support the German workers who are going to jail for refusal to obey British orders to destroy or remove the machinery on which other Germans depend for their livelihood, the Communists will inevitably win the leadership of the German workers, in spite of German fear and hatred of the Soviet Union.

The British, so far, have derived great profit from the trusting attitude of the German labor leaders. But in the long run the advantage they have taken of the German Socialists' faith in the British Labour Government is likely to rebound to the advantage of the Communists. Just as the British are deriving temporary profit from the sale to Soviet Russia and her satellites of armaments and planes or the materials and machinery with which to manufacture them, but are likely in the future bitterly to regret their exclusive preoccupation with the accumulation of dollar funds to the detriment of their defenses, so also in Germany they may come to rue the day when they sacrificed to a commercial motive the good will of those who trusted them and could have become their strongest allies.

My visit to the Ruhr in the fall of 1948 brought home to me not only awareness of the similarity in the victors' treatment of German democracy today and following the first World War, but also understanding of the weakness of German social democracy.

Before Hitler came to power, when German social democracy still held the allegiance of a majority of the German working and professional classes, the German democrats had believed that the Western democracies would not allow them to perish by refusing the concessions which could keep the German people under peaceful leadership. In 1948, in the Ruhr, I found that the German tradeunionists had been convinced that the British Labour Government would not actually carry through the dismantlement program which must drive the German people once again to reject democracy.

Others had apparently been won over to accept dismantlement by a British promise to support socialization of the mining and steel industries against the Americans who favor private enterprise, if the trade-union leaders would collaborate with the British Military Government, or at least take no concerted measures to prevent the removal of machinery from German factories. This apparently accounted for the refusal of Hans Boekler and other old German trade union leaders to accede to the demands of the rank and file for a general strike against dismantlement.

Like Samson, German labor had been shorn of its strength, the temptress being the Socialist ideal. Hoping to establish socialism by collaboration with the British conquerors the old German trade-union leaders had disarmed the working class.

Whether or not a bargain had actually been struck between the British and German Socialists, it was made clear to me in my conversations with Ruhr labor leaders that they were anxious above all not to embarrass or annoy the British Labour Government.

On the other hand I also had to realize that the German tradeunion leaders had little choice but to collaborate with the British. The dependence of the Germans on the food supplied by their conquerors constituted a terrible weapon in the hands of the British and American military governments, and was used with few scruples. No one could forget that in 1947 the Western Powers had threatened to stop food shipments if the German workers went on strike.

As an outsider I cannot judge whether it is the carrot or the stick which plays the greater role in inducing the German trade union leaders to collaborate with the British Military Government. The stick, starvation, is in all probability more potent than the Socialist lure. Starvation as a method of coercion is used less blatantly by the British and American occupation authorities than by the Soviets, but hardly less effectively. It is the dependence of Western Germany on food imports which has cut the ground from under the feet of the German democrats, and placed German labor in an even weaker position today than under the Nazi tyranny.

It was essential for the Nazi government to encourage the Germans to work to the limit of their capacity, since compulsion alone cannot secure maximum production. But the British Military Government has no such interest. The British, to use their favorite expression, "couldn't care less" if German labor chooses to starve by going on strike. Cessation of production in German factories may even be welcome to the British conquerors who are also Germany's competitors. Thus the German workers in the Ruhr have in effect been deprived of their only weapon against the destruction of their means of existence.

Since every German working class family is at all times on the verge of destitution, and dependent for its inadequate food on the good will of the conquerors, no German labor leader can lightly defy the occupation authorities. "A week without work and wages," one of them said to me, "means so many more thousands tubercular children, so many more invalids; we are so undernourished and weak that we can barely keep alive, and have no reserves of strength or food. One little extra push can mean collapse. How can we stand up against the organized might of the conquerors who hold our lives in their hands, and treat us all as criminals, or at best as prisoners on parole?"

Nevertheless, it was hard for me to understand the attitude of such men as Hans Boekler, the William Green of German labor. He had recently returned from London where he had talked to Ernest Bevin. When I asked him what answer Bevin had given to his argument against dismantlement, Boekler made excuses for the British Foreign Minister. "Bevin is so overburdened with other cares," said Boekler, "so absorbed in the difficulties of foreign policy: Palestine, Russia, and the rest, that he simply has no time to attend to our German problems."

After this conversation I was hardly surprised when one of the Ministers in North-Rhine Westphalia, who is himself a Socialist, told me that Boekler was "too much orientated toward Britain." The middle ranks of trade-union officials, this Minister also told me, realized that the German workers were being victimized by the British and the workers themselves wanted to strike against dismantlement, but Boekler had prevented any effective action being taken. Boekler is both head of the metal workers trade union and chairman of the Federation of German Trade Unions.

Arnold Schmidt, the German miners' leader, holds the same pro-British opinions. When I interviewed him in his house near Bochum I had already heard him speak to the British and American Military Government officials assembled at Essen on October 2, and waited in vain for him to protest against dismantlement. So I was hardly surprised when he told me that the German workers were "full of admiration for the Socialist achievements of the British Labour Government." Either from discretion or conviction, he had nothing to say against British policy.

Much as I respect the old-fashioned trade union leaders I met in the Ruhr I found it pathetic to witness their touching faith in the British Labour Government. In spite of the superior attitude adopted toward them as toward all other Germans by British Military Government officials, and in spite of the abundant evidence of British determination to wipe out German competition by ruthless dismantlement, they refused to believe that a British *Labour* Government was not their friend. So, instead of leading the strikes and demonstrations demanded by the rank and file, they continued to argue that if the Germans were patient and submissive the British and French would eventually listen to reason and stop taking the bread out of the mouths of the German workers.

I was accompanied on some of my Ruhr visits by a German from the Social Ministry, recommended to me by Richard Stokes, the English Member of Parliament who has fought hardest to stop dismantlement. Although I speak German, my knowledge of the language is not such as to make it easy to understand every word when technical terms are involved. So Stokes' friend, Zilliken, who spoke English fluently, was of great assistance to me in investigating dismantlement in the Ruhr. He was, moreover, an intelligent, fearless and well-informed young man.

When I expressed my astonishment at the confiding trust which the older generation of German labor leaders appeared to place in the British Labour Government, Zilliken remarked, "Yes, the relationship which the British Labour Government has managed to establish with the Social Democrats of the Ruhr is similar to that between the English aristocracy and the British working class."

This comparison is not as apt today as fifty years ago. It would be truer to say that the Social Democrats in Western Germany stand in much the same position in relation to the British Labour Government as the Socialist Unity party (SED) in the Russian zone to Moscow. Both are dependent for such power as they have on the occupation authorities. Certainly the Social Democrats have more popular support than the SED, but they are well aware that if the occupation forces were withdrawn they would in all probability be swept from office. This is not a reflection on the integrity of the German Socialists, but a result of the identification of democracy in German eyes with subservience to the will of the conquerors.

In spite of its weak position German Social Democracy does not lack leaders who advocate a bolder course than that pursued by the Boeklers and Schmidts. There is a militant opposition which argues that effective direct action against both dismantlement and the conversion of the Ruhr into an Anglo-French colony, is possible; and that if the Socialists fail to fight for the rights of German labor and the German people, the Communists will take the lead. This militant wing of the German Socialist and trade-union movement advocates mass strikes and demonstrations against dismantlement, believing that the British will not dare, at this stage, to crush the German working class by naked force, seeing that the only beneficiaries must be Communists.

Early in 1949 the militants appeared to be assuming the lead in the Ruhr, no doubt because the Communists had begun to take the lead in opposing dismantlement, and because the number of registered unemployed has risen to a million in the combined British and American zones.[12]

In Dortmund I visited an outstanding personality among the militant Socialist trade union leaders, who was in hospital after losing his right hand in a street accident a few days before. Herr Meyer had started life as a miner, been a trade-union organizer before Hitler came to power, and subsequently earned his living in such various occupations as a film company publicity agent, electric-bulb salesman and hotel manager, and had been both a soldier and a draftee in a glass plant during the war. But he looked like Beethoven. His massive torso, pale face, aquiline nose, generous mouth and massive forehead, shock of black hair streaked with grey, and burning black eyes made an unforgettable impression, and I was no less struck by his outspoken and fearless attitude, and the contrast between his views and the narrow sectarian Socialist attitude of such men as Boekler and Schmidt.

Meyer told me how, after being redrafted into the army, in spite of his age, in the last desperate weeks of the war, he had been taken prisoner by the Americans but had been lucky enough to be interrogated by a former trade-union colleague who had emigrated to the United States and

---

[12] These unemployment figures do not include the mass of German expellees living in camps.

become an American citizen. This friend of Weimar Republic days had at once released him, and he had thereupon joined up with his former trade-union chief, Boekler, in reconstituting the German trade-union movement.

Meyer did not, however, agree with Boekler in his present tactics. In the summer of 1948, when dismantlement on a big scale began in the British zone, he had proposed that the German trade unions, chambers of commerce and guilds of artisans, executives and owners of German factories, together with the Protestant and Catholic clergy, should all simultaneously go on strike and refuse all co-operation with the British Military Government.

Meyer's proposal, he told me, had been squashed by Boekler's lieutenants who had said that Boekler did not want any disturbances or threats to mar the good results he expected from his talks in London and Paris. It was also probable that Boekler was averse to taking any action which involved forming a united front with "the capitalists" and the churches in defense of the whole German people.

Fritz Hentzler, the Socialist mayor of Dortmund, whom I interviewed the same day, although not a young man, was also a militant man of broad outlook. Like Ernst Reuter of Berlin he represented the interests of all his people, and was more concerned with human needs, freedom and justice than with "state ownership of the means of production and distribution." He shared none of the illusions of the Boeklers and Schmidts who like Rip Van Winkles in a changed world, continue to believe that the Socialists of other countries are as internationally minded as themselves.

Hentzler told me that the German trade-union leaders had at first refused to believe that a British *Labour* Government would ever deprive the German workers of their means of existence, and that the majority of German workers had accordingly never imagined that dismantlement on a big scale would actually be carried out. They had ascribed the outcry of the employers and executives as merely a capitalist or nationalist reaction against disarmament measures. Thus the trade unions in the Ruhr, voting to restrict their activities to particular objectives, refrained from causing difficulties for the British occupation forces. Later when the full effect of the planned dismantlement was becoming obvious, the German workers had been confident that the Marshall Plan meant that it would stop, and that a higher level of industry would be permitted to Germany. Having first vainly placed their trust in the British Labour Government, they were now looking for justice from capitalist America.

Hentzler and a few others had realized from the beginning that dismantling was a serious menace and had little hope that America would stop it. For, in his view, dismantlement on a big scale had been planned by the United States and Britain as the means to bring about an accord with France; and he thought that in 1948 they had promised to carry it through, whatever its cost and however disastrous the consequences to the German workers and the German democrats.

Hentzler also told me that when he had first spoken to General Robertson about the financial consequences, the British Military Governor had been sympathetic but now was "ice cold." Evidently there was a firm Anglo-French-American agreement on steel, designed to destroy Germany's productive capacity and double French and Belgian production.

"Since antidemocratic and destructive are synonymous terms, the net result of dismantlement," said Hentzler, "is the '*demontage*[13] of democracy.'"

"Every economic difficulty," he continued, "is a reflection on democracy and is welcomed by the Nazis and other extreme nationalists in Germany, as well as by the Communists."

The Ruhr is the center of Communist influence in Germany and the Communists take every possible advantage in their propaganda of the ruin brought about by dismantlement. They play upon nationalist sentiment almost as effectively as the Nazis did, proclaiming that dismantlement and the Anglo-American-French agreement on control of the Ruhr, are planned to turn Germany into a colony of slaves working for

---

[13] The German and French term for dismantlement.

the profit of the Anglo-Saxon and French imperialists. Their propaganda contains sufficient truth for it to be effective. Seeing their Social-Democratic leaders failing to protect their livelihood and Germany's basic interests, the German workers would naturally follow the Communists, were it not for their firsthand experience of the Russian terror.

When I asked Hentzler how it was possible for any German to fall for Communist propaganda, since all knew or heard of the terrible treatment Germans received in Russia and in the Eastern zone, Hentzler smiled sadly and said:

"You underrate the stupidity of the masses. Roosevelt and Churchill were both hoodwinked by Stalin, so why shouldn't the German people be?"

He went on to tell me that some German nationalists believe today that they can rearm Germany with the help of the Soviets. "They are ready to be Russian mercenaries today in the hope of creating an independent Germany in the future."

As an example, Hentzler pointed to the case of Graf Einsiedel, Bismarck's grandson, who today plays an important role in Russia's "Free German" movement, because he wants to revert to his grandfather's policy of friendship with Russia.

I asked Hentzler whether he thought that such German nationalists really believed that Germany could regain her independence by collaborating with Russia against the West, or whether they were preparing to betray the Russians when they got the chance. He replied: "People on the negative side are always more apt to unite than progressives."

I asked Hentzler if he thought that many former Nazis were now Communist collaborators, and he replied, "Very few with the idea of winning Germany for the Russians. A great many on the basis of the belief that they must win Russia's aid to rebuild Germany and free her from Western domination." He went on to point out that only a minority, such as the Nazis had been, was needed to swing a country. "The former high Nazis and many former *Wehrmacht* officers," he continued, "will never be satisfied with low positions. They long above all for a system in which they can once again occupy the seats of power."

Arnold, the president of North-Rhine Westphalia, whom I interviewed in Düsseldorf, drew my attention to the aid and comfort given to the German Communists by Bevin's reported statement to General Marshall that dismantlement in the Ruhr should be continued "on security grounds," since otherwise the Soviets might capture intact plants which could be put to their service.[14]

Naturally, he said, if it was expected that unarmed Germany would not be defended, but surrendered to the Russians in the event of war, many Germans would feel that there was no choice but to get on good terms with the Communists in advance.

"The anti-Communist sentiments of the Germans," said Arnold, "are good and strong." If only England and America would draw up an occupation statute giving the Germans freedom, self-government, and responsibility, there would be a solid basis for a democratic development. "Then," he continued, "we could speak to the East zone with a strong voice."

The effect of a declaration that dismantlement was to be stopped at once would have an electrifying effect on the Germans. "Germans are so ready to cooperate in European reconstruction," said Arnold, "that *'Europa über Alles'* would then supplant *'Deutschland über Alles'*[15] in German hearts."

It is easy to dismiss such statements as this as unworthy of belief and to argue that the Germans under the pretext of being good Europeans plan to dominate the Continent. Such distrust ignores the "all or nothing" nature of the German character. Since they are inclined to pursue a line of policy to its logical conclusion, the Germans today, given the chance to utilize their brains, skills, and capacity for hard work in peaceful ways are perhaps more, not less, likely to become good Europeans than other nations with less singleness of purpose.

---

[14] Cf. *Newsweek*, XXXII (September 27, 1948), 11.
[15] "Europe over (or above) all" instead of "Germany over (or above) all."

War propaganda has obscured the true facts of history, otherwise Americans might realize that the German record is no more aggressive, if as aggressive, as that of the French, British, and Dutch who conquered huge empires in Asia and Africa while the Germans stayed at home composing music, studying philosophy, and listening to their poets. Not so long ago the Germans were, in fact, among the most "peace-loving" peoples of the world and might become so again, given a world in which it is possible to live in peace.

Mistaken as the Boeklers of Germany may be in believing that concessions can be won from the Western powers by negotiation, their attitude proves the willingness of many Germans to trust to peaceful means to obtain their ends.

There is unfortunately little prospect that they will be able to do so. Again, as in pre-Hitler days, the German Social Democrats are between two fires. Twenty years ago they had to struggle against the Nazis on the one hand, and the Communists on the other. Today they are weakened in their struggle against the Communists by British and American Military Government.

"We are compelled to go softly in the Ruhr," I was told, "because there are strong Communist groups among the German workers, who interpret any action we take against dismantlement as opposition to the Western democracies."

The force of this remark had already been borne in on me by what I had read in the Russian-licensed press in Berlin, which inveighed against dismantlement in the Ruhr (though not of course in the Russian zone), and the treatment of Germany as a colony by the Western Powers. But it seemed to me that the German Social Democrats had no hope of maintaining their leadership of the workers, or any other Germans, if they were so afraid of seeming to be on the side of the Communists that they failed to lead Germany's struggle for national freedom and the right to work. This was notably the case with regard to the so-called internationalization of the Ruhr agreed upon by the British, French, and Americans early in 1949. This agreement provides for the permanent, or long-term, control of Ruhr industries by Germany's conquerors with only a minority voice for the Germans in the disposal of the product of their labors. There is no question that it does, in fact, reduce the Ruhr to the status of a British Crown Colony under tripartite control. The leaders of German labor in the Ruhr, however, have seemed to display more interest in ensuring the appointment of their nominees as trustees of the Ruhr coal mines and iron and steel industries, than in opposing the virtual detachment of the Ruhr from the German economy.

So in January 1949 the Communists took advantage of the wonderful opportunity presented to them to pose as the champions of the conquered and oppressed German people. Max Reimann, the Communist leader in the Ruhr, struck a powerful blow for the Communist cause when he said in a public speech:

"German politicians who today co-operate with the occupation forces under the international Ruhr statute should not be surprised if they are considered quislings by the German nation. They may one day have to face reprisals."

The British hardly helped their Social-Democrat friends by arresting Max Reimann for this statement and turning him into a hero of the German resistance. The Communists turned his trial into a mass demonstration against the conversion of the Ruhr into an Anglo-French-American colony.

The crowd assembled by the Communists sang the *"Internationale"* so loudly during Reimann's trial that it forced a recess, and compelled the British public-safety officer, Colonel Pollock, to beg the Communist leader to calm the crowd and tell them to go away. Max Reimann was thereupon reported to have "smiled broadly" and answered, "I didn't call them here."

Finally German police dispersed the crowd, but when Reimann emerged from the court room he was carried for miles on the shoulders of cheering crowds. As a high British official is reported to have ruefully admitted: "It looks like the trial is backfiring. It has made the Communists the champions of all Germans who oppose the control given to the International Ruhr Authority over German coal, coke and steel."[16]

Reimann was nevertheless sent to prison by the British court on the charge of having broken a Military Government law against "interference with persons who give aid and sustenance to the occupying powers," that is, persons who collaborate with the conquerors. Nothing could have suited the Communists better. Their leader was now able to pose as the champion of the oppressed German nation. Anti-Communist German politicians were compelled to come to Reimann's defense. Kurt Schumacher, chairman of the German Social-Democratic party, stated that if the principle of "obedience" to Military Government was applied as a protection for German politicians, it would prove helpful to the Communist cause; and Heinrich Hellwege, chairman of the right-wing *Deutsche Partei*, declared that Reimann's conviction appeared to confirm the Communist charge that non-Communist German politicians were "performers of the will of the occupation power," and that those who openly criticized measures of the Western Powers were subject to punishment.

Subsequently Military Government officials reported privately that they were again having trouble in getting Germans to take responsible administration positions.[17]

Unfortunately for the democratic cause, when some German workers at Essen were arrested by the British for their refusal to dismantle the Bochum Iron and Steel Works, or to permit its being dismantled, there was no such powerful popular support for them as the Communists had organized for their leader, Max Reimann. They were sent to jail unheralded and unsung. Nor did the SocialDemocrat trade-union leaders do anything effective to prevent the use of British troops to compel the Bochum workers to give way, after the British had announced, on January 5, 1949, that "there will be sufficient British troops standing by to insure that the job will start, and that if the Bochumer Verein workers try to interfere this time, we are prepared to take counter measures."

---

[16] *New York Herald Tribune,* January 19, 1949.
[17] *New York Times,* February 4, 1949.

A year earlier, in January 1948, the Social-Democratic leaders in the British zone had been intimidated by the double threat of starvation and British tanks into preventing the general strike demanded by the rank and file. The Ruhr workers had been literally starving that winter of 1947-48 when for a long period the daily ration had been reduced to 800-900 calories, which is less than the Nazis gave their concentration camp victims. Finally the trade union leaders had been called into a conference by the Minister of Food of North-Rhine Westphalia and told that there were only 3,000 tons of fat in the whole Ruhr area. The question was whether to divide it so as to give a four-week fat ration to the miners, on whose labors all industry depended, or to give each worker an ounce a month for two months.

The trade-union leaders had refused to decide this awful question. Then the Minister of Food, having referred the decision to the Economic Council at Frankfurt, was told that even the 3,000 tons did not exist—that in the whole of North-Rhine Westphalia there was only 460 tons of fat, which constituted a bare week's supply for the miners if no other Germans received any fat at all.

In this desperate situation an appeal was made to Bavaria, which came through and supplied some fats.

"If we had allowed a general strike as was demanded by a third of the Ruhr workers," one trade union official said to me, "the last possibility of acquiring fats would have been destroyed by the stoppage of transport."

"We told the workers the truth," he continued, "and asked them to continue working without any fat ration. We prevented riots believing that if they occurred, the British would have used tanks, and there was a real danger that the Russians would then have come as our 'liberators' from Anglo-American tyranny. Anything was preferable to that."

In that terrible month of January 1948 Boekler had told the British and American authorities that they had better use their troops to get food from the German peasants, rather than send their tanks against the Ruhr workers.

It was hard in the Ruhr to resist the conclusion that by their law-abiding nature, their pacifism, and the mixture of respect, trust, and fear with which they regarded the British Labour Government, the German Social Democrats had indeed made themselves appear to be quislings. As in the late twenties, they were losing popular support and preparing the way for their own demise.

If most of the Ruhr's trade-union and Social-Democratic leaders appeared to have learned no more than the Occupation Powers from the tragic history of the past thirty years, the same could not be said of other Social-Democratic leaders in Germany. In an earlier chapter I have spoken of the clear-sighted and courageous Berlin Socialists. The views of Carlo Schmidt, the Social-Democratic leader from the French zone, offered a similar contrast.

Carlo Schmidt is an outstanding personality. The son of a French mother and a German father, he combines Teutonic strength and determination with Gallic wit and fire, and love of life and beauty. A poet, a philosopher, and a professor of international law, as well as an eloquent speaker, Carlo Schmidt is too well known in the European literary world, and too influential, for the French to dare imprison him. Lesser German "heroes of the resistance" against French tyranny are summarily disposed of by the Sûreté. But Carlo Schmidt, who ruled a French province during the days of the German occupation, and achieved an enviable reputation for justice and fair dealing and courage in protecting the French from the Gestapo, is a man who can neither be smeared nor easily repressed.

I met Carlo Schmidt first in October 1948 in Bonn, where he was a delegate to the Parliamentary council endeavoring to hammer out a Constitution for Western Germany. In late November I met him again in Berlin where he had come to help his SocialDemocratic colleagues in the elections. On both occasions I was impressed, not only by his intelligence and understanding of the problems of our time, but also by his humanity and freedom from class, racial, or national prejudices. Like Ernst Reuter of Berlin, and unlike most of the Socialists I met in the Ruhr, Carlo Schmidt represents a new, nondoctrinaire, Socialist movement, which is more liberal than socialist, more concerned with the preservation of freedom and the basic values of Western civilization than with economic theories.

"If the Allies decide to let us live," Carlo Schmidt said to me in Bonn, "they must be reasonable, they must leave us the means to earn our bread. If not, they should announce that they intend us to die of hunger, and, if they are merciful, they should provide the necessary gas chambers for our painless extermination."

The least harm, he said, was being done by the Americans, who took account of economic realities. But the British were determined to wipe out German competition whatever the political and moral cost, while in the French zone destruction had been carried to such lengths that the exports of major industries had been wiped out, and there was no longer any possibility of self-support.

Carlo Schmidt thinks it is a mistake to believe that Communist propaganda in Germany today falls on deaf ears. "If the Germans are driven to despair," he said to me in French, "they will follow the Communists, if only with the hope that the others will also die like dogs."

Later, at a factory in the French zone, I was told that some of the workers were already saying, "Let the Russians come. Whatever they do to us, we shall at least be able to cut the throats of the French first."

I had no reason to doubt the value of Carlo Schmidt's warning that the day might come when the masses would get out of control. Like other German democrats, he also told me that the day after victory the Western Allies could have done anything they liked with the Germans.

"America," he said, "was like Almighty God in those days. Had she known what she wanted and announced it, she could have shaped Germany and Europe to her will. Today this is no longer the case, not only on account of Soviet Russia, but because the Germans have been disillusioned by the wide gap between democratic pretensions and practices, and the vacillation, weakness, and contradictions in American policy."

When later in our conversation I commented on the contrast between the heroism of the Berlin Social Democrats and the weakness of their Western colleagues in dealing with British and United States Military

Government, Carlo Schmidt said this was not due to the cowardice of the latter, but to bitter experience. In Berlin the Germans could look to American support, but in the Western zones they were alone and defenseless. Moreover, the fact that they realized that all open and strong criticisms of the Military Government played into the hands of the Communists, put them in an extremely difficult position.

In Berlin the German democrats had the Western democracies on their side; in the Western zones they had no support since they refused to accept the Communists as allies, or play off Russia against the West.

Nor could the German democrats in the Western zone count on having grievances and injustices remedied by publicity or appeals to the Congress of the United States and the British Parliament. The Germans have no government to speak for them. They are without rights and live in what is in many respects a vast internment camp. Very few Germans are allowed to travel abroad; foreign newspapers and books are generally unobtainable; their contacts with foreigners outside the Military Government are few, and they are not even informed about the debates in Congress on Germany, or given the official texts of documents, such as those relating to ECA, which most intimately concern them.

After fifteen years of semi-isolation under Hitler, the Germans under Western Military Government are still cut off from the free world outside.

At a meeting of Generals Clay and Robertson with German industrialists, officials, and trade-union leaders which I attended at Essen on October 2, 1948, I was astonished to hear neither Hans Boekler nor Arnold Schmidt speak up strongly against dismantlement. Here was a meeting open to the press of the world in which the Germans had had a rare opportunity to cry out loud and be heard. But only Kost, the representative of the coal owners, did more than give utterance to polite platitudes. When a few days later in Düsseldorf, I asked for an explanation from an official of the metal-trades union, he said:

"Boekler and the others have for so long had dealings only with the Military Government authorities that they didn't realize that for once they had an opportunity to speak to the outside world. We are rather like prisoners brought suddenly into the light of day, blinking and unable to believe we are free."

Nor are they free. Although the Germans are today allowed far greater freedom of speech than in the first years of the occupation, the press is still controlled, and any editor who publishes articles or comments reflecting the real opinions of the Germans is liable to be slapped down and told he is encouraging "nationalism." Even Americans are not exempt from this charge as was proved when Kendall Foss, the former correspondent of the New York *Post* who was made editor of the United States Military Government's newspaper, *Die Neue Zeitung*, in 1948, was reprimanded in January 1949 and placed under the supervision of three representatives of the Information Services Division. This action was taken by Colonel Textor as a means of assuring that "a strong American staff would control the editorial output of the paper."

Mr. Foss, who is that *rara avis*, a real liberal, had made the mistake of assuming that freedom of the press meant that a newspaper should be "a forum for the expression of German ideas." He learned, rather later than most Germans, that the "freedom" the United States Military Government allows means only the expression of opinion favorable to itself. Since *Die Neue Zeitung* is privileged with respect to paper allocation, communication, and transport facilities, it has a much larger circulation than other German-language newspapers. So the curbing of its freedom of expression was particularly harmful and its German editors resigned in protest.

With respect to freedom of speech and opinion, it would be more honest and less discreditable to democratic principle, to proclaim openly that such freedom is not permitted in Germany, than to pretend that it exists. As one German said to me, "We should have more respect for America if she stopped preaching what she does not practice, since we now no longer have much hope of her practicing what she preaches."

The Germans are today a little better off than in the first years of the occupation, only because of the disagreements among their conquerors. While the Russian-licensed press exposes us, we expose the

Russians; and Anglo-French-American antagonism makes it possible for British-licensed German newspapers to criticize the American Military Government, American-licensed papers to criticize the British, and the French to criticize both.

If the German people have been permitted to raise their heads again on account of the quarrels among their rulers, this right is not unquestioned. Every time the Germans dare to protest against their intolerable situation and claim the rights of free men, a spate of articles is let loose in the United States press concerning this dangerous manifestation of "nationalism."

An article published in the excellent and outspoken *Wirtschaftszeitung* of Stuttgart on January 29, 1949, concerning Allied complaints of German "arrogance" is very much to the point:

As long as the Germans were pulling their hand wagons and had no idea in their heads other than getting to the country to "organize rucksacks of potatoes," the Germans seemed more agreeable than today. They were then too engulfed in misery, physically weak, and overwhelmed by the catastrophe which had befallen them and the revelation of the atrocities committed by the Nazi regime, to arise and plead their case. They were too discouraged and apathetic then to have much interest in the future. They grumbled, but they did what they were told.

But since they are now a little better off, they are becoming more active—perhaps sometimes even rebellious. Above all they are now industrious and filled with a pathetic desire to reconstruct their country.

The Allied occupation authorities, having permitted the Germans to be a little better off, are now surprised and indignant that there is no gratitude for the improvement. The Germans complain that there is insufficient improvement and demand more opportunity to develop their strength and have become "too bold."

One might say with some exaggeration that, as compared with the former apathy which prevailed, the smallest expression of the will to live on the part of the Germans is now regarded as "arrogance."

Not only is the German press under military government still kept in a straight-jacket; the Germans are not allowed any direct communication with the outside world, or any press representation abroad, so they are entirely dependent on American, British, and French correspondents for the expression of their grievances, which are therefore rarely brought to the attention of their conquerors.

Officially the Germans may have no communication with any authority outside and above the Military Government.

As one German Social Democrat said to me: "The American people are far away but General Clay is very near. We have little faith in the effectiveness of the principles and good will of the American people, as against the power of General Clay. Since General Clay is badly advised, especially on economic questions, we have more reason to fear him than to trust to the good will of the American people."

When at a meeting of the Minister Presidents of all the German states, one bold German proposed to address an appeal direct to Congress on the dismantlement question, begging for help, the majority voted against the proposal saying that the result was uncertain and it would anger the American occupation forces.

"Hoffman does not exist for us," said Carlo Schmidt. "The ECA people will have to come to us, for we are not allowed to communicate with them."

It caused much resentment that the Military Government should use the situation of the Berliners as a means to blackmail the Western German democrats. In effect, the Germans were told on more than one occasion that protests against dismantlement might result in the starvation of Berlin. The threat was, of course, made in more veiled terms. The German authorities in the Western zones were told that if American, British, or French people were antagonized by active opposition to dismantlement, it might be impossible for the Military Government to obtain the means to supply and hold Berlin.

This seems to the Germans not only a denial of the unity of interests between the Western powers and the German democrats in face of Soviet aggression and Communist crimes against humanity. It also recalled the early days of the occupation when the Americans had not scrupled to coerce individual Germans by the threat of handing them over to the tender mercies of the Russians. To hint that Berlin might have to be surrendered to the Communist terror, if the Germans of the Western zone refused to submit quietly to the loss of their livelihood through dismantlement, was both dishonorable and politically stupid.

While in Germany I was often reminded of the story told by a South American ambassador to a New York audience. I cannot vouch for its authenticity but it illustrates my point.

The Foreign Minister of San Marino, the story ran, came to Washington to try to get a loan. At the State Department the first question put to him was: How many Communists are there in San Marino? The diplomat answered that San Marino was a very small state and a happy one and had no Communists. "Very sorry," said the State Department; "in that case we can't give you a loan."

So the Foreign Minister of San Marino went to Paris, and said to Monsieur Bidault, the Foreign Minister: "France and San Marino have always been friends, would you do us a favor and lend us a few Communists in order that we may get a loan from America?"

"I regret it exceedingly." replied Monsieur Bidault. "I would be delighted to help the good people of San Marino if I could. But unfortunately we cannot spare you a single one of our Communists since we need them all for the same purpose."

The sequel to this story provides the moral. Today the Republic of San Marino has a Communist-dominated government.

If there had been a strong Communist movement in Germany, as in Italy, the Germans would be receiving far better treatment at our hands. The great majority of Germans, having met communism in Russia face to face, or having suffered under it following Germany's defeat, or having relatives in the Soviet Union's concentration camps, or having seen the living skeletons of the former soldiers who return from Russian imprisonment, or being immune to Communist blandishments on account of their experiences under Hitler's similar regime, are anti-Communist. This has led the British, French, and American authorities to believe that however badly we treat the Germans they must take our side. We seem to act on the theory that we should bribe those whom we fear may become our enemies, while we can safely maltreat those most certain to be on our side.

Thus the Germans who, for good or ill, are a consistent and straightforward people, suffer today in consequence of the belief that, however hardly we treat them, they will never join our Communist enemies.

While seeking by endless subsidies to maintain the weak forces of French democracy, we insult and browbeat the German democrats, and cut the ground from under their feet by appeasing France, as we formerly appeased Soviet Russia. It is therefore hardly surprising that Communist influence in the Western zones is far from being negligible. Although very few Germans have any illusions about Communism, a considerable number are beginning to think that "it couldn't be worse" under the Russians, and that perhaps in the long run it might be better. A more powerful incentive to coming to terms with the Soviet Government is the refusal of the West either to guarantee Germany's defense or allow her to defend herself.

A former high German administrative official under the United States Military Government said to me in Munich: "If the Germans continue to be told that the United States is only concerned with the defense of France, England, and the Low Countries, and doesn't care a damn what happens to Germany, Western Germany may be forced to join up with Soviet Russia."

A young German employed by the Military Government in Munich said that more and more Bavarians were saying: "If after being disarmed by the United States we are also going to be abandoned in the event of war, we had better not offend Russia."

This same young man told me that he was reproached by everyone, including people who had always been anti-Nazi, for working for the Military Government, so complete is the disillusionment with America among liberal circles which had first welcomed us as liberators.

Moreover, he said, it was considered very dangerous now to work for the Military Government, since anyone who did so could expect to be liquidated "when the Russians come."

"Everyone is now looking for a Communist friend who will protect him, and wants to be able to say to the Russians. 'I never collaborated with the Americans.' Factory owners who refuse contributions to the other parties give money to the Communist Party as a form of insurance."

Dr. Mauritz, a German working in the Public Opinion Section of Military Government, said that the uncertainty of United States policy and the fear that Germany would be left defenseless before Russian attack played into the hands of the Communists. American Military Intelligence, however, seemed to ignore the danger because it took the election returns as proof of the small number of Communist sympathizers. It ignored the fear and the desperate search for security which led men to try and establish "good relations" with the Communists.

"Men who have lived through both the Nazi terror and the Communist terror and have come here after losing everything they possessed," said Dr. Mauritz, "are now in deadly fear that the Russians will come, and are seeking for any kind of security."

Some, he continued, think that they can win only with the Communist Party, not against it. Others, whose houses and furniture have been taken from them for the use of the occupiers, or who have been rendered destitute by currency reform, say: "The Americans have stripped us of everything we possessed; what more can Russia do to us?"

These sentiments were not confined to the former middle classes who are now paupers. They were also expressed to me by a considerable number of workers. At Lindau on Lake Constance, for instance, where the train on which I was re-entering Germany from Switzerland stopped for an hour, I spoke to some of the men working on the railway. When I asked how people felt here about Russia, one of them shrugged his shoulders and said, "What can they do to me? I have nothing more to lose."

The feeling that there is no hope on either side, is reviving the belief that "only a strong man can save us." Whereas the Nazis were utterly discredited by the end of the war, many Germans now think that, after all, Hitler was right. The success of Military Government in creating Nazis, is illustrated by the joke about the German who came to the denazification office to register as a Nazi. "Why the h—— didn't you come three years ago?" he is asked. "I wasn't a Nazi then," he replied.

After spending a few weeks in Bavaria, I could appreciate the force of Carlo Schmidt's speech at a Social-Democratic party meeting in Berlin which I attended on November 27, 1948. He said that thousands of marks had been collected in Bavaria for the Communist Party by people who were "laying in stocks of Persil[18] for the next cleaning." People who were preparing for any eventuality were trying secretly to insure themselves against a Communist victory while voting for "reaction," meaning the Christian-Democratic party (CDU)

"I wish," Carlo Schmidt said, "that I could take some of the strength of Berlin back with me to the West. In the Western zones—where, as compared to the East, we enjoy some freedom and peace—there is defeatism. The future seems to offer us nothing but suffering, and hope is almost dead. But here in Berlin you are showing that we Germans can still make history as well as suffer—here a glorious chapter is being written in the record of man's struggle for freedom. The Berliners are showing the world how a brave people can behave in defeat under alien occupation."

"The German name," he continued, "has been rehabilitated in Berlin. It is honored once more. We have only Berlin to thank for the fact that there is today some sympathy for the German people.

"We in the Western zones are sending you a few calories, but we are receiving from you something infinitely more precious: our moral calories

---

[18] A well-known brand of soap flakes.

come to us from Berlin. We owe it to you that Germany has regained its self-respect, and that we can hope that at last Germans will again be at home in their own country."

The hall was icy cold, unheated except for the body warmth of the thousands assembled. Carlo Schmidt had fired them; Ernst Reuter, who spoke next, evoked a warmth of affection which few democratic leaders in the world today can inspire. Looking like a sad sea lion, in his overcoat and with a muffler around his neck, hoarse and tired and with a bad cold, Reuter spoke to the crowd as their elected mayor rather than as a leader of the Social-Democratic party. Schmidt had spoken against the Christian-Democratic party in the Western zones, although he had been careful to distinguish between the Berlin Christian Democrats fighting together with the SPD for liberty, and the Bavarian CDU leaders whom he called "hard-faced men" who "mean money when they speak of God." But the only part of Reuter's speech which could be construed as Socialist appeal was also a plea for unity. "Adenauer,"[19] he said, "is a foreigner to Berlin which he does not visit. He lives on the lovely *Rhine*, but he should remember that Berlin is also German and that the *Rhine* belongs to us too."

"The Communists," continued Reuter, "will never win power if the Germans remain united against them."

Carlo Schmidt had appealed to the Berliners to "free us of the West" from the domination of the reactionaries who "deny the right of the masses to be a subject instead of an object in the economic process." The people, he had said, see no value in democracy if it means that they have to "endure despotism in the factories six days a week, and become free men only once in every four years when sticking a paper in the ballot box."

Reuter, however, addressed this Socialist meeting in much the same terms as I had heard him speak to the hundreds of thousands of Germans of all parties assembled outside the Reichstag in September.

"We are the only people in Europe still forced to live in war conditions," said Reuter. "We cannot rebuild our besieged city; we still live

---

[19] The leader of the CDU who was also chairman of the Parliamentary Council at Bonn engaged in drawing up a constitution for Western Germany.

in fear and deprived of the possibility to work and reconstruct our devastated homes."

And again, as on every occasion on which I heard him speak, Reuter insisted: "We are not enemies of the Russian people. We are fighting against the policy of the Soviet occupation power."

"We cannot help it that our women will never forget what happened to them at the hands of the Russian soldiers." Reuter continued, "but we are haters of no people, race, or nation."

Both speakers emphasized Berlin's position as the capital of Germany, and Schmidt assured the Berliners that the Germans of the Western zones would insist on Berlin's being represented in the Parliament of Western Germany.

I did not meet Kurt Schumacher, the chairman of the SPD, who was in the hospital recovering from the amputation of a leg while I was in Germany. So Ernst Reuter and Carlo Schmidt are the two outstanding Social-Democratic leaders I got to know. I cannot say which is the greater man of the two, since their experience and the problems they face today are so dissimilar. Reuter spent the war years in exile in Turkey; Schmidt was an officer in the German Army, although never a Nazi. Reuter is leading the German resistance in Berlin against Communism with some Anglo-American support. Schmidt is fighting a battle on two fronts: against Communism *and* against the Western Military Governments which still treat the Germans as unworthy of the rights of free men.

Both men are brave, sincere, and unflinching in their defense of democracy. Both are physically strong and dynamic personalities. Reuter, the Prussian who used to be a professor, and Schmidt the *poet* who was a soldier, are at one in their repudiation of the narrow, doctrinaire socialism of the past. The basic aims and values of both men are primarily liberal. They have both assimilated the experience of the past decades and understand, far better than most Western Labour and Socialist leaders, that the economic organization of society is secondary to the preservation of basic liberties, justice, respect for the dignity of man, honor and truthfulness and fair-dealing between men and groups and nations. They are also realists who refuse to accept words for deeds, and know that all the fine proclamations of the United Nations mean nothing, if denied by actions contrary to the principles professed by the democracies.

As I sat listening to Reuter in my seat next to his wife, I sensed her fears as well as her love and pride. Few others have thus defied Soviet terror at close quarters and escaped death. Frau Reuter lives in perpetual fear that the Russians will murder, or kidnap and execute, her brave husband. She also had good reason to dread that his health will break, since he never spares himself and works night and day without sufficient good food, for the Western occupying powers, unlike the Soviets, give no material aid to those who fight our battles.

Three months earlier I had sat with the Reuters in the little garden of their house in Zehlendorf, where in his "spare time" Ernst cultivates his vegetables like any other Berliner lucky enough to have a small plot of land to produce some food to supplement their inadequate rations.

We had discussed the chances of continuing American support of German democracy, and I had expressed my horror and disgust of the conqueror versus conquered attitude of the British and Americans in Berlin, which reminded me of the behavior of the "whites" toward Asiatic and African peoples. Reuter had replied that all that was "your business," not his. He had made me understand, without precisely saying so, that just as he, like all Germans had to suffer the consequences of Nazi crimes, so we in the West would similarly be held responsible before the bar of history for our government's "crimes against humanity" in defeated Germany. It was our affair, not his. He was concerned with Germany's present fight for freedom against the Communist totalitarian tyranny which threatened to supplant Hitler's.

Reuter told me that it was he who had first formulated the slogan "Berlin is not Prague." He was expressing the feeling of the Berliners that if they could stand firm, in spite of hunger and cold and Communist terror, they would eventually be able to win freedom and "make it impossible for the West any longer to treat us as natives."

The world, having seen the fall of Czechoslovakia without a struggle, had merely watched and said, "Who will be the next victim of Communist aggression?" But Berlin had shown that even an unarmed people, given the will and courage to resist, could withstand the Communist assault.

Reuter was amused, instead of bitter, about the British. While not at all flattering in his remarks about the United States occupation authorities, he said that the Americans were less self-confident, more curious and somewhat more human in their contacts with the Germans than the British, who are "the real master race." Conversations with the Americans in Berlin were "possible"; although he and other Germans were still treated as underlings, they could at least discuss with the Americans the situation caused by the blockade. But the British continued to be "stiff." The British knew their business and made fewer mistakes than the Americans, but the latter at least behaved as human beings. The behavior of British officers, on the contrary, seemed similar to that of the stiffnecked German officials who respected nothing but force.

One day, Reuter said, he had got really angry with the British and told them that he would no longer obey their orders unless they changed their attitude. "Tell your general," he had said, "that he can expect complete disintegration of the administrative machinery." The result of this defiance was a call to visit the British general in command.

"Is it true," Reuter was asked, "that you have said you will no longer obey us."

"If the situation continues as at present, I cannot obey," Reuter replied.

The British general thereupon smiled and terminated the interview. He had wanted to make it clear that the Germans must obey under any circumstances. Confronted with a blunt refusal, he had climbed down.

The Communist menace had forced the Western Powers to start treating the Germans with more politeness. After the Soviet blockade of Berlin began, both the American and British representatives in the Allied

Kommandatura had actually got up when the German representatives arrived.

Reuter was convinced that the Social-Democratic party's majority in Berlin had been won through the confidence engendered by its behavior. Eventually this confidence would enable it to become the leading party in Germany as a whole, and thus enable it to carry out its economic and social program. But, he said, "we shall never try to establish a socialist economy by force. We shall endeavor to lead Germany to socialism, but not to force it upon our people. We don't think of economic problems in the old terms. So many things formerly believed impossible have been proved possible; and so many simple solutions have proved fallible. We are no longer doctrinaire Socialists, for according to theoretical writings we all ought to be dead. We know, from our terrible experiences, that reliance on absolute theories can lead us to ruin; we must experiment and judge by trial and error what are the best forms of economic organization, but always conceiving of freedom and respect for individual rights, justice, and human dignity as the criteria of progress."

It had been warm and peaceful in Reuter's garden, and he had stilled my fears that Western civilization was doomed, by his calm and confident belief that in the end right and decency and reason would triumph. Afterwards, in the Western zones, it had been far harder to believe in the victory of democracy than in Berlin. In the West instead of the sound of American planes flying in supplies to defend democracy, there was the sight of factories being torn down to discredit it.

How long would German fears of the Communist terror prevent their coming to terms with the Russians if we continue to demonstrate that there is no hope for Germany on our side?

In Berlin no one is ever likely to forget the murder and rape and pillage of the Russian occupiers when they held the whole town, and everyone knows what is going on now in the Eastern zone. But in the Western zones they are mainly concerned with their own grievances under Western occupation.

One of the German Defense Counsel at Nuremberg who has a French wife and lives on Lake Constance under French occupation, said to me:

"Russia could create a powerful pro-Russian movement in Germany in a few weeks, if she would give even the smallest practical proof of good will in deeds, instead of words. She would only have to offer to give back our lost territories and give us a national government. The Russians have this chance to play on German patriotism while the Americans haven't. Moreover, the Americans want us to have no patriotic feelings at all.

"Although almost all Germans are anti-Communist and terrified of what the Communists would do to them, if the Russians came with patriotic slogans and ceased to use the German Communists, they would be wonderfully successful.

"Most Germans would think twice before becoming soldiers of America. Not only is there little faith left in your democratic professions after the way you have treated us. The very fact that we still recognize that you are more humane and civilized than the Russians plays into their hands. Having little confidence that America will defend Germany or win the war quickly, it seems safer to go along with the Russians who will kill everyone who opposes them if they occupy Germany. We know, on the other hand, that those who fight for Russia won't all be killed after America's victory.

"Since the West offers us nothing to fight for and we have no illusions left about anybody or any political creed, don't expect us to think nowadays about anything but our personal security. Having been both Nazified and denazified with equal disregard for justice and honesty, and having also observed America's benevolent attitude toward the Communists so long as it suited her interests, we Germans are today disinclined to believe anything or fight for anybody."

This young German lawyer, although anti-Communist, had conceived a great affection and respect for the Russian people while on the Russian front in the early stages of the war. He had marched on foot from the Polish frontier to the Sea of Azov and been very much moved and impressed by the kindness of the people and the virtue of the women. When the German soldiers arrived footsore, hungry, and weary at the end of a long day's march the villagers would come with milk and make them comfortable.

"Their instinct was to help the suffering because they themselves have suffered all their lives. Yet the women who tended to us were extremely virtuous. They were friendly, but they would have no sexual intercourse with us. They were human beings helping other human beings and unconcerned with national hatreds and passions."

"Coming from Nazi Germany where everything was action, it made a tremendous impression on me to come to Russia where suffering is constant and borne with passive courage. Many of us who were soldiers in Russia now feel that we have more to learn from Russia than from the West.

"By being so active and working hard, we Germans have made the whole world unhappy. Our greatest need is to develop our contemplative faculties, and here we can learn much from the Russian people.

"We Germans are always either too hostile or too friendly to other people, whereas the Russians take people as individuals, and know that principles are just principles, and that it is human behavior which counts. We ask, What has he done, but the Russian people ask, What kind of a man is he?"

This is a romantic view. But there is no doubt that many Germans feel sympathy for the Russian people, who are as miserable, oppressed, and poor as themselves.

A few of the returned prisoners of war I talked to in Germany, without having any such philosophical concepts as those I have just quoted, felt friendly toward the Russians who had suffered as much or more as themselves. And down in Munich where I met a whole group of Russians who had been prisoners of war or "slave laborers" in Germany, I found a reciprocal friendliness toward the German people. The maxim that suffering makes all men brothers may yet bring the Germans and

Russians together against the rich, comfortable, and complacent West. The Germans and Russians are held apart only by the cruelty and stupidities of the Soviet Government. Should the latter be able or willing to reverse its policies, I have no doubt that it is true that Russia could win immense influence in Germany. Fortunately for the Western world the crimes and follies of the Soviet dictator are greater even than ours. Nevertheless our belief that however badly we treat the Germans they must remain on our side, is a dangerous delusion.

The fact that the United States Military Government has its headquarters in Berlin probably gives it an unduly optimistic view of German sentiments. As a well-known German politician in Bavaria said to me: "The sentiments of the Berlin population are quite different from those of the Germans in the Western zones. Not only do the Berliners know better what to expect from Russia: they are also terrified at the prospect of the revenge the Soviet Government will exact if Berlin is abandoned by the West. But in the Western zones where the people have experienced only the injustices perpetrated by America, Britain, and France, and where there has been no such strong opposition to Communism as in Berlin, the people are less afraid of Russia."

6

THE NUREMBERG JUDGMENTS
IS GERMANY OUR COLONY?

THE MATERIAL COST OF VENGEANCE IS HIGH ENOUGH, BUT THE MORAL and political consequences are incalculable. It is as urgently necessary to revive the German people's faith in democratic justice as to cease destroying their assets and capacity to work for the rehabilitation and defense of Europe.

Four years after their unconditional surrender the Germans are still *rechtlos*: without civil or political rights and without the security offered by a government of laws not of men.

As one prominent German lawyer said to me at Nuremberg: "We have merely exchanged one dictatorship for another; after twelve years of Hitler's lawless rule, we have had four years of military government with its similar arbitrary decrees and denial of justice."

The basis of democracy is government of laws not of men, and this means that the law is known and applied to all. But at Nuremberg we not only applied ex post facto law but also stated that it applied only to Germans. According to the judgments of the United States tribunals at Nuremberg the will of the conquerors is absolute, and the vanquished have no right to appeal to international law, American law, or any other law against it.

Instead of teaching the Germans that "crime does not pay," we have enunciated the theory that the victors are entitled to do anything they please to the vanquished once the war is over. According to the logic of our judgments at Nuremberg, the Germans are punished, not for having committed war crimes, but for having lost the war.

The belief that Might makes Right is clearly stated to be the basis of the trials the United States has conducted at Nuremberg. "We sit," said the American judges, "as a Tribunal drawing its sole power and jurisdiction from the will and command of the four occupying powers. In so far as Control Council Law No. 10 may be thought to go beyond established principles of international law, its authority, of course, rests upon the exercise of the 'sovereign legislative power' of the countries to which the German Reich unconditionally surrendered."[20]

Few Americans at home may be aware of it, but their representatives at Nuremberg have expressly stated that the victors are not bound by the same laws as the vanquished. When the German defense counsel argued that if it was a crime against international law for the Germans in occupied Poland and Russia to confiscate private property, use civilians and prisoners of war as forced laborers, and starve the people in the occupied territories, then why is it not also a crime for American, British, French or Russian Military Government to do the same thing, they were told:

"The Allied Powers are not subject to the limitations of the Hague Convention and rules of land warfare."

Why?

"Because," said the American judges and prosecutors at Nuremberg, "the rules of land warfare apply to the conduct of a belligerent in occupied territory so long as there is an army in the field attempting to restore the country to its true owner, *but these rules do not apply when belligerency is ended, there is no longer any army in the field, and, as in the case of Germany, subjugation has occurred by virtue of Military conquest.*"[21] (Italics added.)

In other words, if Germany had won the war, she would have ceased to be bound by international law, and none of her nationals could be held

---

[20] P. 14 *et seq.* of the Judgment in case No. 3. See also the Krupp case (No.10 and other trials where the same thesis is repeated.
[21] *Ibid.*, p. 10.

guilty of having committed war crimes or "crimes against humanity." Since we won it we are not limited in any way by the provisions of the Hague or Geneva conventions, or by any international or recognized law.

The argument that what is a crime during war ceases to be one as soon as the fighting stops, is surely the choicest bit of legal sophistry thought up by Mr. Justice Jackson, or Brigadier General Telford Taylor who succeeded him as chief United States Prosecutor at Nuremberg. It is tantamount to saying that you must not hit a man below the belt while you are fighting him, but you can kick him in his most sensitive spot once he is down and out.

The argument that the Hague and Geneva conventions ceased to be binding on us the moment the Germans surrendered unconditionally was continually repeated by the American judges and prosecutors at Nuremberg: "A distinction is clearly warranted," it was stated in the Judges case, "between the measures taken by the Allies prior to destruction of the German Government, and those taken thereafter. Only the former need to be tested by the Hague Regulations, which are inapplicable in the situation now prevailing in Germany."

This theory was given immediate application after Germany's surrender. Many German prisoners of war in American hands, who had hitherto been decently treated, suddenly found themselves transformed into rightless men liable to be forced to work long hours for a pittance in consequence of a disposition made in Washington. Instead of being sent home at the war's end, according to the Geneva Convention, their American captors handed them over to the French to be used as slave laborers in mines and factories. The French thereupon deprived them even of their warm clothing and the dollars they had earned as prisoners of war. The British similarly kept German prisoners of war as forced laborers for years after the end of the war.

President Truman's agreement at Potsdam, that "reparations in kind" should be exacted from Germany in the form of labor conscripted to work in the victor countries, gave Stalin the right to add hundreds of thousands more German slave laborers to the gangs of prisoners of war already working in Russia.

This imitation of Nazi practices was given a "legal" basis by the convenient thesis that international law ceased to be binding upon the victorious "democracies" on May 15, 1945, when Germany surrendered unconditionally.

The fact that only the Germans are liable to punishment for war crimes, because they were defeated and have no government to protect them, was expressly stated at Nuremberg:

"It must be admitted that Germans were not the only ones who were guilty of committing war crimes; other violators of international law could, no doubt, be tried, and punished by the state of which they were nationals, by the offended state if it can secure jurisdiction of the person, or by an International Tribunal of competent authorized jurisdiction."

"The apparent immunity from prosecution of criminals in other states," the Germans were told, "is not based on the absence there of the rules of international law we enforce here" [at Nuremberg], but is due to our exercise of sovereignty in Germany as against the impossibility of any international authority assuming power "within a state having a national government exercising sovereign power."[22]

In other words, the conquest of Germany and elimination of her government makes German nationals liable to prosecution while the nationals of undefeated countries are not so liable. The fact that only the defeated are liable to punishment for breaches of international law was expressly stated in the Generals case (No. 7). When the German defense counsel argued that such acts as "devastation unwarranted by military necessity"; the seizure of private property; the infliction of general penalties, "pecuniary or otherwise," upon the population of occupied territories; "requisitions in kind and services demanded from municipalities or inhabitants except for the needs of the army of occupation," and "out of proportion to the resources of the country"; seizure of "cash funds and realizable securities which are not strictly the property of the state"; compulsory recruitment from the population of an occupied country for labor in the occupying country; and other acts

---

[22] *Ibid.*, p. 22.

expressly forbidden by the Hague and Geneva conventions had all been committed by the victors as well as by the Germans, the American Tribunal replied:

> "It has been stated in this case that American occupational commanders issued similar orders. This Tribunal is not here to try Allied occupational commanders, but it should be pointed out that subsequent to the unconditional surrender of Germany, she has had no lawful belligerents in the field.[23]

In their anxiety to prove that only Germans should be punished for war crimes, the American judges and prosecutors at Nuremberg with their theory concerning the difference between what is permitted under a "nonbelligerent" occupation, but not permissible while fighting is going on, have got the Americans and the British into an ambiguous position. Mr. Richard Stokes, the English Labour Member of Parliament, argued in a speech made in the House of Commons on June 30, 1948:

> I doubt very much if we are legally entitled to take reparations until there is a peace treaty. I should like to hear the opinions of an international lawyer about that. I believe that reparations form a part of peace terms, and are not a consequence of the cessation of hostilities, even if this involved unconditional surrender. *I believe that reparations taken before a peace treaty are loot, and nothing else.* Honorable Members may not like the term, but that is what I believe it is in international law.

Such legal and moral scruples have not troubled the American prosecutors at Nuremberg, who have felt secure in the knowledge that the American public has been left completely ignorant by its press and Congress of the moral and legal issues at stake. Some of the United States Judges sent to Nuremberg, however, have felt qualms in applying an unprecedented law based on nothing but the power and will of the conquerors. In the "Judges Case" where the basis for the judgments pronounced at Nuremberg was most clearly expressed, the United States Tribunal endeavored to reassure itself by saying: "Surely Control Council

---

[23] Statement by the Tribunal on "The Hague and Geneva Conventions."

Law Number Ten, which was enacted by the authorized representatives of the four greatest powers on earth, is entitled to judicial respect."

The will of the Big Four Powers was thus held to provide the sanction reserved to the Deity or to a rational concept of the Rights of Man in other legal systems.

While maintaining that international law does not apply to our occupation of Germany because her unconditional surrender transferred sovereignty to the occupying powers, it was also stated at Nuremberg that "the fact that the Four Powers are exercising supreme legislative authority in governing Germany for the punishment of German criminals, does not mean that the jurisdiction of this Tribunal rests in the slightest degree upon any German law, prerogative or sovereignty."

This latter statement is obviously in direct contradiction to the first, which claims that the transfer to us of sovereignty in Germany justifies our repudiation of international law. We have the Germans both going and coming. We refuse to observe international law because we are the "sovereign" power; and we refuse to apply American or German law because our tribunals derive their power from "international authority." The Germans are left *rechtlos*—without the protection of any law and subject to the arbitrary decrees issued by their conquerors. We have, in fact, outlawed the whole German "race" as Hitler outlawed the Jews. In the name of democracy we have subjected the German people to the rule, not of laws but of men.

Since no peace treaty has been signed and yet our occupation of Germany is held to be "nonbelligerent," the question arises: "What is its legal basis?" Is the United States ruling its zone in Germany as a colony in theory as well as practice? In that case should not either "native" law or American law be applied, since international law has been ruled out? The answer given to the German defense counsel was in the negative.

Neither international law, nor German law, nor American law, nor the basic principles of Anglo-Saxon jurisprudence were the basis of the indictments, procedures, and judgments of the Nuremberg Tribunals.

The British, French, and Russians withdrew from Nuremberg after the first and only "International Military Tribunal" (I.M.T.) had tried and condemned Goering and other top Nazi leaders. The other twelve trials which subsequently took place at Nuremberg and only came to an end in November 1948, were all-American shows. The judges and prosecutors were all American citizens; the trials were held under the American flag; the proceedings began each morning by the Marshal of the Court asking God's blessing on the United States of America; and the indictments ran: "The United States of America, plaintiff *versus* the defendants." Nevertheless the tribunals were supposed to be "international" and to derive their authority from the Allied Control Council even after the latter ceased to exist.

Neither the principles nor the procedures of American jurisprudence were followed, and the defendants were debarred from appealing to the Supreme Court or any higher authority than the United States Military Governor. The verdict of the American judges who constituted the Tribunal was absolute, except for the right of General Clay to mitigate the sentences.

The "legal" basis for these trials was Control Council Law No. 10, drawn up by the United States, the Soviet Union, Britain, and France for the "Punishment of Persons Guilty of War Crimes, Crimes Against Peace and Against Humanity."

Far from being the beautiful child of International Justice as Mr. Justice Jackson still maintains, CC Law No. 10 is the monstrous offspring of Communist "Peoples democratic justice" and the savage principle of "Woe to the Vanquished."

It is based on the totalitarian concept of collective guilt and punishment. It decrees that anyone, who in any capacity, military or civilian, aided or abetted the German war effort, is guilty of the crime of waging aggressive war. Its scope is so wide that it defeated its purpose. American judges sent to Nuremberg to judge war criminals have not known where to draw the line without incriminating the whole German population and creating a precedent for the incrimination of all Americans in any future war designated as "aggressive" by the Communists. For CC

Law No. 10 can be held to mean that the peasant or farmer who produced and sold food, the industrialist who continued to give employment and the workers employed, the civil servant and the soldier who obeyed orders, are all guilty.

CC Law No. 10 seems in fact to have been a "legal" attempt to indict the whole German nation and thus justify the Morgenthau Plan. But such was the reluctance of most American judges to administer totalitarian "justice," that none but the top policy makers condemned by the International Military Tribunal have been sentenced on this count, in spite of the passionate efforts of the American prosecution to secure convictions.[24]

Unfortunately, however, the articles of Control Council Law No. 10 relating to "war crimes" and "crimes against humanity" which are equally wide in their scope have been the basis for the sentences imposed at Nuremberg by American Tribunals.

According to CC Law No. 10 you are accounted guilty of a war crime or atrocity if you "took a consenting part therein" (i.e., obeyed orders); were "connected with plans or orders involving its commission"; were "a member of any organization or group connected with the commission of any such crime"; "held a high position, civil or military" (including General Staff), or "held a high position in the financial, industrial or economic life" of Germany or its allies or its satellites.

This latter provision suggests the influence of the Communists in drawing up the CC Law No. 10, since it indicts most of the capitalist class.

The American judges at Nuremberg insisted on drawing a line and would not apply the principle of collective guilt in the manner demanded

---

[24] Since this was written von Weizsäcker has been convicted on the aggressive-war charge as concerns Czechoslovakia. It is an ironic commentary on the Nuremberg trials that the man whom Lord Halifax and British Foreign Office officials testified had done his utmost to try to stop Hitler from going to war, and who, as a leader of the German opposition, escaped death after the July 20, 1944 plot only because he was Minister to the Vatican, should have been convicted by the United States Tribunal on an aggressive-war charge. Judge Powers, of Iowa, wrote a dissenting opinion, but the views of the prosecution were accepted by the other two judges.

by the prosecution. They insisted, for the most part, on proof of some direct responsibility or overt act, and thus modified the law, instead of acting like Soviet judges. Nevertheless, in many cases the judgments at Nuremberg have no basis in international law and bear the imprint of a Communist conception of justice. This was notably the case when Alfred Krupp was indicted and condemned in place of his father, although the younger man had never been in control of the Krupp enterprises.

It was strange and horrifying to sit listening to the proceedings in the Ministers case (No. 11) in the same courtroom in which the representatives of the Soviet dictatorship had formerly shared the bench with American, British, and French judges, and to hear American jurists in November 1948 refer to the judgments of the International Military Tribunal as precedents. When one reflected that General Rudenko, who was the chief Russian prosecutor at the International Military Tribunal trial, is now commandant of the Sachsenhausen Concentration Camp in the Russian zone, one could appreciate what kind of "justice" was being administered by American judges at Nuremberg.

The powers and procedure to be followed by the American Nuremberg Tribunals were laid down in United States Military Government Ordinance Number Seven. This ordinance specifically states that American rules of evidence are not to be applied by the judges. Hearsay and double hearsay evidence is permitted, and it is left entirely to the discretion of the judges whether or not the defense be permitted to question the authenticity or probative value of evidence. It is worth reproducing Paragraph VII of Ordinance No. 7, since it is one of the bitterest complaints of the German defense lawyers that all known rules of evidence were jettisoned by the Nuremberg Tribunals:

The Tribunals shall not be bound by technical rules of evidence. They shall adopt and apply to the greatest possible extent expeditious and non-technical procedure, and shall admit any evidence which they deem to have probative value. Without limiting the foregoing general rules, the following shall be deemed admissible if they appear to the tribunal to contain information of probative value relating to the charges: affidavits, depositions, interrogations, and other statements, diaries, letters, records, findings, statements and judgments of the military tribunals and the reviewing and confirming authorities of any of the United Nations, and copies of any document or other secondary evidence of the contents of any document, if the original is not readily available or cannot be produced without delay. The tribunal shall afford the opposing party such opportunity to question the authenticity or probative value of such evidence as in the opinion of the tribunal the ends of justice require.

The Judges were also given the right to be informed beforehand of any evidence to be presented by the defense, and could refuse to allow it if they did not consider it "relevant." Considering the close proximity in which the judges and prosecutors lived in the small closed American community in Nuremberg, this proviso was taken by the Germans to mean that the prosecution would always be informed beforehand of the defense's evidence. The assumption that the judges and the prosecutors had an identity of interest was justified in at least one trial by the spectacle of the prosecutors shaking hands with the judges and congratulating them on their verdict.

The defense counsel were in any case in a very weak position. The accused had all spent a long period in prison before being brought to trial and their papers had been seized and searched by a large American staff. Whatever was useful came into the hands of the prosecution, while the defense lawyers had the utmost difficulty in securing any documents. Only in the last trial, that of Baron von Weizsäcker and other Foreign Office officials, was the defense allowed to peruse the files of captured documents in the possession of Military Government, and even in this case only a few weeks were allowed in comparison with the years during which the prosecution had prepared its case.

In the Krupp case the German lawyers never had an opportunity to search the files carefully and didn't even know if all the files had been made available.

The accused, weakened by long imprisonment and insufficient food before being brought to trial, had to rely for the most part on their memories, instead of upon documents, for their defense.

The gravest handicap of all under which the defense labored was the difficulty of finding witnesses, obtaining access to them, and inducing them to testify at Nuremberg. The prosecution had all Military Government information and facilities at its disposal for locating witnesses, and the right to imprison them, interrogate them endlessly and exert fearful pressures to induce them to testify as the prosecution desired.

The defense lawyers had neither access to Military Government information, nor communication and transport facilities, nor funds to spend on searching for witnesses, since the property of all the accused was sequestered before they were proved guilty.

At the time of the International Military Tribunal trial of major war criminals, nearly all the witnesses were in jail, and could not be interviewed by the defense if the prosecution claimed them as its witnesses. By 1947 the situation had improved so that most witnesses were free, although some were still in prison and could be interviewed by the defense counsel only in the presence of a representative of the prosecution.

Naturally, witnesses whose release from imprisonment depended on the favor of the United States Military Government were reluctant to give any testimony contrary to the desires of the prosecution. Moreover, even those not in custody were frightened by the close connection between the prosecution and the denazification authorities.

There was a "Special Projects" branch of Military Government in the Palace of Justice at Nuremberg, which analyzed all the documents presented at the trials with a view to uncovering such evidence as might convict the witnesses in denazification courts. Thus many witnesses found themselves hauled off to prison to be tried by denazification courts supplied with evidence against them by the "Special Projects" branch.

The fear of all witnesses that they would land up in prison themselves if they came into the United States zone to testify at Nuremberg was so great that in the fall of 1947 Military Government had to give "safe conducts" guaranteeing their return home to witnesses living in the British and French zones.

Witnesses at Nuremberg were never subject to the horrible tortures used at the Dachau Military Tribunal trials, which I deal with in the next chapter. At Nuremberg the pressures exerted on witnesses by the prosecution were mental rather than physical. It was often possible to get the testimony required from a witness by keeping him in prison for two or three years in terrible anxiety for the fate of his family, left unprovided for, or by threatening him with being arraigned as a war criminal himself if he refused to testify against the accused.

In some cases the all-too-familiar weapon of Military Government in Germany was employed: the threat of handing over an un-co-operative witness to the Russians. This practice was dramatically revealed in the trial of Baron von Weizsäcker and other German Foreign Office officials, in the fall of 1948.

Van Weizsäcker had so many eminent liberal friends abroad who testified to his innocence that it was possible to raise funds to hire an American lawyer for his defense. Mr. Warren Magee of Washington, D.C., came to Nuremberg and, being an American, was able to obtain access to documents denied to the German defense counsel. He managed to get hold of a transcript of the interrogation of Friedrich Gaus, who although designated as the "Grey Eminence" of the German Foreign Office, and as "Ribbentrop's evil spirit," had become the prosecution's chief witness. There was a sensation in court when Mr. Magee read out the transcript of Gaus's first interrogation which showed that Mr. Kempner, the American prosecutor, had threatened to hand Gaus over to the Russians, if he did not help the prosecution.

The highhanded manner in which the American Tribunal treated the defense counsel in several of the trials, and the denial to the defense of the right to examine or cross-examine many witnesses, led to one of the biggest scandals of the Nuremberg trials, and finally discredited American justice in German eyes.

The American judges in the Krupp case were from all accounts more prejudiced and un-American in their method of conducting a court of law than any others who came to Nuremberg. They continually overruled the defense counsel, while allowing the prosecution to shout and rant at the witnesses and the German lawyers. Finally, Judge Daly drove the defense counsel to leave the court in a body in protest. He first overruled the German lawyers' objections to the examination of witnesses out of court by a commissioner, and then arranged for the examination to take place while the Tribunal was sitting, so that the defense lawyers would have no opportunity of being present unless they could arrange among themselves which of them would stay in court and which of them be present at the commissioner's examination.

When one of the defense counsel started to ask for an adjournment in order that this could be done, he had hardly opened his mouth before Judge Daly, then presiding, said to him: "Take your seat or I'll order you out of the courtroom." The German, Dr. Schilf, having started to say, *"Ich bitte darum"* ["I beg you"], Judge Daly told him to "remove himself." Thereupon the other defense counsel followed him out of the court in a spontaneous protest.

Not having been permitted to speak, the German lawyers sat down to draft a written statement asking to be allowed to exercise their right to be present at the examination of witnesses. Before they could present it to the Tribunal, they were all arrested and taken into custody. They were kept in prison over the week end and then asked to apologize for their "contempt of court," although the apologies would seem to have been clearly due to them, not from them.

Dr. Kranzbuehler, who was Krupp's counsel and a brilliant jurist, had been absent on a case in the French zone when this incident occurred. On his return, which coincided with the release of his fellow defense lawyers from prison and the demand that they all apologize to the court, he made a statement to the Tribunal, part of which I reproduce below. Because of the contempt of American justice shown by this Nuremberg Tribunal applying the bastard law based on CC Law No. 10 and United States Military Government ordinance No. 7, Kranzbuehler was able to shame the American judges.

Referring to the question of whether or not the German lawyers had been guilty of "contempt of court" he said:

I am in the unfortunate position of not knowing according to which law this decision is to be taken. Yesterday the Tribunal through Judge Wilkins explicitly refused to apply American law. It has rather tried to base its decision, or based its decision, on Ordinance Number Seven which gives the authority to the Tribunal to have a summary proceeding "with contumacy," as it is said there.

I would like to comment on this as follows: The question of which law is to be applied is of fundamental importance. The attorney has grown up and is trained in the legal concepts of his country. When, in a task that he has undertaken as a German lawyer, judgment is suddenly passed under the legal system of a country which is foreign to him, or according to a legal system which does not belong to any country at all, but the significance and interpretation of which is entirely up to the discretion of the Tribunal, then there is great danger that decisions are passed which in his eyes are a grave injustice.

The German defense counsel is already surprised to ascertain that his conduct is considered according to the same procedural regulations as apply to the trial of alleged war criminals, that is, rules which are drawn up for a specific purpose, and that this is the opinion of the Tribunal has definitely been confirmed to me when I moved that Judge Daly should be excluded because of prejudice. Therefore, without regard to which law the Tribunal will finally consider using, I state the principles which would be guiding for such incidents as occurred here under German law. Only then will the Tribunal understand the basis of the instinctive reactions of the defense attorneys present here.

According to German procedural law, it is first of all a breach of duty for a judge not to hear a motion by defense counsel. Such a breach of duty entitles a German defense counsel, among other things, to complain to the superiors of such a judge. Furthermore, a German defense counsel has the possibility, when he deals with a tribunal which is made up of several judges, to object against the ruling of one of the members of the tribunal and to appeal beyond that to the decision of the whole of the tribunal. Therefore, according to German procedure, it was right for Dr. Schilf to do what he did. In addition, a German judge is not permitted to dismiss a defense counsel from the courtroom so long as he performs his duty.

Under German law there are very often long and heated discussions between the tribunal and the defense counsel, and no judge would think that he could hold a defense counsel guilty of contempt of court because of objections on the part of the defense counsel to the statements of the tribunal. For such a conception, Your Honor, is not included in German law. The judge has no disciplinary authority against a defense counsel. If the tribunal believes that the defense counsel has not fulfilled his duty properly, then it can appeal for a decision to the bar association having jurisdiction. On the other hand, however, the defense counsel has the right to complain about the tribunal if he believes that their attitude caused him to be dismissed from the courtroom.

With biting sarcasm, Kranzbuehler observed:

These in large outlines are the fundamentals of German law. Your Honors will probably agree with me that under such legal training the events look entirely different than they look from your point of view under the legal training of an American Judge.

While making his oblique denunciation of "American" justice as applied at Nuremberg, Kranzbuehler made good use of his opportunity to protest against the unfairness of the whole proceedings; and he was heard through to the end, perhaps because Judge

Schick, United States president of all the courts, had told Judge Daly and Judge Wilkins that they had got themselves into a mess and warned them to behave with more circumspection.

This is the third trial [Kranzbuehler said] which I am experiencing at Nuremberg. I cannot say that I am spoiled in my expectations of Nuremberg trials which is partly caused by the nature of the whole procedures. Many and grave anxieties have overshadowed the defense counsel in this trial to an enormous degree.

After protesting the kind of evidence decreed as inadmissible by the Judges, he concluded by saying:

> I would ask the Tribunal to consider that these defendants have been in an almost hopeless position from the beginning, and are entirely dependent upon our being able to assure a fair trial for them. I know the Tribunal will probably say or perhaps think: "That is our business as judges, to safeguard a fair trial." But, Your Honors, you will probably have to admit that—I still remember the words which were said at the beginning of the session yesterday—that "ultimately this is a trial of the victors against the vanquished." In the judgment in the Flick case, right at the beginning, this fact was mentioned specifically. The Tribunal deduced from this its duty to safeguard all the rights and privileges of the defendants in every detail; but in these trials, here in Nuremberg, such a guarantee is only valid if either the Tribunal itself creates all the prerequisites for a fully fair trial, or if the defense counsel is in a position, because of their motions and objections, to insist that the trial be a fair one.
>
> If you consider for a moment, Your Honors, that you have here the unlimited authority of an American judge, which you know from your own home country, but that we have not all the guarantees here which you have in your country to prevent a wrong or, in the eyes of the defense counsel, unjustified use of such authority. These defendants have no constitutional rights. It has been confirmed again and again to them that guarantees as given in American procedure are not applicable to them. Neither is there a powerful press, which in complete independence, can see to it that no misuse of power can occur."

Dr. Kranzbuehler, also referred to the enormous responsibility of the German defense counsel at the Nuremberg Trials owing to the fact that there is no higher court of appeal. He had himself, on February 27, 1948, sent a telegram to President Truman saying that "all endeavors to secure a fair trial" had been frustrated "on account of rules originating from American military authorities," and appealing to the President of the United States for "help and relief." His appeal was not answered. It was referred back to the United States Military Government on the ground that the "international status of the Nuremberg tribunals based as they are on quadripartite agreement precludes any responsibility or duty resting upon any executive agency of the United States Government to entertain any such petition or plea." Kranzbuehler was further informed that no such German petitions would in future be transmitted by Berlin.

Thus, by the hypocritical pretense that the American Nuremberg Tribunals were "international," the United States washed its hands of responsibility for the conduct of its own judges. If this is the way we expect to teach respect for justice and democracy to the Germans, we must be among those whom the gods mark out for destruction by first making them mad.

The subject of the Nuremberg trials requires a book, not a few pages. I have endeavored here only to present the basic assumptions of the trials, so that the American public may know how justice is mocked in their name.

A Swiss journalist pointed out the disservice which these trials have rendered to the interests and reputation of the American people. Writing in *Die Weltwoche* of Zürich in October 1948, Robert Ingrim, quoted what Alexander Hamilton had said in 1788:

To establish an act as a crime after it has been committed, or in other words to punish people for things which did not violate any law when committed, and the practice of arbitrary detention, were at all times the most favorite and also most horrid tools of tyranny.

Many of the condemned at Nuremberg were, no doubt, guilty of hideous crimes and deserved their sentences. But, as the Swiss journalist pointed out, the effect of verdicts based on ex post facto legislation violates the sense of justice so that even justified convictions leave doubts among a large number of people. We have made martyrs of criminals by the Nuremberg trials, and given a new lease on life to Nazi doctrines by our own transgressions against fundamental democratic principles.

Lastly the Nuremberg trials have aroused a justified suspicion, not only in Germany but also in other European countries, that the real objective of the Americans responsible for them was to "level the social structure of Germany." The aim of the prosecution at Nuremberg seemed to be to prove that "the capitalists and landowners" were the main support of Nazism, and to obscure the resemblance of the Third Reich to Stalin's Russia. Hence the endeavor to indict Flick and Krupp and other German industrialists as war criminals. Hence also the trials of German generals, some of whom had in fact opposed, not encouraged, Hitler's mad ambitions. Hence also, and far more unjustly, the arraignment at Nuremberg of Baron von Weizsäcker, the aristocratic diplomat who had continued in office under the Nazis, but whose endeavors to prevent war and to save the victims of Nazi terror were attested at his trial by such persons as Lord Halifax and other Englishmen in other responsible positions; the former French Ambassador François-Poncet: Carl Burckhardt, former High Commissioner of the League of Nations in Danzig; von Steiger, the President of Switzerland; Bishop Berggrav, the leader of the Norwegian resistance movement under German occupation; the Pope; the American Catholic Bishop Muench, of Fargo, North Dakota, now Apostolic Visitor in Germany; the Protestant Bishop Wurm of Stuttgart, who was persecuted by the Nazis: and many of the relatives of Hitler's blood purges, including Jews.

As the afore-mentioned editor of the Swiss *Weltwoche* suggested, "by dragging the Junkers, militarists and industrial barons in the dust, not on the basis of individual guilt but collectively," the prosecution at Nuremberg was endeavoring to pave the way for Stalin by obscuring the fact that Nazism was akin to communism, and by falsely representing it as a "concoction of the German upper classes." They were endeavoring to destroy, not the Nazis but the pre-Nazi social structure of Germany, based on private property, free enterprise, and the European tradition.

The Kempners of Nuremberg [wrote Robert Ingrim] cannot get over the fact that the list of those executed after [the plot against Hitler of] July 20, 1944, looked like an excerpt from the Almanach de Gotha. Deep down in their hearts those who adored the masses were much closer to the Führer than to Moltke, and Stauffenberg: for Hitler was spirit of their spirit, the most common of all common men, the national socialist, the owner of the miraculous formula which offers selfadoration in the nation as compensation for the inferiority complex of common men.

There are grounds for suspecting that Brigadier General Telford Taylor, who as Chief Counsel for War Crimes directed the Nuremberg Trials after Justice Jackson's departure, was sympathetic to the Soviet Union. For instance, he refused even to apply to the

Soviet Government for the extradition of German witnesses in Soviet territory, such as the notorious Nazi, Martin Bormann, suspected to be still alive, because it might be "embarrassing to the Russians."

When asked by the correspondent of the *London Evening Standard* whether the Russian campaigns in Poland, Finland, Roumania, Lithuania, Latvia, and Estonia could be considered as "aggression" under the International Military Tribunal findings, General Taylor replied: "Whether a particular episode constitutes a crime against the peace is not determined solely by legal definitions, but by the evidence relating to 'action' and 'state of mind.' " And he went on to say that it was not his function as chief prosecutor to comment on "episodes outside his competence."

Asked before leaving Germany on September 25, 1948, whether the transfer of German workers to slave labor in Russia is in contravention of the laws established at Nuremberg, General Taylor said that the evidence concerning this was only "lay" evidence and that Russia's action ought, in any case, to be considered "in relation to the existing situation."

These remarks are not conclusive proof of where General Taylor's sympathies lie, and since he had left Nuremberg before I got there, I had no opportunity to interview him myself. But the consensus among the correspondents devoid of Communist sympathies supported the German and Swiss conviction that he was a sympathizer, or dupe, of the Communists who have derived such great benefits from the travesty of American justice at Nuremberg.

In spite of the 115 convictions at Nuremberg, including 18 death sentences, which he had secured out of a total of 144 completed cases, General Taylor was not satisfied with the result of his efforts. For he not only failed to secure the conviction of any German capitalists on the aggressive war count, but he was also unsuccessful in trying to persuade the

British to stage any trials similar to the political trials conducted by America. The British sense of legality led them to try Germans only for abuse of recognized international law, or for atrocities which would be punishable under German or Anglo-Saxon law.

General Taylor's only success was to induce the French to set up a tribunal, complete with a Polish Communist, as well as a Dutch and French judge, to indict and sentence a German industrialist, Roechling, on the aggressive war charge. But even in this case, General Taylor, who attended the trial, was said to have been disappointed that Roechling was sentenced to seven years' imprisonment, not as a capitalist, but as the German official in charge of steel production.

Whether or not German and neutral opinion was right in believing that the aim of the American prosecution was to "level the social structure of Germany" by proving that "capitalists and landowners" were guilty as a class, and that a big German executive was *ipso facto* a Nazi, the trials gave good grounds for the suspicion.

Not only did the prosecution direct its fiercest invective against German industrialists and the *Wehrmacht* generals, and try hardest to convict the former of the aggressive war charge. The fact that Alfred Krupp was indicted and sentenced for his father's "crimes" make these trials seem designed to punish a class, not individual guilt.

As regards "landowners," it was noticeable that the prosecution used the most notorious Nazi murderers as the main witnesses against the titled *Wehrmacht* generals who had opposed, and in some cases failed to carry out, Hitler's orders for the liquidation of Poles, Russians, and Jews.

In the Generals' case the chief witnesses for the prosecution were Oswald Pohl, the former administrative chief of the SS who testified in fetters; and Otto Ohlendorf, *Gruppenführer* (major general) in the SS in charge of the *Einsatzgruppen*, formed in 1941 for the purpose of following the German army into Russia to exterminate Jews and Communist officials. Otto Ohlendorf, admitting at his own trial that he had killed 90,000 people, had been condemned to death. But he was not executed because the prosecution valued him for his bitter hatred of the *Wehrmacht* generals who had despised and hated him and his kind. He was kept as the prosecution's star witness against the "officers and gentlemen" it wished to convict.

This use of men condemned to death or long years of imprisonment as prosecution witnesses was a particularly unsavory feature of the Nuremberg Trials. Naturally such men could easily be induced to bear false witness in the hope of saving their lives or regaining their freedom. The case of Ohlendorf was particularly revolting since he was and remains a fanatic Nazi ready to say anything to convict the *Wehrmacht* generals whom he loathes.

Reading the indictments and judgments in most of twelve cases of "The United States *versus* the defendants," one is struck by the anomaly that we should have spent so much time, money, and energy, and so tarnished America's reputation for impartial justice, prosecuting Germans for having committed war crimes in Russia, while the Soviet Government itself refused to have any part in the trials. The Soviets for their part were busy inducing the German "war criminals" to become their collaborators. So it frequently happened that American judges at Nuremberg sentenced those who had carried out the orders of their superiors, while the superior officers themselves were occupying high positions in the Russian zone. For instance, General Vincent Müller who drafted the order for the liquidation of Russian civilians in the way of the German army, is now Chief of Staff to von Seydlitz who commands the Soviet-German "police force" in the Russian zone. But General Hans von Salmuth who was the staff officer who distributed the order was condemned to twenty years' imprisonment by the American Tribunal at Nuremberg. And many an obscure sergeant or corporal has already been hung for carrying out the orders of his superiors, while those responsible for the orders have not been punished.

It might satisfy the American prosecutors and judges at Nuremberg to say that a crime was only a crime when committed during a war, and that in peacetime crimes against humanity could be committed with impunity. But to me—and I felt sure to most Americans also, as well as Englishmen—this doctrine is repugnant.

Unfortunately most Americans and most Englishmen have no knowledge of the crimes against humanity which we have committed or agreed to let our allies commit.

The American press reported little beyond the indictments and statements of the prosecution in the Nuremberg trials. At the United States Public Information Office in the Nuremberg Palace of Justice I found that, whereas copies of the indictments, judgments, and statements made by the prosecution were available in unlimited quantities, I could not secure copies of the statements made by the defense counsel. I had to spend hours copying them myself from the single copy available in the office.

The attitude of the American Public Information officials appeared to be that it was impertinent of the Germans to put up any defense. "When these lousy kraut lawyers get through with their dirty tricks," was the answer given to an inquiry when Case No. 11 was likely to end.

When I asked the Chief Public Information Officer, who was supposed to arrange appointments for correspondents, to put me in touch with one of the German defense counsel, he said he didn't know how to contact them and made me understand that I was guilty of a breach of good manners, if I was not positively a suspicious character, because of my wish to talk to the German lawyers.

Betty Knox, an American newspaperwoman who hails from Kansas, but is now a correspondent of the British Beaverbrook press and has spent three years in Nuremberg, told me that at the International Military Tribunal, although hundreds of copies of the prosecution documents to be presented to the court were available to the foreign press before the proceedings, only two copies in German were provided for the thirty-five defense lawyers, and these only after each day's proceedings. When Betty Knox asked Justice Jackson why more copies were not supplied to the German defense counsel, he said that in the United States there was no exchange of documents. When she insisted that in international law courts it is done, Jackson got furious and exclaimed: "That would be too good for these bastards!"

The Nuremberg Trials are now at an end. The only function they have fulfilled is that of making a mockery of American justice and filling the Germans with hatred and contempt for our hypocrisy. It is to be hoped that Congress, which has begun to interest itself in the miscarriage of justice in Germany under the American flag, will order a review of the sentences passed at Nuremberg, so that the innocent may be released from prison and only the guilty punished.

7

OUR CRIMES AGAINST HUMANITY

COMPARED WITH THE RAPE AND MURDER AND LOOTING ENGAGED IN by the Russian armies at the war's end, the terror and slavery and hunger and robbery in the Eastern zone today, and the genocide practiced by the Poles and Czechs, the war crimes and crimes against humanity committed by the Germans condemned at Nuremberg to death or lifelong imprisonment appeared as minor in extent if not in degree.

It was impossible to travel through the devastated towns of the Western zones without it seeming strange and horrible that we should sit in judgment on the Germans who had never succeeded in killing nearly so many civilians as we did, or in perpetrating worse atrocities than our obliteration bombing of whole cities. Were the German gas chambers really a greater crime against humanity than our attacks on such nonmilitary objectives as Dresden, where we inflicted the most horrible death imaginable on a quarter of a million people in one night, by dropping phosphorus bombs on this undefended cultural center crowded with refugees fleeing west before the Russian advance? This atrocity was among our greatest war crimes, since we demonstrated that our objective was the murder of civilians. We even machine-gunned from the air the women and children fleeing into the countryside from the burning city.

Nor was Dresden the only example of horrible death inflicted on the people of towns which had neither war industries nor any "military importance."

The story of Hiroshima has been written up in American magazines and books, but who has told the story of Dresden, or that of Cologne, where the cathedral stands in the midst of acres of rubble, demonstrating the fact that we knew how to avoid destruction of nonmilitary objectives if we wanted to?

As the British Major General J. F. C. Fuller wrote in his book, *The Second World War*: "For fifty or a hundred years, and possibly more, the ruined cities of Germany will stand as monuments to the barbarism of their conquerors. The slaughtered will be forgotten, the horrors of the concentration camps and gas chambers will dim with the passing of the years; but the ruins will remain to beckon generation after generation of Germans to revenge."[25]

A thoughtful American professor, whom I met in Heidelberg, expressed the opinion that the United States military authorities on entering Germany and seeing the ghastly destruction wrought by our obliteration bombing were fearful that knowledge of it would cause a revulsion of opinion in America, and might prevent the carrying out of Washington's policy for Germany by awakening sympathy for the defeated, and realization of our war crimes. This, he believes, is the reason why a whole fleet of aircraft was used by General Eisenhower to bring journalists, Congressmen, and churchmen to see the concentration camps; the idea being that the sight of Hitler's starved victims would obliterate consciousness of our own guilt. Certainly it worked out that way. No American newspaper of large circulation in those days wrote up the horror of our bombing, or described the ghastly conditions in which the survivors were living in the corpse-filled ruins. American readers sipped their fill only of German atrocities.

Whether most Americans in Germany have developed a mental defense mechanism, or really believe that an atrocity ceases to be one when committed in a "good cause," that is, our own, I do not know. But I found many Military Government officials who considered it bad taste, if not almost treasonable, so much as to refer to our war crimes and those of our allies.

In Berlin, for instance, I found myself in disgrace after having remarked, at a cocktail party in Harnack House, that I thought it was high

---

[25] New York, Duell, Sloan & Pearce, Inc., 1949.

time we stopped talking about German guilt, since there was no crime the Nazis had committed, which we or our allies had not also committed. I had referred to our obliteration bombing, the mass expropriation and expulsion from their homes of twelve million Germans on account of their race; the starving of the Germans during the first years of the occupation; the use of prisoners as slave laborers; the Russian concentration camps, and the looting perpetrated by Americans as well as Russians.

The effect of my remarks, which seemed to me only a plain statement of fact, produced first a shocked silence, and then a stream of rather silly remarks, such as that of a Captain Spear, of Military Intelligence, who said: "Do you mean you wish we had not won the war?" Next morning came the pay-off. A certain Mrs. Van Delden, in charge of the libraries which the Information Division of Military Government has established in America Houses in various cities as part of the program of teaching the Germans democracy, had been particularly incensed at my remarks. So I was hardly surprised to find that she had got in touch with Mr. Panuch, one of General Clay's special advisors and a very decent and intelligent fellow, to urge the cancellation of the lecture I was scheduled to give on Russia at Berlin's Amerika Haus. The following day I was informed that the automobile placed at my disposal by Military Government on my arrival in Berlin, was now needed by someone else; and asked to please leave Harnack House where I had originally been invited to stay "as the guest of General Clay." To make it quite clear that I not only was no longer a VIP, but that there had been a mistake made about me from the beginning, I was presented with a bill charging me $2.50 a day for my room for the time of my stay in Harnack House as "the guest of General Clay."

I certainly had no claim to VIP status and it was in most ways an advantage to move over to the Press Camp, where I was free of social or other obligations; and my fear that Mrs. Van Delden, Captain Spear, and others of their kind would prevent my getting my military permit extended proved groundless. General Clay, whom I met and had a long conversation with a few days later, welcomed me warmly and recommended the extension of my military permit originally granted to me only for three weeks. Either General Clay did not know what "dangerous thoughts" I had expressed, or did not share the narrow-minded sentiments of lower officials in Military Government.

My experience in Berlin was only one among many in which I learned that referring to our "crimes against humanity" is simply "not done." Yet it seems to me that if the Germans are ever to be "taught democracy" we must start judging our own actions by the same standards as we apply to them. Otherwise we must appear as hypocrites and convince the German people that Hitler was justified in his belief that "might makes right," and that democracy is a delusion and a sham.

The terrible consequences of the different ethical standards prescribed for victors and vanquished, and of the Nuremberg dictum that we have the right to do anything we please in Germany because ours is a "nonbelligerent" occupation, were displayed at the "Dachau trials."

These were the trials conducted by the United States Army Tribunals (as distinct from the civilian and ostensibly international trials at Nuremberg) of the privates, corporals, sergeants, and junior commissioned officers involved in the Malmédy case: of civilians accused of having lynched Allied airmen shot down during the bombing raids; and of the Germans held responsible for the atrocities committed in the Nazi concentration camps.

The methods employed by the investigators and prosecutors in these cases were worthy of the GPU, the Gestapo, and the SS. The accused were subjected to every kind of physical and mental torture to force them to write dictated statements; witnesses were tortured and bribed, and the procedures of these American courts bear unfavorable comparison even with those of the Hungarian and Bulgarian ones which are today sentencing the Catholic and Protestant clergymen who have defied the Communist terror.

On the other hand, the fact that America is still a democracy has resulted in the exposure of the horrible methods employed by United States Army representatives to secure the "confessions" of the hundreds of men already executed, or now being executed, at Landsberg.

Lieutenant Colonel Willis N. Everett, Jr., an American lawyer who had served as defense counsel for the seventy-four Germans accused in the Malmédy case, petitioned the United States Supreme Court, after his return to America, charging that the Germans had not had a fair trial.

The Supreme Court refused his petition, saying it lacked jurisdiction over the acts committed by the United States Army in Germany, a statement which means that the United States Military Government is above the law, and the "sovereignty" we claim in Germany is that of a lawless despot.

Colonel Everett's action, nevertheless, forced the Army to take notice, and Secretary Royall appointed a commission to investigate his charges. This commission, sent to Germany in 1948, consisted of Judge Edward Leroy van Roden, of Delaware County, Pennsylvania, and Justice Gordon Simpson, of the Texas Supreme Court.

The report made by these two American judges following their investigation, like so many other reports pertaining to Germany, has been kept secret from the American public. But Judge van Roden, after his return to the United States, gave a series of lectures and after-dinner speeches in which he stated that such thirddegree methods as the following were used to obtain the conviction of the Germans condemned to death, many of whom have already been hung:

Beatings and brutal kickings; knocking-out of teeth and breaking of jaws; mock trials; solitary confinement; torture with burning splinters; the use of investigators pretending to be priests; starvation; and promises of acquittal. Speaking to the Chester Pike Rotary Club on December 14, 1948, Judge van Roden said: "All but two of the Germans in the 139 cases we investigated had been kicked in the testicles beyond repair. This was standard operating procedure with our American investigators."

He told of one German who had had lighted matchsticks forced under his fingernails by the American investigators to extort a confession, and had appeared at his trial with his fingers still bandaged from the atrocity.

Another case mentioned by this American judge in his speech was that of an eighteen-year-old boy who, after a series of beatings, agreed to write a statement dictated to him by the American investigators. After they finished sixteen pages, the boy was locked up for the night. During the night the prisoners in the adjoining cells heard him saying, "I will not utter another lie," and when his jailers came in the morning, he had hung himself from the cell bar. Nevertheless, the statement he had begun to write, and had killed himself rather than sign, was offered in evidence at the trial of other accused.

"Sometimes," continued van Roden, "a prisoner who refused to sign was led into a dimly lit room, where a group of civilian investigators, wearing United States Army uniforms, were seated around a black table with a crucifix in the center and two candles burning, one on each side. 'You will now have your American trial,' the defendant was told.

"The sham court passed a sham sentence of death. Then the accused was told, 'You will hang in a few days, as soon as the general approves this sentence; but in the meantime sign this confession and we can get you acquitted.' Some still wouldn't sign.

"We were shocked by the crucifix being used so mockingly.

"In another case, a bogus Catholic priest [actually an investigator] entered the cell of one of the defendants, heard his confession, gave him absolution, and then gave him a little friendly tip: 'Sign whatever the investigators ask you to sign. It will get you your freedom. Even though it's false. I can give you absolution now in advance for the lie you'd tell.'"

In some cases solitary confinement or the threat of reprisals on the prisoner or witness's family were sufficient to persuade him to sign a prepared statement involving others. In others, "the investigators would put a black hood over the accused's head and then punch him in the face with brass knuckles, kick him and beat him with a rubber hose."

Judge van Roden also told his audience that Lieutenant Colonel Ellis and Lieutenant Perl, of the American prosecution, pleaded, in extenuation of the atrocities they were responsible for, that it was difficult to obtain evidence by fair means. Perl said: "We had a tough nut to crack and we had to use persuasive *(sic)* methods." Lieutenant Perl admitted that the "persuasive methods" included "some violence and mock trials," and that the Malmédy cases rested on statements obtained by such methods.

"There was no jury," concluded van Roden. "The court consisted of ten officers sitting as judge and jury, and one law-member, the only person with legal training, whose rulings as to the admissibility of evidence were final.

"The statements which were admitted as evidence were obtained from men who had first been kept in solitary confinement for three, four, and five months. They were confined between four walls, with no windows, and no opportunity of exercise. Two meals a day were shoved in to them through a slot in the door. They were not allowed to talk to anyone. They had no communication with their families or any minister or priest during that time."

"The tragedy," said van Roden, "is that so many of us Americans, having fought the war with so much sweat and blood, and having defeated the enemy, now say 'All Germans should be hung!' We won the war, but some of us want to go on killing. That's not fighting. That's wicked. The fact that there were atrocities by the Germans during the war against Americans, or by Americans against Germans, would not in the least lessen the disgrace to this country of ours, if such peacetime atrocities were to go unchallenged they would be a blot on the American conscience for eternity."

Unfortunately the investigation made by Judges van Roden and Simpson, and their exposure of the whole sorry business, did not stop the hangings of the Germans condemned on "evidence" obtained by torture. General Clay had previously commuted the sentences of a few of the condemned, but it seemed as if the outcry in the American press forced him to continue the executions instead of having the cases of all the condemned men re-examined.

In November 1948 fifteen men were being hung every Friday, instead of seven hung each previous week, presumably on the theory that the more victims of the miscarriage of justice who could be done away with, the less evidence of injustice would remain. Among the first batch hanged following the van Roden-Simpson investigation five were among those whom they had stated had been convicted on questionable evidence.

Betty Knox, whom I have already mentioned, and "Jose" of the United Press, had attended the previous week's hangings just after I first met them in Nuremberg. Neither of them were ever likely to forget their terrible experience. The Protestant and Catholic chaplains at the Landsberg prison where the executions take place were both convinced of the innocence of several of the men hung. They were in despair at their inability to do anything to stop the crime of killing men, several of whom had convinced the priests or pastors that they were innocent, and all of whom had been condemned by confessions extorted by torture or on the testimony of witnesses proved to have perjured themselves.

One of the men Betty Knox saw had been told on the preceding Wednesday that he was reprieved pending a reinvestigation of his case, and then dragged out of his cell on the Friday to be hung.

Another had been promised he should see his wife before dying, after not being allowed to see her for three years. But when she arrived at the prison at the appointed time she was told, "Sorry, he's already dead; he was hung first instead of last by mistake."

These are the last words of three of the men Betty Knox saw executed:

Cornelius Schwanner:

"No, I have nothing to say. Only my relatives I should have liked to see. I am sorry that I could not see my relatives one last time."

Fritz Girke:

"I protest against this execution of my sentence. According to official information given by American officials the time for filing petitions expires tonight at 2400 hours. On account of postal service delays, my petition, filed on September 20, cannot have been taken into consideration when they approved my sentence and ordered my execution. As an officer I did my duty for my people and my country when I obeyed my orders to execute those terror flyers who had shot down women and children on open roads. International law was also violated by my sentence.[26] I call upon Germany to witness. I call Lucia, Renate, *you murderers!*"

Willi Rieke:

"I do not want to accuse, nor do I want to pay back what I have received. I want to say that I am innocent. The one really guilty in my case hanged himself when he was taken prisoner. Because I was involved I was condemned. I am dying as a free German man. My last greetings go to my dear family, my dear wife, my dearly loved boy, my daughter-in-law, my little grandchildren and once more I greet all my dear relatives and friends. I forgive everybody who was unjust to me and I also forgive those who have rendered false oaths upon which such a sentence could only have been said. May God be a merciful judge for them. My last greetings also go to my beloved sport which is the basis for interior and exterior recovery of our youth. May in the next years the best men of the world meet in a fight, not to win but to be together no matter what nation and what race."

How many of the men America has hung, and is hanging now week by week, were innocent, will never be known. Only one thing is certain: they never had a fair trial and their interrogation, condemnation, and execution are a disgrace to democratic justice.

Some readers will be inclined to turn away and say all this does not concern them, not realizing that the honor and dignity of the United States are involved. Others may say that, after all, it doesn't much matter because the men hung were all Nazis or only Germans. But how can the kind of world Americans have died to preserve be saved, if we ourselves destroy belief in the justice which is the foundation of democracy?

Judge van Roden's testimony carries weight because he is an American—nowadays we refuse to hear the voice of Germans, however

---

[26] This man had been subjected to a mock trial "under the black hood."

unimpeachable their record. But the Dachau trials have aroused such widespread horror and protest in Germany that America should not ignore the appeal of the twenty-five German Catholic bishops who wrote: "Will not the tortures at the preliminary inquests at Schwäbische Hall and Oberwesel, and the mass executions at Landsberg, later on do more harm to victorious America than a lost battle?"

In their so far unheeded appeal to America, these representatives of twenty million German Catholics say:

"When the survivors who were in the martyrlike heat cells of Oberwesel are released, they will be able to tell the world in detail what inhuman treatment they received. Until now only a few of them have been able to reveal anything from their prison."

The Catholic appeal then quotes the following from an affidavit signed by Hans Schmidt on June 25, 1948, concerning his treatment in the period September 17 to October 3, 1945:

Seven of us were transported from the camp at Bad Aibling to Oberwesel, where we were thrown into small cells stark naked. The cells in which three or four persons were incarcerated were six and a half by ten feet in size and had no windows or ventilation. The walls, ceiling, and door were covered with tight asbestos plates. On one wall there was an electric stove with a four-grade switch (type-plate 2,000 watts) which was switched on from outside.

When we went to the lavatory we had to run through a lane of Americans who struck us with straps, brooms, cudgels, buckets, belts, and pistol holders to make us fall down. Our head, eyes, body, belly, and genitals were violently injured. A man stood inside the lavatory to beat us and spit on us. We returned to our cells through the same ordeal. The temperature in the cells was 140° Fahrenheit or more. During the first three days we were given only one cup of water and a small slice of bread. During the first days we perspired all the time, then perspiration stopped. We were kept standing chained back to back for hours. We suffered terribly from thirst, blood stagnation and mortification of the hands. From time to time water was poured on the almostred-hot radiators, filling the cells with steam, so that we could hardly breathe.

During all this time the cells were in darkness, except when the American soldiers entered and switched on electric bulbs of several hundred candle power which forced us to close our eyes.

Our thirst became more and more cruel, so that our lips cracked, our tongues were stiff, and we eventually became apathetic, or raved, or collapsed.

After enduring this torture for several days, we were given a small blanket to cover our nakedness, and driven to the courtyard outside. The uneven soil was covered with pebbles and slag and we were again beaten and finally driven back on our smashed and bleeding feet. While out of breath, burning cigarettes were pushed into our mouths, and each of us was forced to eat three or four of them. Meanwhile the American soldiers continued to hit us on eyes, head, and ears. Back in our cells we were pushed against the burning radiators, so that our skin was blistered.

For thirteen days and nights we received the same treatment, tortured by heat and thirst. When we begged for water, our guards mocked us. When we fainted we were revived by being drenched with cold water.

There was dirt everywhere and we were never allowed to wash, our inflamed eyes gave us terrible pain, we fainted continuously.

Every twenty minutes or so our cell doors were opened and the soldiers insulted and hit us. Whenever the doors were opened we had to stand still with our backs to the door. Two plates of food, spiced with salt, pepper, and mustard to make us thirstier, were given us daily. We ate in the dark on the floor. The thirst was the most terrible of all our tortures and we could not sleep.

In this condition I was brought to trial. I fainted and was brought back to my cell. A sergeant with dirty fingernails tore my skin around the nipple, and I developed blood poisoning. The doctor treated me brutally and did not even disinfect the wound.

This is only one of many accounts of the Gestapo-like tortures inflicted on German prisoners by Americans, *before* their guilt had been proved. I forbear to inflict on my readers the full tale of horror I heard in Germany, knowing that "atrocity stories" constitute popular reading only when the torturers, instead of the victims, are Germans.

It is, nevertheless, essential that the American public should have the opportunity to learn the facts so long withheld from them by the Administration and the press. For if we hold the German people accountable for Nazi crimes, then we are responsible for those committed by the United States Government or its agencies. The fact that Americans are free, and that no one here can be sent to prison for protesting against injustice, increases our responsibility.

Baron von Schlabrendorff, the man "who almost killed Hitler" by placing a bomb in his plane, supplied me in Wiesbaden with copies of the affidavits made in the case of Willi Schäfer, a non-commissioned officer sentenced to death at Dachau for the shooting of American prisoners at Malmédy during the Battle of the Bulge. Schäfer's sentence was commuted to life imprisonment but Baron von Schlabrendorff, who is acting as his counsel, has appealed, so far in vain, for his case to be retried.

Schäfer was charged with having "watched and not to have taken action against shootings of U.S. prisoners of war at crossroad Engelsdorf, south of Malmédy, on the 17th December 1944," and to have "forwarded an order" to have five American prisoners shot.

According to the evidence in the possession of von Schlabrendorff and Colonel Everett, Schäfer is innocent of both charges and was not even present when the shooting of American prisoners took place. The chief witnesses against him have all sworn that their evidence was false and was given only under duress, and Schäfer himself "confessed" to the crimes he could not have committed only after prolonged torture.

Below I reproduce part of Sergeant Schäfer's affidavit:

On April 7, 1946, Mr. Harry W. Thon asked me at Schwäbisch Hall to write out an affidavit accusing myself, and showed me an affidavit signed by Sepp Dietrich admitting that there had been an order to murder the American prisoners. Mr. Thon said that what was wanted was the heads of the generals and that we little men had nothing to fear. I told him that I was prepared to write a report of my experiences in the Eiffel offensive, but that I was not aware of any offenses committed against the laws of war. Thereupon Mr. Thon gave me paper and pencil, told me I had a respite of one night and that, should I fail to make a statement admitting my guilt, my family would be deprived of their ration cards. He then had me shut up in the death cell.

That night I wrote a report of my experiences but it did not include any self-accusations.

Next morning Mr. Thon appeared in my cell, read my report, tore it up, swore at me and hit me. After threatening to have me killed unless I wrote what he wanted, he left. A few minutes later the door of my cell opened, a black hood incrusted with blood was put over my head and face and I was led to another room. In view of Mr. Thon's threats the black cap had a crushing effect on my spirits. Four men of my company: Sprenger, Jaenckel, Neve, and Hoffmann accused me, although later they admitted to having borne false testimony. Nevertheless I still refused to incriminate myself. Thereupon Mr. Thon said that if I continued to refuse this would be taken as proof of my Nazi opinions, and he would have me charged together with the generals, in which event my death was certain. He said I would have no chance against four witnesses, and advised me for my own good to make a statement after which I would be set free. I still refused. I told Mr. Thon that although my memory was good, I was unable to recall any of the occurrences he wished me to write about and which to the best of my knowledge had never occurred.

Mr. Thon left but returned in a little while with Lieutenant Perl who abused me, and told Mr. Thon that, should I not write what was required within half an hour, I should be left to my fate. Lieutenant Perl made it clear to me that I had the alternative of writing and going free or not writing and dying. I decided for life and said I would sign anything they wanted. Mr. Thon then dictated a statement to tally with Sprenger's and ruled out all objections I raised.

On the 8th or 9th of April after I had apparently not replied in the manner the investigators desired, I was kicked in the hollow of the knee and on my backside and beaten with a stick across my shoulders and the back of my head. A black hood was again placed over my head and face so I cannot testify as to who inflicted this punishment.

I hereby testify that I never took part in any shootings of Prisoners of War, nor issued any such orders, nor watched any shootings. I stated this to the Military Court at Dachau.

The methods employed to obtain the false evidence used against Schäfer are described in an affidavit, dated January 20, 1948, at Landsberg prison, signed by Joachim Hoffmann, who states that:

For 3½ months I was kept in solitary confinement without either writing or bathing allowed. Even when taken for a hearing a black hood was placed over my head. The guards who took me to my hearing often struck or kicked me. I was twice thrown down the stairs and was hurt so much that blood ran out of my mouth and nose. At the hearing, when I told the officers about the ill treatment I had suffered, they only laughed. I was beaten and the black cap pulled over my face whenever I could not answer the questions put to me, or gave answers not pleasing to the officers.

In March, 1946, I was taken before a Summary Court. Prior to this I was beaten and several times kicked in the genitals. At my trial I was sentenced to death and then locked up in a cell which contained nothing but a wooden chest and one blanket. Here I remained three weeks, after which the investigating officers came to my cell and promised me I should be released within two months, if I would write what they dictated. I was unable to resist the pressure. I often witnessed the ill treatment suffered by my comrades. Finally I agreed to write the false statement required. I believed that if I wrote it I would be set free, but this was an illusion.

Another of the witnesses against Schäfer, Siegfried Jaenckel, made a similar sworn statement concerning the methods used to force him to bear false testimony. He too had been placed in solitary confinement while a prisoner of war and tortured until he agreed to sign a dictated statement.

He was also one of those given a mock trial with a black hood over his face lifted to show him the crucifix, black cloth, and candles. The prosecutor, as usual, was Mr. Henry Thon and Jaenckel's "trial" lasted some twelve hours, after which he was told he would be "taken for a ride" in a jeep and hung from a tree since he was "not worth a bullet." Two days later he was again taken before a court and told by Lieutenant Perl that "in consideration of his youth" and the fact that he had acted in obedience to an order, he would be pardoned if he would "tell the truth." At this second "trial," according to Jaenckel's affidavit, Lieutenant Perl told him, "So you still don't want to confess? You have no money to pay for your defense so you will hang. Look at your comrades, they are to be released because they spoke the truth."

In his affidavit, signed two years later, Jaenckel says he can no longer remember how often he was questioned but he thinks a dozen times. And always he was told: "If you confess you will go free; you need only to say you had an order from your superiors. But if you won't speak you will be hung."

I was beaten and I heard the cries of the men being tortured in adjoining cells, [writes Jaenckel] and whenever I was taken for a hearing I trembled with fear. I was then only nineteen years old and had never had anything to do with courts or the law. Subjected to such duress I eventually gave in, and signed the long statement dictated to me, and copied the sketch maps as ordered. I could never have done it otherwise, as I have insufficient education. Captain Schumacher said to me: "The streets are to be the same as in the statement of the other witnesses, but the other details should be different because otherwise it will look too much like a copy."

Jaenckel concludes his affidavit as follows: "My charges against my comrades according to the statement dictated to me at Schwäbisch Hall which I was forced to sign are not true."

In the Malmédy trials the objective of the investigators seems to have been to force the young German prisoners of war to incriminate their commanders, failing which they were themselves to be hung. The concentration-camp trials were worse because in these cases it seemed that the American Prosecution acted on the Nazi-Communist principle that the aim was to bring a sufficiently large number of people to the gallows, rather than to apprehend the real criminals. For the chief witnesses for prosecution were the former criminals and the Communists in the concentration camps who had been used as *Kapos* (trusties) by the Gestapo after most SS men had been withdrawn from supervision of the camps to fight at the front. Thus the Dachau trials of those accused of being responsible for the atrocities in Nazi concentration camps offered the horrible spectacle of former political prisoners being accused and condemned on the "evidence" of the criminals who had hated them, or on that of Communists given the opportunity to condemn their political enemies to the gallows.

It is impossible to avoid the conclusion that some of the men condemned to death or lifelong imprisonment at these trials were innocent of any crime or atrocity and were sentenced because while inmates of Hitler's prisons they had incurred the enmity of the criminal or Communist inmates.

The innocent could have little hope of acquittal since the American investigators promised immunity to the most guilty if they would incriminate others, and threatened witnesses with reprisals on their families if they refused to sign dictated statements. The cycle of horror and injustice started by the Nazis was completed when their victims were forced by Americans to perjure themselves to escape death, or condemned on the evidence supplied by tortured witnesses.

The names of the American investigators in these cases. Kirschbaum, Metzger, Enders (alias Andrews), Colombeck, and Egger, like those of Lieutenant Perl and W. Harry Thon, will be remembered in Germany as long, and with as much loathing, as the names of Himmler, Bormann and other Nazi bullies and criminals are remembered in America.

In one famous instance Kirschbaum brought forward a certain Einstein to prove that the accused Menzel had murdered Einstein's brother, but the prisoner pointed to the said brother sitting in the witness box. Kirschbaum, deeply embarrassed, turned to Einstein and hissed,

"How can we bring this pig to the gallows, if you are so stupid as to bring your brother into the court."

Sebastian Schmidt, a former farmer, states the following in an affidavit:

I was questioned by Mr. Metzger if I knew the most ill famed and brutal beater, the greatest sadist of Dachau, the former prisoner Karl Mayer.

Thereupon Mr. Metzger submitted to me a ready-made statement of several pages, to be signed by me at once, without reading it, since Mr. Metzger was in a great hurry. Nevertheless I began to read and saw that the statement said: "Mayer being Kapo for the building of a garage at the camp of Dachau, daily killed with a cudgel about 100 prisoners, to be pressed by a steamroller into a new road that was under construction."

I did not continue to read further on and refused my signature, since a thing like that never happened. I called Mr. Metzger's attention to the impossibility, whereupon Mr. Metzger said to me: "It is all the same, since Mayer has already been hanged for a long time and is lying 5 feet under the earth." But nevertheless I refused my signature.

Mr. Metzger grew furious, stripped up his sleeves and approached me threateningly saying he would kill me unless I signed. Seeing that his threats were lost on me, he added: "Well, surely I shall find an accusation against you. I shall succeed in bringing you before an American military court; and if you are hanged you owe it to me as surely as I am called Metzger."

According to the well-known methods of Metzger and his companions this also happened.

I am thankful to God that I remained firm against Metzger's threats, for by such a perjury I might have plunged into distress an innocent man and his family. I have known Karl Mayer only as a quiet, honest man, whose behavior in the KZ must be called unobjectionable. Karl Mayer was a political prisoner at Dachau.

Martin Humm, another prisoner at Landsberg, reveals in his affidavit, signed on May 30, 1948, why Mr. Metzger was so determined to get evidence against the unfortunate Karl Mayer. Mr. Metzger asked Humm in July 1947, whether he had ever heard Mayer say that he, Metzger, had formerly been a leader of the Hitler Youth who had been prosecuted for moral delinquency and had afterwards escaped to America. Humm replied that he had heard such talk about Metzger at Dachau. Metzger then started asking Humm for evidence against Mayer, assuring him that he did not want it for Mayer's trial but because he, Metzger, "had a personal quarrel with Mayer." When Humm said he had already made a statement at Dachau a year earlier saying he knew nothing against Mayer, Metzger rose and said "Oh, Humm, how beautiful life is and yet you will be hanged, although you are so young."

Humm being an epileptic and a consumptive lacked the stamina of Sebastian Schmidt. He finally broke down and promised to write what was required of him. He was then taken back to the hospital in an exhausted condition and a pneumatic compress put on his lungs. Since Metzger insisted on getting the statement by the next day Humm got a fellow prisoner to write it for him as he was too ill to write it himself.

In his May 1948, affidavit Humm repudiates the false evidence extorted from him by Metzger, saying that he had never seen Mayer hang a prisoner, or steal food from Red Cross parcels, or do anything "unnatural or unchaste" in the camp.

The use of duress in obtaining "evidence" has been explicitly admitted by American Army authorities. Colonel A. H. Rosenfeld, on quitting his post as chief of the Dachau War Crimes Administration Branch in 1948, was asked at a press interview whether there was any truth in the story about the mock trials at Dachau.

He replied: "Yes, of course. We couldn't have made those birds talk otherwise."

Colonel Rosenfeld did not consider such measures as duress since the victims were Germans. He was quite proud of his cleverness and said: "It was a trick, and it worked like a charm."

Such methods as torture, mock trials, blackmail, false evidence, and the rest may indeed have "worked like a charm," but the odor with which they have surrounded American "justice" in Germany is anything but charming. The net result is to have convinced most Germans that there is little to choose between "democratic" and Nazi or Communist "justice."

The majority of the accused in the Dachau trials were not only tortured; when finally brought to trial in the weakened state induced by beatings and starvation, they were usually denied any possibility of defending themselves. They were not informed of the charges against them until a few hours, or at best a few days, before their trials and had no possibility of calling witnesses in their defense. With rare exceptions they had no German lawyer to defend them, either because they could not pay for one, or because the American authorities would not permit it. When a German lawyer was admitted, he had to act under the orders of the American officer detailed for the defense, and was not even allowed to confer with his client except during the short recesses during the trial.

In the concentration-camp cases, the indictments failed even to indicate the specific crime of which the prisoner was accused, or the time and place where it had been committed.

According to the appeal sent to General Clay on July 30, 1948, by the German lawyer, Dr. Georg Fröschmann, in these cases:

In the predominant number of concentration camp trials, the prosecution contented themselves with enumerating in a single sentence of twenty-four typewritten lines, the war crimes and crimes against humanity, that is, "killings, beatings, torturings, starvings, violent infringements and humiliations," *in general*, which the defendants were supposed to have been guilty of as perpetrators, accomplices, abettors, accessories or otherwise "participants," on nationals of fifteen different countries.

The date of the crimes was left similarly vague, being given as any time between January 1942 and May 5, 1945.

The American officers who acted as defense counsel usually had no legal training, could not speak German, and did not trouble to discuss the case with the defendants. The accused were unable to question the witnesses against them because the proceedings of the court were conducted in a language they did not understand and no competent interpreters were provided.

The whole proceedings resembled those of a staged Moscow trial. According to Dr. Fröschmann:

Many defendants could not avoid the impression that the advice given them by the defense counsel was the result of his wish to comply with the desires of the Tribunal to hurry up the proceedings.

Some of the American defense counsel maintained a close contact with the prosecution. They consented to peculiar compromises with the prosecution. They failed to make necessary applications for an adjournment of the trial for the preparation of the defense their pleas seemed to be drawn up in accordance with the prosecution, and in some cases they appeared to be prosecutors themselves.

Whereas the prosecution had ample time and opportunity to call for witnesses from the whole of Europe, and to torture German witnesses into giving the evidence required, the accused, incarcerated in their dark cells and denied any contact with the outside world, were, of course, unable to summon anyone to their defense. Moreover, the "Association of Persons Persecuted by the Nazis" through the press and radio forbade any former concentration camp inmate to appear for the defense.

In spite of the free travel, good food, handsome daily allowance, and ample supplies of cigarettes to sell on the black market promised by the prosecution to former political prisoners, few of them came to testify against the accused at Dachau. The fact that the prosecution relied in the main on those who had been sent to the concentration camps for criminal acts in itself suggests that some at least of the men condemned to death at Dachau were innocent. The use of "professional witnesses" who appeared in dozens of trials and whose affidavits unsupported by other evidence were sufficient to secure a sentence of death, have invested these American trials with an odor repugnant to the most elementary sense of justice.

It is hard to avoid the conclusion that the prosecution was not in the least interested in convicting those actually guilty of atrocities, but wanted only to secure a maximum number of convictions in order to demonstrate the mass guilt of the German people. The natural result is that many Germans, knowing how the trials were conducted and on what kind of "evidence" guilt was proved, now say that there never were any atrocities, and that the whole story of the concentration camps is an American invention. Thus the use of Nazi methods to establish Nazi guilt has resulted in obscuring the reality of Nazi crimes.

This was notably the effect of the Ilse Koch case. The Germans know that no evidence was produced by the American prosecution to prove the existence of "human lampshades" popularly believed in America to have been found in Ilse Koch's home. Ilse Koch was exactly what General Clay described her as, when he commuted her sentence, a prostitute and a pervert of a low type, but not a war criminal.

The atrocities committed by the Nazis were horrible enough without the need to invent stories about human lampshades. By attempting to prove lies, we have obscured the reality of the gas chambers, and it is probable that within a few years the truth will be dismissed as an atrocity story spread by the victors to justify the inhuman treatment of the conquered.

The damage done is irreparable, but the reputation of the United States could still be cleared if the executions were stopped, a full and independent investigation ordered, and the Americans responsible for the torture of prisoners and miscarriage of justice brought to trial themselves in Germany on the charge of having committed "crimes against humanity."

Although the Supreme Court of the United States professes itself disinterested in the crimes committed by American citizens in Germany, the Senate in March 1949 showed its concern by voting for an investigation. It is to be hoped that the Administration and the Department of the Army will not stop the Congressional action which alone can reestablish the reputation of the United States for justice. Since the investigators who adopted Nazi-Communist methods at Dachau were not Regular Army officers, but civilians with temporary military rank, it would seem that the American Army itself has an interest in punishing those who have disgraced it. This must also have been the view of Lieutenant Colonel Everett, the brave man who first drew America's attention to the shameful acts committed in her name.

It may be easier to expunge the horrible record of the Dachau trials than to make the German people forget the brutal and unjust treatment they received in the first years of our occupation. Young men and women who had obeyed Hitler from a mistaken but sincere conviction that no patriotic German could fail to follow his lead; workers who had joined the Nazi party believing it would give them "bread and work"; the defeated men of the German army who bore no responsibility for the atrocities committed by the SS and the Gestapo, but who had fought bravely to the last to save their country from Communist terror; even the victims of the Nazis emerging from hiding or released from concentration camps, were all punished by the victorious democracies. Some were held in prison for years without trial; others had all their own and their family's property confiscated; others were denied their rights as prisoners of war and used as slave labor. Even today, four years after the war's end, there is a Control Council ordinance (No. 3) in force under which *any* German can be recruited for forced labor—a plain infringement of the United States Constitution which forbids slave labor in *all* territories under United States jurisdiction.

Nor were the prisoners of war and civilians tried at Dachau the only Germans subjected to physical torture. At the war's end we arrested generals, SS men, government officials, and Nazi leaders en masse and subjected them to varying degrees of ill treatment without waiting to find out who was guilty and who innocent.

One German of my acquaintance connected with the Reich Foreign Office told me how he had been pushed into a freight car so crammed that no one could sit down, and transported without food and water for thirty-six hours. One man in the car, he said, was a general eighty-two years old who had retired long before the war but had been arrested because of his rank. The mixed company of officers and civilians subjected by the Americans to the same treatment as Soviet Russia metes out to its enemies, had managed to squeeze themselves even tighter to enable this old man to sit down.

Many of the prisoners were ill and some were wounded and they were not allowed out of the car during the whole journey. Subsequently, in prison, the German generals were forced to polish the boots of their guards, set to cleaning latrines with their bare hands, and in general treated like the inmates of Nazi or Communist concentration camps.

Everywhere you go in Germany you hear such stories. No doubt some are exaggerated, but there is little doubt that a perverse pleasure was taken in subjecting the officers of the defeated enemy army to every conceivable indignity.

In every army there are bound to be some sadists and cads. The horrible thing was that the orders given to the American Army in the early period of the occupation encouraged the brutal and unchivalrous minority, and prescribed imitation of Nazi methods in the treatment of the vanquished.

The shock to the Germans was all the greater because, although they had expected Russian lawlessness and brutality, they had believed that America would treat them fairly. Many had welcomed the end of the war which, whatever punishment it might bring, they expected to establish a rule of law in place of Nazi lawlessness and tyranny. But today belief in democratic justice is almost dead.

The atrocities we have ourselves committed in Germany are not the only ones for which posterity will hold us guilty.

President Roosevelt at Yalta and President Truman at Potsdam agreed in the name of the American people to one of the most barbaric acts recorded in the long history of man's inhumanity to man. According to these agreements, some twelve million people were expropriated and driven from their homes for no other crime than that of being Germans.

In past ages when territory was annexed by a victor nation, the inhabitants were not all robbed and they were allowed to continue living in their ancestral homes. America and England, however, agreed that Germany was not only to be deprived of territory inhabited by Germans for hundreds of years; the Russians, Poles, Czechs, Yugoslavs and other nations were given the right to expropriate and drive out all people of German ancestry.

The proviso that the expulsions should be conducted in a humane manner merely added a revolting aura of hypocrisy to this crime against humanity.

The Poles, who were given possession of the territory "east of the Oder-Neisse line," drove out the inhabitants with the utmost brutality, throwing women and children, the aged and the sick, out of their homes with only a few hours' notice, and not sparing even those in hospitals and orphanages.

The Czechs, no less brutal, drove the Germans over the mountains on foot, and at the frontier stole such belongings as they had been able to carry. Having an eye for profit as well as revenge, the Czechs held thousands of German men as slave laborers while driving out their wives and children.

Many of the old, the young, and the sick died of hunger or cold or exposure on the long march into what remained of Germany, or perished of hunger and thirst and disease in the crowded cattle cars in which some of the refugees were transported. Those who survived the journey were thrust upon the slender resources of starving occupied Germany. No one of German race was allowed any help by the United Nations. The displaced-persons camps were closed to them and first the United Nations Relief and Rehabilitation Administration (UNRRA) and then the International Refugee Organization (IRO) was forbidden to succor them. The new untouchables were thrown into Germany to die, or survive as paupers in the miserable accommodations which the bombed-out cities of Germany could provide for those even more wretched than their original inhabitants.

How many people were killed or died will never be known. Out of a total of twelve to thirteen million people who had committed the crime of belonging to the German race, four or five million are unaccounted for. But no one knows how many are dead and how many are slave laborers. Only one thing is certain: Hitler's barbaric liquidation of the Jews has been outmatched by the liquidation of Germans by the "democratic, peace-loving" powers of the United Nations.

As the Welsh minister, Dr. Elfan Rees, head of the refugee division of the World Council of Churches, said in a sermon delivered at Geneva University on March 13, 1949: "More people have been rendered homeless by an Allied peace than by a Nazi war."

The estimate of the number of German expellees, or *flüchtlinge* as the Germans call them, in Rump Germany is now eight or nine million. The International Refugee Organization (IRO) takes no account of them, and was expressly forbidden by act of Congress to give them any aid. It is obviously impossible for densely over-crowded Western Germany to provide for them. A few have been absorbed into industry or are working on German farms, but for the most part they are living in subhuman conditions without hope of acquiring homes or jobs.

In Bavaria, while we, the occupiers, have requisitioned thousands of hotels, chateaux, barracks and private houses for our exclusive use, and while the IRO's dwindling DP population occupies comfortable quarters also provided by the Germans, the German DP's are crammed into draughty huts and receive no gifts of food and clothing from international organizations. Having agreed that they should be expropriated and driven from their homes, the United States professes itself uninterested in their fate. Military Government tells the German *Länder* administrations that German refugees are entirely a "German concern."

In effect, we say in Germany that anyone who was a victim of Nazi crimes is to be succored, but that those whose sufferings are our own responsibility can rot and die. We also make a careful racial distinction between the various categories of Communist persecutees. Thus a Czech who escapes from the Communist terror is entitled to enter the DP camps and be fed on American food. But a Russian, Rumanian, Hungarian, or Yugoslav who manages to slip across the border into Bavaria, has to live on the German economy. Members of these nations may not enter the DP camps, unless they were in Germany before the end of the war. In effect we say that with the sole exception of the Czechs, only Nazi victims are entitled to help, not Communist victims. Thus Germany not only has to provide accommodation for Hitler's former victims, the German economy is also now forced to support hundreds of thousands of Stalin's victims. Nor is this all. Germany acts as a receiving center and transit camp for many thousands of Jews who have left Poland, Rumania, Hungary, and Czechoslovakia since the Communists took over. In one Jewish DP camp near Munich every single person I spoke to had come to Germany after 1945 in hopes of getting to Palestine.

Although the number of displaced persons in Germany is continually diminishing and many of the camps are half empty, the Germans are not allowed either to regain possession of the many houses, barracks, and other buildings occupied by the DP's, or to place their own refugees in them. Exact information is not available since the German authorities are not allowed to enter the DP camps but, according to the estimate of the Bavarian Minister for Refugees, between twenty-four and twenty-eight thousand beds are now unoccupied. While this accommodation is wasted the German refugees are crowded into unsanitary huts and other accommodation unprovided with the most elementary comforts and decencies, and frequently have to sleep on the floor.

Before coming to Nuremberg I visited several of the *flüchtlinge* camps in Bavaria. The contrast between their living conditions and those of the majority of non-German DP's demonstrated how fortunate are the former victims of the Nazis as compared to those who suffer the consequences of the crimes against humanity committed by the "victorious democracies."

In the Dachau camp near Munich I found fifty or more people—men, women and children—to each wooden hut 26 x 65 feet in size. There were no partitions, but the inmates were using some of their precious blankets to screen off their cubicles. The huts were cold and damp. It was raining and one woman with a little girl suffering from a bad cold showed me the wall behind their bed where the rain seeped through.

Four hundred people at Dachau shared one washroom and one outdoor latrine and there was no hot water. No one had any linen or sheets, and some had neither shoes nor overcoats.

Those of the *flüchtlinge* who have found employment have to continue living at places like Dachau since there is no other accommodation to be found. In Bavaria as a whole, there are already two people on an average in every room or cellar, and the situation is little better in the rest of the United States and British zones. So the *flüchtlinge* who get jobs often have to travel four or five hours a day, partly on foot, to reach them. One woman I talked to at Dachau told me her daughters left home at 5:30 a.m. and returned from work at 9:00 p.m. after walking two and a half hours each day.

For the most part, however, the *flüchtlinge* have no hope of work, especially since the currency reform which wiped out many small enterprises which had formerly given some of them employment. Moreover, a large proportion of the German refugees are women with young children.

I visited the two schools at the camp, one for Protestants and the other for Catholics. The schoolroom was an unheated wooden barrack without desks. The children sat on benches and had no books and hardly any paper or pencils. The two schoolmasters gave instruction by writing on the blackboard. One of them was a Social Democrat from the Sudetenland who had spent the war years in a Nazi concentration camp, and had been liberated only to be thrown out of his home by the Czechs. The children looked thin and pale, but somehow clean and neat, as almost all Germans somehow manage to be even when living in the most miserable conditions.

In both schoolrooms the children stood stiffly at attention and shouted *"Grüss Gott"* in unison when I came in. Formerly they would have said *"Heil Hitler"* in the same manner, and I could hardly imagine that at Dachau they thought "democracy" was an improvement on the Third Reich.

I spent the greater part of a day at Dachau, and spent several hours in Barracks No. 14 getting the history of each family there. The oldest inhabitants of the barrack were a Dr. Werner, aged 64, and his wife. He had been a judge in old Austria and then a state's attorney in the Sudetenland for twenty years. The Werners' only son had been killed on the Russian front. In May 1945 Dr. Werner had been arrested by the Czech Government and kept in prison for two years where he was himself starved and beaten, and witnessed the torturing of many fellow prisoners. When finally released he was a wreck and of course all his property had been confiscated. Meanwhile his wife had been driven out of Czechoslovakia and been robbed of everything she possessed, even her wedding ring. She had first been transported with thousands of others in open freight cars as far as Teplitz, and then literally driven by the Czechs on foot over the Erz Mountains. After five weeks of wandering hungry over the roads she had found a place as a farm worker in Saxony. Dr. Werner finally found her there after his own expulsion and was also hired by a farmer. But in August 1947 he was deported back to Bohemia as a slave laborer. Finally he was allowed to go to Bavaria to rejoin his wife who had managed to escape from the Russian zone.

These two old people had no hope at all. They were by now too worn out to do physical labor, and there was no other. They had been robbed of their home and their clothes, their furniture and their linen, and could expect gradually to rot away in Dachau. But they were brave old people and not merely concerned with their own troubles. Frau Werner was helping the women with young children and Dr. Werner clearly enjoyed the confidence and respect of all the other fifty-three people in the barracks. Thanks to him I got each of their case histories, and later when I managed to send him some food and clothing, and got friends in America to send a few CARE packages, Dr. Werner distributed them all around, as I know from letters I received.

Each family or individual in the barracks had had the same kind of experience as the Werners, and some had suffered far worse treatment. The case of Fritz Bernglau and his wife Melitta was typical. After fighting on the Russian front and being taken prisoner, he had escaped and got home to Czechoslovakia. There he had "eagerly awaited the arrival of the American troops, who unfortunately remained outside Karlsbad." The Russians came and under their protection the Czech Communists looted the town of Bodenbach where the Bernglaus lived. Later the whole population was expelled in a veritable March of Death. In one day the twentyfour thousand inhabitants of the town were thrown out and then driven like cattle into Saxony. The women and children and old people who could not keep up the pace were beaten with clubs and many dropped by the way. All baggage had to be abandoned. After being unable to obtain shelter in Russian-occupied Lower Saxony, and wandering the roads there for three weeks, the Bernglaus turned back to Bodenbach hoping to be able to retrieve some clothes and linen they had hidden in their house before being expelled. Both were discovered and arrested and Melitta was brutally beaten. They spent ten weeks in prison where thirty-two people were penned into cells for two, and the women had to listen to the screams of men being tortured, for the prison was full of "political" prisoners, meaning "capitalists and landowners." The wife of the banker Adler committed suicide because she thought the screams she heard were those of her husband in the next cell. Some prisoners were literally beaten to death.

"Having learned the horror of Bolshevism on our own bodies," as Fritz Bernglau expressed it, he and his wife, after their release from the Czech prison, now had only one idea: to get out of the Russian zone. So today they are in Dachau, which, bad as it is, is preferable to being under Communist rule.

I will mention only one more case, that of Erika Bruno whose pretty little daughter Renate caught my attention when I entered the barracks. She was a farmer's wife in Silesia but had been caught by the surrender visiting her brother in Czechoslovakia. Although pregnant she was banished to her home and had to walk two hundred miles on foot, over the Riésen Mountains, living on roots and what she could get by begging. But as soon as she got home, the Poles threw her out and robbed her of all she possessed, even her coat and shoes. In an advanced state of pregnancy she walked barefoot until Christmas 1945 from town to town as far as the March of Brandenburg, where she was admitted to a hospital and her child was born.

It was somewhat more cheerful to visit the Wagoner "factory" which a group of Sudeten expellees had managed to set up near Munich. They had been driven out with two thousand others on foot, and had the fifty-five pounds of baggage each had been allowed to carry stolen from them by the Czechs at the frontier. One of them had even been deprived of the little pushcart on which he was transporting his two-year-old son and had to carry him on his back. But the workers from the Wagoner Factory had kept together and had managed to get hold of a few machines from the American authorities who let them use dismantled reparation machinery for a time. Then the Norwegians had given them a couple of reparation machines in return for their services in repairing others. In this and other ways, being highly skilled workers, they had pieced together sufficient means of production to be able to earn their living once again, and were producing boring machines in a little factory. Visiting this enterprise one realized the stupidity of the Czech Government in throwing out skilled workers to satisfy their lust for revenge, or their greed.

But a sword of Damocles hung over the *flüchtlinge* who had ceased to be paupers. At any moment the United States reparations authorities might order the dismantlement of the transformers which supplied power to the Wagoner workshops and other small enterprises in the vicinity.

If this should happen, the Wagoner workers would be flung back into the misery of life at Dachau or other camps, as had already happened in the case of others who had established small productive enterprises only to be mined by the currency reform which wiped out their small capital resources.

It was not surprising to find that the Communists have considerable influence in the huge Dachau camp where people are living in such terrible conditions. The unofficial leader of the Dachau *flüchtlinge* was a Communist who by organizing a hunger strike and mass-protest meetings had forced the Bavarian administration to improve conditions in the camp, by "winterizing" the wooden buildings and providing somewhat more food.

The Bavarian authorities held responsible for the inadequate accommodations and food in the camps are not, however, the real culprits. Bavaria has been forced to take far more German expellees than any other part of Western Germany, and since so much housing has been requisitioned for DP's and the occupation forces, the problem is insoluble.

According to Military Government estimates, in 1948 a quarter of the more than nine million inhabitants of Bavaria were not Bavarians. There are over a million expellees from Czechoslovakia; 606,000 from east of the Oder and Neisse rivers; 51,500 from Hungary; and another 170,000 from various other places. In addition, there are nearly 300,000 Germans from the other zones or other Western states; and 164,000 foreigners living on the German economy. To these figures there has to be added uncounted thousands of unregistered persons who have entered Bavaria illegally. In this respect Bavaria has the worst problem of all the Western *Länder* because of her long frontier, which vast numbers of people cross under the cover of night, coming from Czechoslovakia, Rumania, Hungary, and Yugoslavia, as well as the Russian zone of Germany. Whatever efforts are made to find work and adequate shelter for the refugees, so many more keep on coming that Bavaria is like a Sisyphus pushing uphill a stone which continually rolls down again.

Only half of the total population increase in Bavaria is accounted for by expellees "legally" brought in under the Potsdam agreement. By the first of January 1948, the Bavarian population which in 1939 was seven million had increased to nine and a quarter million; 1.8 million were refugees and 292,000 were evacuees from other parts of Germany.

Seventy thousand foreigners, not cared for by UNRRA, entered Bavaria in 1945-46. In 1947 another seventy-five thousand "border trespassers" were registered in the German camps in Bavaria. The currency reform in 1948 which entitled everyone to receive forty of the new D marks revealed the existence of a hundred thousand additional illegal immigrants in Bavaria who had never registered and had not received ration cards but had presumably existed on the black market.

An increase of two and a quarter million in Bavaria's population makes it physically impossible for the German administration to provide adequate housing, for in addition there are 330,000 people who were rendered homeless either by the bombing of their houses or their requisitioning by Military Government. A million rooms were destroyed and another million seven hundred thousand damaged by bombing during the war. The United States Military Government has requisitioned another 115,000 rooms. Excluding the comparatively ample space reserved for the

IRO's DP's and the far more than adequate accommodation taken over by the Military Government for the housing and recreation of Americans and their guests, Bavaria is today so overcrowded that the average "living space" is one room to each two persons. In Nuremberg, Regensburg, and other badly damaged cities there are nearly two and onehalf persons per room or cellar.

This average housing space includes barracks, wooden summer camps unfit for living in winter, the dungeonlike bunkers (air-raid shelters) with damp cement walls in which thousands live, stables, and other structures unfit for human habitation.

Some refugees are housed in dance halls and gymnasiums and other quarters without sanitation or heating. The transit camps are so packed with humanity that newcomers often have to be kept in the freight cars in which they arrive, or left to sleep in the fields without cover.

The majority of the German refugees are women and children, but it is not even possible to find employment for the men and others fit to work. Of the 1.9 million German refugees in Bavaria, 1.2 million are sheltered in agricultural communities with fewer than four thousand inhabitants, and they cannot make use of refugee labor to any considerable extent.

The cost to the Bavarian state of feeding the refugees and providing them with beds, blankets, clothing, and household utensils is out of proportion to its resources. In 1948, it was providing three and a half million D marks a month for the maintenance of the camps, not counting the clothing and beds initially supplied.

In 1948 Herr Jaenicke, the Bavarian Minister, who is himself a refugee from Silesia, appealed to the United Nations for help, saying that it is impossible for Germany to house and feed the German and non-German refugees denied help by the International Refugee Organization. He appealed in particular for *a)* the release of unoccupied housing accommodations by the IRO; *b)* speeding up the repatriation or emigration of DP's; *c)* extension of IRO care to the large number of foreign refugees who now escape from Soviet territory to Germany and have to be provided for by the German economy; *d*) consideration of the need to provide employment for German and other European refugees in the allocation of Marshall Plan funds.

Bavaria is the land of refuge for all who succeed in escaping from the countries ruled by the Communists. But when the Germans appeal for help in coping with this great influx of fugitives from Communist terror, they are told that it is not the concern of the Military Government, but entirely a German responsibility. It is not funny, however ridiculous, that, while insisting that expellees and refugees are a German responsibility, the Military Government should smugly announce that it has "directed that adequate reception and distribution facilities be provided." For it knows as well as the Germans that this is impossible.

8

OUR UN-AMERICAN ACTIVITIES IN GERMANY

IF THE UNITED STATES ADMINISTRATION HAD BEEN DOMINATED BY Communists it could hardly have done a better job in preparing the way for Communist rule in Germany, than the Military Government during the first two years of the occupation. The denazification law was used to expropriate the capitalists, pauperize the middle classes, and bring democratic justice into contempt; Communists were appointed to leading administrative positions and put in control of newspapers and radio stations; and Germany was confined in an economic strait-jacket which precluded the revival of free enterprise and created the chaos, misery, and despair, calculated to drive the Germans into the Communist camp.

The Nuremberg and Dachau trials directly affected only a small number of people, but the principles enunciated there, combined with the directives given to the Military Government by Washington in JCS 1067/6, deprived the majority of Germans in the United States zone of liberty, property, and other civil rights.

JCS 1067/6 suspends habeas corpus indefinitely, and told the Military Government it had authority to arrest and hold in prison without trial anyone who might endanger Allied objectives, including, of course, those of Soviet Russia.

It also instructed the United States Army authorities to dismiss both from public office and from positions of importance in private enterprise, not only Nazis but "all other persons hostile to Allied purposes." If this instruction had been applied in its full rigor, it would have allowed practically no Germans, except the Communists, to hold administrative or executive positions, since few other Germans could have been expected at that time not to be hostile to Allied policy.

The "Law of Liberation from National Socialism," as the denazification decree was humorously, or cynically, named, affected some twelve million people out of the total seventeen million in the United States zone. For it penalized not only all members of the Nazi party, but also their families, and members of affiliated organizations. It was based on JCS 1067/6 which instructed the United States Army authorities to arrest, among others, all persons holding "important" positions in the national and local civil and economic administration down to and including village mayors, and in "industry, commerce, agriculture and finance."

"It may generally be assumed," said the Washington directive, "that in the absence of evidence to the contrary, any persons holding such positions are Nazis or Nazi sympathizers."

Thus in effect the United States adopted the Communist theory that capitalists were *ipso facto* National Socialists, and as late as the fall of 1947 the United States Military Government was still holding in prison without trial men whose only crime was that of having been the owners of industrial enterprises or executives of large corporations.

So great was the influence of the Communists in Washington at this time, and so closely did the United States follow Moscow's class-war directives, that the United States Commander in Germany was also ordered to "take under his control all property, real and personal, owned or controlled by all persons subject to arrest."

Since several years were required to process the tremendous number of people affected by the denazification law, this meant that the property of the accused and their families was confiscated for an indefinite period whether they were guilty or not.

In Bavaria the United States Military Government went so far as to appoint a known Communist as Minister of Denazification. Many *Spruchkammer* (denazification boards) were dominated by the Communists who utilized their position to get rid of their political opponents. For the terrible thing about denazification in the United States zone was that if anyone denounced you as a Nazi you had your job and your money taken from you until you could prove your innocence. Many people were kept waiting in prison, or "free" but deprived of the right to earn a living, for years before they so much as had an opportunity to prove their innocence.

Since anti-Communist and Nazi were synonymous terms in the Communist vocabulary, many non-Nazis and even anti-Nazis were deprived of their jobs, or penalized in other ways by the Communist-dominated denazification boards. For instance, I was told by the students at the University of Munich that Professor Adolf Weber, who is one of Germany's best economists and never a Nazi, was persecuted and prevented from teaching for a long time by the denazification authorities because he is anti-Communist.

Of course it was not only the Communists who took advantage of the unlimited right given by the United States to anyone to ruin innocent men by denouncing them without evidence. Anyone who had a grudge against someone else for personal as well as political reasons could cause his enemy injury by informing against him without proving the charge. Even if the victim of the denunciation was eventually able to prove his innocence, he would have suffered loss of his job, sequestration of his property, and a long period of mental anguish. This was the inevitable consequence of America's destruction of the foundation of democratic justice by decreeing that in Germany innocence, not guilt, had to be proved.

Another case worth citing which was brought to my attention by the students at Munich was that of Professor Voerlzer, a well-known architect who had been driven into exile in Turkey by the Nazis in 1933. In 1946 while holding the position of Rector of the Munich Technical College and Chairman of the Commission for Reconstruction, he was accused by an obscure architect of having spied for Turkey during the war. He was thrown out of his job and subjected to all sorts of restrictions and indignities for a whole year. During this period reconstruction in Munich was at a standstill.

The Nazis as well as the Communists were able to use the denazification law to get rid of their enemies. In fact, the Communists and the Nazis had a joint interest in utilizing the denazification law to penalize everyone of liberal or conservative tendencies.

After denazification was abandoned in the Russian zone in favor of the present Soviet policy of courting the Nazis and encouraging them to join the Communist Party, the Communists in the Western zones withdrew from the *Spruchkammer*, and held large meetings for the "little Nazis" to tell them how badly treated they were by the United States authorities.

The turnabout of the Communists left few Germans interested in implementing the denazification law which had not only identified Nazism with opposition to Communism, but had placed a premium on dishonesty and was regarded by most Germans as merely a method of exterminating the German professional classes, "capitalists," and qualified administrative and technical personnel.

Meanwhile the United States Military Government had been forced to admit that it had bitten off more than it could chew by attempting to process some twelve million people. It had also begun to realize not only that a democratic Germany could never be established under its original directives, but also that no kind of a viable economy could be reestablished in Germany if no one who had ever been a Nazi was allowed to work except as a laborer. The fact that the Nazi regime had insisted that administrators, technicians in important positions, and executives of industrial and business enterprises must join the Nazi party in order to retain their jobs, made it impossible for the German economy to function so long as all former Nazis were debarred from working except as "hewers of wood and drawers of water."

Unable or unwilling to admit the absurdity and futility of the original denazification law, the United States Military Government tried to escape from its predicament by proclaiming a series of amnesties. First there was a "youth and poverty" amnesty; next a disability amnesty which wrote off veterans and others fifty per cent disabled. A distinction was further drawn between those who had joined the Nazi party in 1933 or before when its character was unclear, all of whom were held guilty, and those who had joined it later who were held to be less culpable.

Finding that in spite of all its efforts to escape from the predicament into which its original directives had landed it, it was still stuck with three million seven hundred thousand unprocessed "Nazi criminals," the Military Government wrote off a million and a half of them as only "nominal" Nazis. It also released most of the men and women who had been kept for years in prison without trial, and allowed many others who had been tried but had appealed their sentences to go home.[27] Wishing to wash its hands of the whole silly business, the Military Government finally declared that denazification was a German concern. Its pressures were subsequently exerted under cover, being used to ensure the institution of denazification proceedings against those who were acquitted at Nuremberg in spite of the efforts of the prosecution, and against those witnesses who had refused to testify as the prosecution required.

Since the Military Government had started out with the idea that the "little guys" should be tried first, the net result of America's attempt to process nearly half the population and then giving up the whole project is that the minor offenders who were tried in the first years of the occupation received very stiff sentences, while many major offenders have escaped with light sentences or have been acquitted because their cases were tried recently by local German courts. Thus those least responsible for Hitler's crimes have lost everything, while the major offenders and offenders (Groups 1 and 2) who were not tried until later, have recently been "denazified" after the payment of a small fine. It became a matter of luck how a former Nazi was classified and what penalties were inflicted. Where those who believe the German name can be cleansed by inflicting stiff sentences are in charge of denazification, former Nazis receive maximum sentences. Elsewhere they have escaped with nothing more than a small fine, or are put in Group 5 and let off. Moreover, a man's fate has largely depended on his influence as well as the locale in which he is tried.

---

[27] In February 1947 Military Government ordered that all those who had appealed against their sentences should be held in prison; but in March 1948 it rescinded the order and left it up to the Germans to decide who should be set free. So in 1948 most of the former Nazis who had appealed their sentences were allowed to go home.

Whereas many Gauleiters, Gestapo chiefs and other leading Nazis have either been exonerated or classified as minor offenders, and are now at liberty, I found a miserable collection of former industrial workers, craftsmen, peasants and minor party functionaries in the Langwasser prison near Nuremberg, which I visited in November 1948. Here were the last remaining Nazis in Bavaria still held in prison while awaiting trial, and those already condemned but not permitted like others to go home while awaiting the result of their appeals.

Out of a total of 240 men interned at Langwasser 70 were manual workers, fifteen farmers or peasants. 40 minor civil servants, and 35 intellectuals. The prisoners included 41 people who were not even party members and three former inmates of Nazi concentration camps. The majority of them had been in prison without trial for years; many were old and sick. They were for the most part a pitiful collection of forgotten men who had no money and no influence and had lost all hope. The exceptions were such former important figures as von Papen, shoved into prison by the Bavarian denazification authorities after his acquittal by the International Military Tribunal, although he is not a Bavarian; and Fritzsche, the Nazi Propaganda Minister, who had been condemned to nine years imprisonment by a denazification court also after having been acquitted by the I.M.T.

I was taken to Langwasser prison at my request by Camile Sachs, who is chief of denazification in Bavaria, presumably because he is half Jewish, since he seemed to have no qualifications for the job. He had not himself suffered imprisonment under the Nazis and he insisted passionately that it was a German concern to punish all Nazis. Sachs was certainly an improvement over his predecessor Lorenz, who as Minister of Denazification had condemned hundreds of thousands of people to prison but had now been arrested himself as a common criminal. Lorenz, I was told by American correspondents, was a sinister type and a potential new Hitler, but no one knew whether he had been subsidized by the French or the Russians.

The trouble with Sachs seemed to be his subservience to the Military Government. His son was employed in the "Special Projects Division" attached to the Prosecutor's Office, and there was thus perfect coordination between the Nuremberg prosecution and the Bavarian denazification authorities. The latter have pounced upon witnesses and such of the accused as the prosecutor failed to convict and sent them to German prisons in place of Military Government ones. In Germany under United States rule the legal principle that you cannot be tried twice for the same crime has been jettisoned like so many others.

Camile Sachs' thick Bavarian accent and voluble inconsequential meanderings made it very difficult for me to understand him, so the prisoner, Fritzsche, former Propaganda Minister of the Third Reich, translated what he said into good German, or what Sachs called Prussian German, so that I could understand.

Fritzsche had come to Sachs' office to plead for a re-examination of the cases of the minor offenders in the camp, because as he stated to me frankly, if the little people were not released, he had no hope of ever getting out of prison himself. It struck me, however, that the indifference of German and other democrats to the fate of the workers who had got themselves in prison merely because they had believed Nazi propaganda or despaired of democracy, was enabling former Nazis to retain or regain the confidence of the German "common man."

Fritzsche, very tall and straight, polite but not subservient in his manner in talking to Sachs, inspired the respect which courage evokes whatever a man's antecedents and views may be. He was thin to the point of emaciation but he had not been broken by his ordeal at the hands of the Russians, who had put him in the Lubianka prison in Moscow after he surrendered Berlin to them and interrogated him day and night; nor by his long incarceration at Nuremberg where the prisoners had been kept under brilliant lights day and night, watched every moment, forced to sleep with their arms outside the covers, and never given enough to eat.

He also had a sufficiently good sense of humor to laugh when I said I thought the propaganda ministers of *all* nations ought to be incarcerated.

Sachs said he was no Gestapo man and told Fritzsche to show me around the prison, which consisted of wooden huts in a large compound. The greater part of this huge camp was empty. It seemed to me a great pity that the German expellees from the Eastern territories could not occupy it, since the huts afforded better accommodations than that afforded to the victims of Yalta and Potsdam. It was a commentary on the postwar world that the imprisoned Nazis held guilty of Hitler's war crimes were living in considerably better conditions than the victims of our war crimes, whom I had visited at Dachau and other places. Not that the Langwasser prison could compare to the prisons of the United States in which common criminals are confined. The huts are draughty and cold and the food as inadequate but not more so than that of the German workers. But the prisoners at Langwasser at least had elbow room, unlike the German expellees from the Eastern territories who are crowded fifty to a room.

I talked to von Papen in the hospital wing of the prison for an hour, during which he told me how close Germany and France had been in 1932 to an accord which would have prevented the Nazis from coming to power. Afterwards I talked to other prisoners. Of these conversations I remembered best the one I had with a former factory worker who had been a social democrat before 1933. When I asked him why he had become a Nazi, he said: "It was the first time in my life I ever had security. No one could fire me."

Almost bald, short, emaciated and grey faced, a bewildered "common man" who had never understood what it was all about, this man now sits in jail for an indefinite period.

On our way through the camp we met a group of prisoners waiting at the locked gate to attend the funeral of a man who had hung himself the night before. The poor devil had been rearrested after having been released from several years in prison, because the Yugoslavs claimed him. He had been torn away from his wife and three young children whom he had had to leave without anyone to provide for them, just when he had begun to hope he could earn a living again. Expecting death at the hands of the Communists, or life-long slave labor, he had committed suicide.

Denazification is today nearing its end, but it has left enduring bitterness and distrust of democratic justice. To punish men for their opinions or political affiliations, not for actual crimes, is bad enough. It is even worse to have let the "big shots" who were the pillars of the Third

Reich go unpunished because they have influence, are useful to the Military Government, or pretend they never were Nazis, and to punish thousands of small fry because they were tried too soon, or were too honest to deny their beliefs, refused to be subservient to their conquerors, or had no power to move their judges.

Fritz Hentzler, the Socialist *Bürgermeister* of Dortmund, who has been a lifelong anti-Nazi, said that denazification was a fundamentally unjust proceeding, and one of the "most appalling things ever done." As he pointed out, one of the essentials of a democratic state is the independence, impartiality, and legal experience of those who administer justice. The man in the street lacks the qualifications to be a judge, and to use him as such on a denazification panel was to imitate the "peoples democratic justice" of the Communists.

According to Fritz Hentzler, the British denazification proceedings were worse than the American. Anyone useful to the British, he said, was tolerated, and a premium put on treachery, as for instance when Diehl (who was the first chief of Goering's Prussian Gestapo and was succeeded by Himmler who formed the Reich Gestapo) was put in Category 5 (exonerated) because at the end he had betrayed the Nazis, as he had formerly betrayed the last Weimar Republic Minister of the Interior for Prussia under whom he had served before Hitler came to power.

In the British zone, Hentzler said, the hearings of denazification boards were not open to the public and the defendants were not even heard. Former Nazis who had "good connections" or were in a position to supply black-market goods, could obtain "certificates of exoneration" to send into the courts. There was at first no Public Prosecutor to call witnesses and ensure the condemnation of the guilty, nor any court to which those sentenced on account of their lack of influence could appeal.

According to other accounts the British denazification proceedings were far more equitable than the American. They picked only such Nazis as would have been tried in a criminal court under pre-Hitler German or Anglo-Saxon law. That is to say, they tried people only for the crimes they had committed, not for their opinions or for membership in the party. So they prosecuted only twenty-five thousand people and released many of them. But Fritz Hentzler was probably right in thinking that some prominent Nazis were released because they would be useful to the British.

The French, like the Russians, regarded ex-Nazis as their most reliable aides since such Germans were completely dependent on their mercy, and to a much smaller degree this may have been true of the British. The point is, of course, that the whole denazification process put a premium on dishonesty, subservience, and treachery and condemned honest men while releasing timeservers, cowards, and clever men who could camouflage their real sentiments and prepare for the day when they could take vengeance on their conquerors by serving them now.

There was no doubt a good deal of truth in the description of denazification given me by Löwenthal, the German-born Frankfurt correspondent of Reuters News Agency.

"In the British zone," he said. "denazification was carried out by the Nazis, and in the United States zone by the Communists."

The Communist Schmidt already referred to was removed from his post "for incompetence" nine months after he took office. But this did not change the fact that the totalitarian concepts of the Communists were the basis of the United States zone denazification law. This law, as German jurists have pointed out, was based on the same principles as Nazi and Communist law. It punished men for their opinions without need to prove any guilty action; it penalized their families; it violated the principle of judicial independence by giving the Denazification Minister the right to re-examine and quash every judgment: it kept men in prison for years without trial and it continued to penalize them after they had been tried and "denazified."

A German attorney, Dr. Otto Gritschneder, in a pamphlet called *Dead End Denazification* demonstrates in detail the Nazi characteristics of the denazification law. He writes:

The law of Liberation by Article 61, combined with Military Government Law No. 52, produces effects which are in full harmony with the Himmler principle, so rightly opposed, of 'liability of kinship.' Not only the respondents' property is blocked, but also that of his wife. It is of no use for the wife to have been officially notified, long ago, that she is "not affected" by the law; nor is it of any avail to her if she was one of the political persecutees of the Third Reich. Together with her children she shares the fate of her husband, in spite of her own clean political record. In addition to undeniable psychic injury, she takes upon herself all the material injuries as well. Not even in the Third Reich was it customary to ban the wife of a political prisoner from her lodgings. Nor was it usual to seize the property of a non-Jewish wife married to a Jew.

The various amnesties proclaimed by the United States Military Government, far from rectifying the abuses of the denazification law, showed up its arbitrary character, and its unjust foundations. It showed no equity to amnesty people on account either of their age or their incomes. In the case of the youth amnesty it was absurd to say that a man who joined the Nazi party at the age of eighteen in 1933 when its aims were unclear, is guilty; whereas a younger man who joined the party in 1942 is innocent.

The poverty amnesty was similarly inequitable, unless one accepts the Communist view that a capitalist, or man of property, and a Nazi are the same thing.

To make an amnesty dependent on either age or fortune is to deny the principle of equality before the law which is the very basis of democratic justice. Thus, both in its application and exemptions the so-called Law of Liberation from National Socialism denied the very basis of liberty, and brought all democratic law into contempt. Politically, as well as morally, the law has been disastrous, since who will disclose his real convictions if tomorrow he may be persecuted once again for his opinions—either by the Communists or the Western democracies?

To quote a German liberal woman writer, Dr. Maria Fritzle of Stuttgart:

A man is never more sensitive than in his feelings for law. if he has to suffer discrimination under the law, which he does not deserve, then abhorrence and internal resistance will arise which gnaw at his mind and make him unfit for reconstruction. We should always bear in mind that Hitler in the years after 1930, could boast so great an afflux, and of decent Germans too, because he fought against the articles of the Versailles Treaty which burdened Germany with the guilt of having started the war. This article violated the German feeling for law because it established a collective guilt of all the Germans and based the demand for reparations upon that guilt. We do not serve peace but work against it if we violate the sound feelings for law of our countrymen by imposing upon them reparations for things which are not a crime in themselves. Numerous young people deny the state and politics their service, although they could give valuable help to democracy. *The fear of the questionnaire of the future kills the honest battle of opinions at the present time.*

Dr. Ludwig Hagenauer, the Socialist Minister for Denazification in Bavaria who succeeded the Communist Schmidt, pointed out the harmful political consequences of the Denazification Law in 1947, when he said that the incrimination of hundreds of thousands of persons for formal reasons had pressed many who were formerly averse to National Socialism "into a sympathetic community with the confirmed National Socialists, due to the common and equal treatment of both." As Dr. Gritschneder wrote: "Instead of purging the German people by punishing the Nazi criminals, National Socialism is being immortalized by the Denazification laws."

Finally, it is worth quoting the statement made by Eugene Kogon who himself spent years in Hitler's concentration camps:

It is not a crime to have erred politically. A political error is not a matter which should be brought before a court. To err is human we have a right to err, if we do not want to be either slaves, marionettes or gods.

The manner in which attempts have been made for two years now to make the German people free of National Socialism and militarism has contributed a great deal to the chaotic state in which we find ourselves today. Everybody with inside information knows that the result is less denazification than renazification. The following bad saying is repeated from mouth to mouth:—

"Since the democratic sun shines above us, we are getting browner every day."[28]

Before one gets brown one gets red. There is little doubt that it was the influence of the Communists, and of those Americans who have knowingly or in ignorance adopted their theories, which led to the denial of fundamental American political and legal principles in occupied Germany. Not only did Americans sit with the representatives of Soviet tyranny on the International Military Tribunal at Nuremberg, thereby bringing the whole proceedings into disrepute, the United States Military Government put Communists and "totalitarian liberals" in a position to discredit democracy and pave the way for a Communist conquest of Germany from within.

The appointment of a German Communist as Minister of Denazification in Bavaria in 1945 was only one among many examples of the Military Government's partiality for the Communists, and acceptance of their definition of democracy during the first years of the occupation. The general use made of Communists to "teach democracy" to the Germans was in fact the outstanding un-American activity which helped discredit democracy in German eyes and made it indistinguishable from Nazi totalitarian rule.

The former political intelligence officer (PIO) in Bavaria for the United States Military Government in its relations with the Germans was a certain Martin, a former DP of Austrian origin and a full-fledged member of the Communist Party, who was refused a visa to the United States. Nevertheless, he continued to represent the United States Military Government as a PIO charged with supplying information to DENA and other German news media. Mr. Martin was also sent by the Military Government on a tour to exhibit the documentary film "People's Court," which recorded the trial of the German resistance leaders who had tried to assassinate Hitler on July 20, 1944.

General Telford Taylor, who sent Mr. Martin on this tour, apparently imagined that the film would demonstrate to the Germans how

---

[28] In an article in the *Frankfurter Hefte* in July 1947. Quoted in *Dead End Denazification*, privately printed as a manuscript by Dr. Otto Gritschneder, Munich.

fair the Nuremberg trials were, in contrast to the horrible treatment meted out to the anti-Hitler conspirators. Taylor was, it seemed, too obtuse to realize the effect of sending a Communist to show the film in Germany and comment on it. Of course, the reaction of the Germans to the movie was to say, "What fine brave fellows those German aristocrats were, and how terrible it is to be ruled now by Communist sympathizers under the American flag."

This same Mr. Martin was held responsible for the continued operation, after the Communist coup in Czechoslovakia, of the Czech short-wave radio station in the former press camp at Stein Castle near Nuremberg. So while thousands of Czechs were seeking to flee the Communist terror, a radio station in American occupied territory was still permitted to broadcast Czech-Communist propaganda!

Thus the communist Martin, in American uniform with American transport and communications at his disposal, was enabled to perform yeoman service for Stalin under the protection of General Telford Taylor, who used him to instruct the German press concerning what they should and should not say.

As Peter Blake, a former United States political intelligence officer in Frankfurt demonstrated in an article published in *Politics* in the summer of 1948, it was not the failure of the "army mind," but that of the "liberal mind" which made the American zone of Germany "ripe for Stalinism."

Mr. Blake's article shows in detail what a "strange collection of American 'liberals,' Stalinoids, and Russia Firsters" were assembled in the Information Control and Political Affairs Divisions of Military Government "to lend the United States Army a helping hand in re-educating the Germans."

Information Control Division (ICD), he wrote, contained such well-known Communist sympathizers or Soviet apologists as Saul K. Padover of *PM*, Cedric Belfrage of Hollywood who subsequently became editor of a pro-Wallace magazine (the *National Guardian*), and a choice selection of other former OWI employees of the same political coloring.

Mr. Cedric Belfrage, according to Peter Blake's account, appointed German Communists as the licensees of the most important newspaper in the American zone: The *Frankfurter Rundschau* with a circulation of 150,000. One of his appointees, Emil Carlebach, who had been in Buchenwald, was subsequently exposed as having collaborated with Hitler's SS in murdering other inmates of the concentration camp.[29]

Another of the men Mr. Belfrage picked to teach the Germans democracy as an editor of the *Frankfurter Rundschau* was Wilhelm Gerst, who later became an active organizer for the Russian Socialist Unity Party (SED).

The Information Control Division rejected the services of such proved anti-totalitarian German liberals as the former editorial staff of the pre-Hitler *Frankfurter Zeitung* and "kicked them around" for so long that some took off for the French zone, and started a fortnightly called *Die Gegenwart* which has established itself as one of the best magazines in Europe.

Dr. Joseph Dunner, who, although former Chief of Intelligence for the OWI in Europe, was neither a Communist sympathizer nor naive, wrote in the June 8, 1946 issue of the *New Leader* how, as an ICD official in Germany, he was approached by the German Communists who evidently expected him to do his duty by Stalin like his colleague Mr. Belfrage. Bruno Goldhammer, chief of the Bavarian Communist Party, came to Dr. Dunner and said:

I understand that you are about to organize a German newspaper in Munich. You know that in Frankfurt, where such a paper already exists, several Communists have been admitted as licensees of the paper. *I have come to ask you, in the name of the Communist Party to follow the example of your colleagues in Frankfurt and to include among the licensees in Munich Communists whom my party will nominate.* (Italics added.)

---

[29] See the August 1948 issue of *Harper's Magazine* for the account given by the Socialist Ernst Federn of how Carlebach murdered, or attempted to murder, fellow inmates of Buchenwald whom he thought might become postwar opponents of Communism.

In another issue of the *New Leader* (May 25, 1946) Dr. Dunner told how the German-American News Agency, DENA, was placed under Communist control.

The Communists and their fellow travelers having established a center in the Information Control Unit for Greater Hesse in June 1945, Brigadier General Robert McClure, chief of the I.C.D. assigned seven civilians of the O.W.I., two lieutenants and four enlisted men, to Bad Nauheim to lay the foundation of DENA. the team was headed by Lt. Edel, a former correspondent for *PM*.

According to Peter Blake's account in *Politics*, the Information Control Division of the United States Military Government, also enlisted the help of a certain Dr. Hans Meyer, a German from Switzerland who was a leader of the Stalinist "Protective League of German Writers," who told Blake that he "thanked God for the Soviet Union."

The top licensee of DENA, as might have been expected, turned out to be Dr. Rudolf Agricola, a Communist Party member since 1933.

The Stalinist Dr. Hans Meyer was subsequently appointed Political Chief of Radio Frankfurt but eventually, according to Peter Blake:

Even I.C.D. found his (Meyer's) denunciation of Churchill and others as "war mongers" a little hard to swallow, and it even penetrated Military Government's consciousness that a Communist political commentator, broadcasting three times a week over one of Western Germany's principal stations, was not the best advertisement the U.S. could produce of the democratic way of life.

So at least, early in 1948, Dr. Meyer was "permitted to resign."

The Munich radio station was also placed under the direction of a Communist: Herr Bentschen.

Heute, an official American German-language magazine, was entrusted to a certain Captain Heinz Norden, who besides being fanatically anti-German was a member of several Communist-front organizations such as the American League against War and Fascism, whose vice-chairman was Earl Browder, and the American Youth Congress. Captain Norden naturally devoted a large amount of space in *Heute* to articles by Ilya Ehrenburg and to picturesque accounts of the happy life of the Poles and of the Germans in the Russian zone.

There have been many and important changes in the past year or two, and the "Stalinists" no longer have the power they once held in the Information and other divisions of Military Government. But the evil they did lives after them. Many Germans no longer believe in American democracy, after having for so long been forced by the United States Military Government to swallow Communist propaganda.

Germans cannot forget how during the first years of the occupation the Information Control Division forbade any criticism of Soviet Russia or its satellites in American-licensed newspapers, periodicals, and radio stations. The American ban on the publication of news unfavorable to the Soviet Union and its satellites was extended to cover such subjects as the cruel expulsions of women and children from Silesia, Russian arms manufacture in the Eastern zone of Germany, and the collaboration of former Nazis and German General Staff officers with the Red Army. Military Government directives not only protected the Soviet Union from adverse criticism but forbade knowledge of its anti-western activities to be published in German newspapers. By its positive and negative actions the representatives of the American people in Germany both discredited Western democracy and destroyed belief in our integrity.

Military Government did not confine its un-American activities to giving unlimited facilities for propaganda to the Communists. It also insisted upon the inclusion of German Communists in state and city administrations. In its zeal to establish a "people's democracy" it insisted on "coalition governments": forcing the Germans to include Communists in the *Länder* administration of Bavaria and Hesse. In Munich, for instance, as late as April 1948, the head of the Economics Office was a German woman Communist who naturally sabotaged production instead of endeavoring to increase it and improve conditions.

It was not until 1947 that the Germans were permitted to get rid of the Communists in state and local government, and as late as the summer of 1948 when I was in Berlin, Communists were still employed in the labor offices, food offices, and health administration of the boroughs of Zehlendorf, Steglitz, Schöneberg, Tempelhof and Neukölln in the Western sectors.

In Munich I asked Hermann Jordan, a particularly intelligent and politically well-informed young instructor in mathematics at the University, about Communist influence in Bavaria. His reply was a revealing commentary on the past un-American activities of the United States Military Government. He said:

"In the early days of the occupation the Communists were very influential because of the key positions they held in the Western zones, their excellent organization, and their long period of training in the Soviet Union before being appointed to their jobs by the United States Military Government. But not now. Since America withdrew its support from the Communist Party, it is no longer a political factor in the Western zones."

Jordan is half Jewish and so escaped military service but he had been elected head of the organization for securing jobs for the students of the University who nearly all have to earn their living while studying, and most of whom are veterans. Thanks to Jordan, I was invited to a big student meeting addressed by Dr. Hans Ehard, the President of Bavaria. Ehard was endeavoring to convince the students that they should not despair of democracy, now that there was hope of the formation of a Western German state, but the loudest applause his speech evoked occurred when he said:

"The mention of the word democracy, or democratic, especially before a young audience, arouses a wave of distrust in Germany today."

Ehard went on to say that this does not mean that the idea of democracy is considered fundamentally bad, or that the years of dictatorship have rendered the German people so unaccustomed to freedom that they have become "obtuse to the principles of democratic life." "The explanation is somewhat different." said Ehard. "Our doubts arise from the contradiction between democratic illusions and the reality of power relationships in the world of today."

Listening to the questions put to Dr. Ehard by the students and talking to some of them afterwards, I got a glimmer of understanding of the attitude of German youth today. Most of them stand aside from politics, having no respect for, or confidence in, any of the parties. Veterans of all the battlefields of Europe, brought up in the Nazi ideology which led Germany to disastrous defeat and now equally disillusioned with democracy, they also have no faith in communism. Several of them, however, told me that in 1945 they had inclined toward the Communists, or had believed that collaboration with them was possible and desirable. It had taken them a year or two to understand the difference between Communist theory and practice, just as they had not at the beginning understood the gulf which divides the professions of the Western Powers and their actions. Moreover, at the beginning of the occupation it was impossible to distinguish between democracy and communism, since the Americans had identified the two and put many Communists in power over the Germans in the United States zone.

When I asked if they thought that many young Germans were still Nazis at heart, Jordan replied: "The drift back to Nazi ideas is mainly the consequence of denazification."

How could it be otherwise since the only difference between "democratic" justice and totalitarian justice appeared to be the categories of people singled out for collective punishment?

The American view that the "followers" of the Nazi party are not dangerous while the former convinced believers should be punished for the rest of their lives, was both unrealistic and harmful to the democratic cause in Germany. For whereas men of integrity and intelligence could have been convinced of the error of their beliefs and converted to our way of thinking, the mob which follows success is as likely to follow Stalin today as it was ready to follow Hitler yesterday.

Many of the "little Nazis" have in fact joined the Communist Party since Germany's defeat. All that was needed, as one former Nazi said to me in Berlin, was "to take the swastika out of the Red flag." On the other hand, those Nazis who were critical of Hitler's policies, and opposed them at the risk of their lives, are precisely the type which refuses to abase itself before the power of Military Government and plead that they never were "real Nazis." Their former doubts of Hitler's policies, instead of bringing them over to the democratic camp, give way to a conviction that after all Hitler was right since the democracies also believe that justice means only the will of the strong, and there is no hope for the weak.

Many Nazis who never committed any crimes, but are too proud to deny former convictions, and who believe that they only did their duty as German patriots, are outcasts in Germany today; while the timeservers, the liars, the self-seeking and unprincipled men who joined the Nazi party for material advantages or the advancement of their careers, are exonerated and allowed to hold office or practice their former professions under Military Government.

Our treatment of the German officer class has been no more intelligent. No former *Wehrmacht* officer above the rank of captain is allowed to hold a job in the state or local administrations, or in the universities and professions. No officer is allowed to receive his pension, even if he is so old that he did not fight in either of the World Wars. The widows and children of officers who died fighting for their country are deprived of their pensions by order of the United States Military Government. No victor ever treated a vanquished foe with less chivalry and humanity than the United States treats the officers of the defeated German army.

When Marshal von Leeb wrote to General Clay begging that the German States be permitted to pay small pensions to the widows and orphans of the German officers who fell fighting, General Clay did not even design to reply himself to the old Marshal who was appealing not for himself but for the dependents of the slain. Instead, on March 18, 1947, a curt epistle signed by an American lieutenant colonel, was sent to Marshal von Leeb, which said:

"In August, 1946, the Allied Control Authority adopted Law Number 34, repealing all legislation granting privilege, or particular status to ex-military personnel or their survivors. The objectives of the above measures were to combat militarism and the prestige and position of the military classes in Germany."

Just as Stalin had condemned the children of kulaks and other capitalists to starvation, so the United States Military Government condemned the children of its slain enemies to a pauper status.

The curious thing is that the Military Government should have imagined that it would extirpate militarism in Germany by making martyrs of the families of those who had died fighting for their country.

Some of the wives and children of the fallen were able to exist on their savings until currency reform. But this measure deprived them of their last resources and reduced them to destitution together with the officers who survived the war but have been debarred from earning a living.

A letter written by the wife of an old friend to an American general who once studied in Germany and now holds a high position in the War Department, shows the plight of the German army wives whose husbands are either dead or prisoners of war in Russia.

HAMBURG, JANUARY 1, 1949

"Unfortunately there is nothing good to report. My husband is still a Russian prisoner. As a result of the currency reform I lost the last of my money. At the Welfare office they told me that officers' families are not allowed to receive anything; that they should be exterminated. They nevertheless allowed me a little relief, although not enough to keep alive my four children, who are all still going to school. From June till October our situation was quite bad. Now I have a job as secretary to an exporting firm, so our situation is better, although it is difficult for me also to look after the children.

"We have had a lot of misfortune with sicknesses which are doubtless due to long years of poor diet. My oldest child has been at the hospital for two months, but he is to be sent to Switzerland. I am very glad on that score. When are the Russians going to release the prisoners? The war has been over four years now and still there are hundreds of thousands who have not returned home. This is very inhuman indeed.

"Please don't be angry at me for having told you my sorrows. I would like to have told you good things. Perhaps it will be possible for my husband to write to you himself next January 1 and perhaps things will be better then.

"And now I wish you and your wife much happiness for the year 1949.

With hearty greetings,"

I. RANCK

The American officer who translated this letter wrote on the margin: "It is hard to read such a letter without being touched by the thought: the common tragedy, the common courage of all humanity, which transcends man-made national boundaries. Christian kindness, sympathy and understanding also, fortunately can transcend them:"

When in the fall of 1948 the former *Wehrmacht* officers of Hesse wanted to form an "Economic Association of former members of the Wehrmacht" to secure their pensions and civil rights, the United States Military Government forbade it.

Meanwhile the Russians offer good pay and special privileges to any former Wehrmacht officers who will join them against us.

As Count von Schlabrendorff (the man who almost killed Hitler) said to me in Wiesbaden, many Wehrmacht officers will have no choice but to join up with Russia, since America condemns them and their families to starvation.

Von Schlabrendorff told me what tempting offers he himself had received from the Russians when visiting Berlin—offers which he himself had rejected but which he realized were hard to resist by others who unlike himself were precluded from earning a living by the United States. Moreover, the Russian appeal is not only to self-interest, but also to German patriotism. The German officers are tempted by the prospect of "freeing Germany from the AngloSaxon yoke."

"It is only one step from National Socialism to Bolshevism," said von Schlabrendorff. Many German officers were anti-Nazi, although America has identified their patriotism with Nazi sympathies. Today many formerly anti-Nazi officers are moved by the Russian appeal to the old tradition of Russo-German friendship. Stalin continually reminds the Germans that in the past they were strong only when Germany and Russia were friends.

However great their dislike of Communism and their former antagonism to Nazism, German officers today remember that after Prussia had been defeated and humiliated by Napoleon, it was restored in alliance with Russia which broke the power of France. Germany's situation today is sufficiently similar for Russian propaganda to evoke a response, in spite of German fears of Communism, and the terrible situation of the Germans under Russia's heel in the Eastern zone. The fact that German officers, like former high Nazis, are much better treated by the Soviet Government than German "common men" cannot but lessen the antagonism of the former officer class to Russia.

The denial by the Western Powers to Germany of the right to defend herself, coupled with our refusal to guarantee her defense ourselves, and the fact that only Russia can restore her lost eastern territories to Germany, all play into Russia's hands.

General Speidel, who was Rommel's chief of staff, said to me in Freudenstadt in the French zone: "If we cannot expect either justice or security under America, we shall be forced to turn toward Russia. It is not yet too late to orientate Germany toward the West, because that is where most of us want to turn; but the last hour is striking. Soon you will have made it impossible for the Germans to find their way back to the West."

9

How Not to Teach Democracy

THE BEHAVIOR PATTERN SET FOR AMERICAN SOLDIERS AND CIVILIAN in Germany is perhaps no less important than our economic policies and repudiation of democratic legal principles, in convincing the Germans that the United States Military Government and the Nazis have much in common.

I have already referred to the behavior of the Western Powers toward "the natives" in Berlin, but it is in the Western zones that the contrast between our actions and our much-boasted democratic principles is most grotesquely displayed. It seemed that the further away the Russians were, the greater the contempt displayed for democracy by the United States and British occupation forces.

It was therefore fitting, however depressing, to find that in Nuremberg, where Hitler first promulgated his racial laws, our Jim Crow regulations should be most in evidence.

Lest any person of inferior race should dare to pass the portals of the Grand Hotel, which we have taken over for our exclusive use, notices have been posted outside forbidding the entry of Germans, DP's and dogs. "Anyone violating the above," it is written, "will be booked by the Military Police for proper disciplinary action."

Recently a line has been added in small red letters at the bottom, saying that it is possible to obtain a guest card admitting Germans and displaced persons by applying to the officer on duty at the billeting office further along the street. However, any German permitted to enter the hotel by special dispensation is continually reminded of his inferior status. On the wine list in the bar, for instance, there is a printed list of instructions concerning the correct behavior of Americans toward what Kipling called "the lesser breeds without the law."

In the Nuremberg-Furth Military Post Officers Club and bars, it is written,

We Do not:

(1) Bring Germans or DP's as guests.
(2) Tip or become familiar with any of the help.

Paragraphs 3 to 8 of this guide for the proper behavior of American officers include the recommendation that they should not gamble, bring in bottles, cut in on people they do not know, dance boisterously, or order an excessive number of drinks. Positive as well as negative instructions are included:

"We do wear class A uniform or the equivalent (coat and tie) and we do believe that a man can drink and enjoy himself and still remain a gentleman."

Kipling in the days when the British bore "the white man's burden" could hardly have done better than the Nuremberg military authorities who were endeavoring to teach American officers the correct behavior of officers and gentlemen in a colonial country.

The Grand Hotel faces toward the ruins of the beautiful medieval city which our bombs have utterly destroyed. Many centuries have passed since Hans Sachs sang, and the memory of the Meistersinger is preserved only in a restaurant in the modern part of the city which our bombs left partly standing. But Wagner lived at a time when Americans believed in liberty, equality, and fraternity, and would have been horrified at the notice outside the Grand Hotel.

Could any satirist imagine a greater contrast between the Statue of Liberty and its welcome to the poor, starved, and oppressed, and the commands now given to Americans to avoid contact with the wretched of the earth?

I saw no such notices outside the hotels and clubs of the British occupation forces in Germany. This is presumably because the British, with their centuries-old experience in ruling over subject peoples, do not need to be told how to behave in a conquered country.

Americans are far less at ease in a colonial country such as Germany has become. While retaining the privileges of a master race they have lowered the barriers to social intercourse with "the natives" in many places. At the PX cafeterias, in the press clubs and in the hotels reserved for visiting businessmen, Congressmen, VIP's and other transients, Germans are admitted as guests, although not allowed to sleep there. But the British, even in Berlin and Frankfurt, still exclude *all* Germans from the clubs, hotels, bars, and restaurants they have requisitioned. British journalists, wishing to entertain German guests, have to resort to the American press clubs, whose only restriction is the necessity to pay for food and drink in dollar scrip.

The British also go even further than the Americans in their washroom regulations. At the Bizonia Coal Commission headquarters in the Krupps' villa in Essen, I was not sure whether I had any right to use the lavatory labeled "For the use only of English ladies."

The United States Military Government, as I have already noted in my account of Berlin, also has separate washrooms for American and "indigenous personnel," but the notices in American offices say nothing about "ladies" and "gentlemen." I am being a bit unfair to the British here, since all lavatories in England are labeled "Ladies" or "Gentlemen," not "Men" and "Women." But in Germany the prefix "English" makes the British Military Government's notices look excessively insular and absurd.

The more liberal members of the United States and British occupation forces explain these particular Jim Crow regulations as due to the fact that toilet paper and soap are so scarce that if Germans were admitted to the same washrooms as their conquerors, there would not be enough of these supplies to go around. They do not seem to realize that it is a shameful reflection on us that four years after the end of the war we do not let the Germans, who have a passion for cleanliness, manufacture enough soap and paper to provide for their minimum needs. We have allowed the British to dismantle the largest soap factory in Germany, the Hänckel Works at Düsseldorf, and German wood has been exported for the profit of the British and French.

Germans working for the Military Government are, of course, also restricted to different eating places and provided with food much inferior to that provided for United States personnel. This in itself can be justified on grounds of economy and the fact that American occupation currency has to be used to buy the good food in our restaurants, most of which is brought from the United States. The unpleasant thing about our treatment of the Germans working with us is the way the meals they buy for marks are served to them. Even highly qualified German employees or advisers of the Military Government had their food served out to them as if they were prisoners.

If our discrimination against the Germans were due only to the belief that, as conquerors, we have a right to enjoy all the material comforts of life, to live in spacious and warm apartments or houses, have plenty of hot water and soap, better food and more personal service than at home, while the Germans are crowded two or three to a room or cellar without the necessities as well as the amenities of life, the Germans would consider this natural, although hardly democratic. But we add insult to injury by our race segregation regulations.

Many picture theaters as well as clubs and hotels are reserved for Allied personnel. In Frankfurt there are three kinds of street cars: Those for Allied personnel, those for "indigenous personnel" working for us, and a third for the mass of the German population. All the first-class, and most of the second-class carriages on the trains are reserved for the master races, and are usually half empty, while the Germans travel in the overcrowded third-class coaches. When, as rarely happens, we permit a German to travel on a plane, he is not allowed any food. All eating places at the airports are forbidden him.

Anti-Nazi Germans returning from exile abroad receive the same treatment as all others. Dr. Alexander Boeker, a former Rhodes scholar who has lived as an exile in the United States for many years, told me how when visiting Germany in the summer of 1948, he had been dumped in the street with his baggage when he arrived at Frankfurt from the airport, and had been unable to get a room in a hotel for the night although he had dollars with which to pay for his accommodations, simply because he is a German. He also told me of his annoyance in Wiesbaden when he found himself debarred from using the swimming pool, the tennis courts, and his favorite café, and found the outdoor dancing place which he had frequented in the past converted into a parking lot for military vehicles.

German youth today is denied simple pleasures and normal recreation by our sequestration of so many sport places, cinemas, cafés and dance halls. Instead of releasing more accommodations for German use as our occupation forces have dwindled, we seem to have requisitioned more and more of the places of entertainment which survived the air raids. In Munich, for instance, during the first year of occupation we had shut the Germans out of only two of the four popular restaurants fronting on the Englischer Garten. In the second year we took over another, and in 1948 we requisitioned the last of them.

Later I give some details of occupation costs, and the manner in which the Western Powers have unnecessarily deprived the Germans of housing space. For the moment I am concerned, in particular, with the racial bias we have displayed. Why should not Germans play tennis on the same courts or swim in the same pools as Americans, or listen to music and watch movies in our company? If we ever seriously meant to teach them democracy and show them how wrong Nazi race prejudices were, we have certainly shown a strange way to set about it.

No doubt, we had some vague idea that sending the Germans to Coventry would "learn 'em." In fact, all we have taught them is that there is little to choose between Anglo-American Military Government and Nazi government. In fact, the *Wehrmacht* in France, Holland and Belgium seems to have behaved better in many respects than we do.

I remember one young German, who had been in occupied France, saying to me, "When I was a soldier in France, I never had a chance to enjoy life and kick other people around as you do. We were strictly disciplined and told to be polite and considerate to the French; we lived with them in their houses, and did not throw them into the gutter as you do us. We have learned our lesson though; if there is ever a next time you have taught us Germans what is permitted to a conqueror."

Other Germans, less cynical and bitter, took pride in the fact that they still corresponded with the French families they had lived with during the occupation, and just thought us silly to stir up unnecessary resentment and hatred.

For the past two years or so we have gradually been abandoning the idea that the way to teach democracy to the Germans is to punish them for the sins of the Nazis by ourselves behaving as ruthlessly, unchivalrously, and with as little regard for democratic and Christian principles as Hitler's bullies. Nevertheless, the old "hate the Germans and kick them in the teeth" propaganda and indoctrination still colors our thinking and our actions.

GI's find ways to make friends with German families as well as to pick up *"Fräuleins,"* but United States officers and civilians have little social intercourse with the conquered people. Many of them are quite satisfied to live after the fashion of the British in India when they ruled there. Military Government officials who have brought out their families can enjoy home life, and be satisfied with the narrow social intercourse provided by mixing only with Americans and with the British and French. But the pilots of the air lift and many a young American officer would be far happier if billeted on German families, and provided with a little of the comforts of home and an opportunity to enjoy social intercourse with decent Germans, instead of being restricted to clandestine "affairs" with such girls as they can pick up on the streets. This was brought home to me by a talk I had with the pilot of the plane flying me to Berlin on the air lift late in the evening of Thanksgiving Day. He came from Chicago, and he talked a lot because, as he said, it was their loneliness in Germany which was the hardest thing to bear for the Air Force pilots whose life consists only of flying, sleeping, and eating. "I have a wife and two kids at home," he said, "whom I hope to get back to soon. I don't want a love affair with a *Fräulein*, and I can't afford to go out with an American girl in my liberty hours, for American women want you to spend too much money."

Then he went on to tell me that he had had the luck a few days before to get acquainted with a nice German girl who had taken him to her house. He had suggested taking her out to a meal and a movie but she had seen he was very tired, and had put him to rest on the family sofa listening to music. He had gone to sleep and woke up to find a rug over him and the light dimmed. He had been touched and grateful and only wished that he were allowed to live with a German family instead of being segregated in an exclusive American billet.

It is indeed a curious fact that United States policy fosters prostitution and makes normal decent social intercourse almost out of the question for the occupation forces. After World War I, the United States and Britain observed international law and billeted their officers and soldiers in German families in the towns we then occupied in the Rhineland. But this time, wishing to punish the whole German people and prevent our soldiers from being contaminated by contact with an accursed people, we threw the Germans out of the houses we requisitioned instead of letting them occupy a part of their old homes.

This practice, which still continues, was not only particularly brutal in view of the bombing which had destroyed so many houses in almost every German town. It also penalized our own soldiers.

Officers and civilian officials on permanent duty in Germany, installed in emptied German houses, with German servants hired to attend to all their wants, and with their social needs cared for by intercourse among themselves, enjoyed more comforts than at home. But the GI's, and also the pilots doing temporary duty on the air lift, are deprived of the homelike comforts they might otherwise have enjoyed in their leisure hours. They are permitted to pick up girls on the streets, but they are carefully excluded from the society of respectable German families. Some of them, of course, break through the Jim Crow barriers, and some of the girls they pick up are no worse than those they knew in their home towns would be if driven by the drab misery and hopelessness of their starved lives in cellars and bombed-out buildings to seek a substitute for love, or some food and a few hours enjoyment of light and warmth at movies or other entertainment.

The fact that many German girls, casually met, win the real love and affection of American soldiers and marry them is a tribute to the qualities of German women, not a reflection on the American GI.

Many of the latter have displayed the best qualities of the American tradition in helping children, giving food to the old and weak, and in general helping whole families to exist, without thought of personal advantage. Others, of course, take advantage of their position as conquerors to take everything and give nothing, accumulate small fortunes by exploiting the acute want of soap, cigarettes, candy and other "luxuries" which can only be bought in the PX stores for American money, and can be disposed of at a huge profit on the black market.

By 1948 it was no longer easy for every American soldier and civilian to make his fortune by importing cigarettes and coffee and exchanging them for silverware and precious china, furs, heirlooms, cameras, and anything else the Germans had left to exchange, but it was still easy for the clever and unscrupulous to trade on the black market. It was quite usual to see huge consignments of coffee arriving at the Frankfurt Press Center for correspondents who knew how to sell what had cost them one mark a pound at the official rate of exchange for fifteen marks a pound. They might use the marks to pay their servants or to dine in German restaurants, or they could buy the German luxury goods which had appeared in the shops since currency reform. Without joining the big racketeers engaged in shipping abroad via the French zone large quantities of German goods needed on the home market, many Americans still did their bit to undermine the value of the new currency, stimulate inflation, and deprive the German workers of the necessities of life.

Although German women can no longer be hired for a carton of cigarettes or some food now that famine conditions no longer prevail, labor is still the cheapest thing in Germany. So Army wives and those of civilians who would do their own work and look after their own children back home in the States have servants to attend to all their wants so long as their husbands work for the Military Government. Some few take an interest in the condition of the German people and organize charities, but for many of them bargain hunting is the favorite pastime. The remark I heard one evening in the Bar of the Grand Hotel at Nuremberg was typical of many conversations among the women of the occupation forces. "My dear!" said a shrill voice rising above the din, "You can get wonderful Madonnas there for a carton."

The contrast between America's desire to teach the Germans to be democratic and the undemocratic treatment they receive at our hands was strikingly illustrated as late as the spring of 1949, when a group of German women was brought over to the United States as "the guests of the Military Government" to study American democratic institutions under the direction of the Carrie Chapman Catt Foundation. The indignities, abuses, privations, and discomforts these women suffered before they arrived in the United States might well have disgusted them with "democracy" for the rest of their lives.

Nora Melle, whom I have already mentioned in my chapter on Berlin, was one of them. She told me in Washington in April 1949 how she was first unable to get her visa to come to America, because the United States consul in Berlin refused to issue it until she could pay ten dollars, which she neither had nor was permitted to possess, since no Germans are allowed to own United States currency. Finally a Military Government official paid the ten dollars out of his own pocket.

When she went to get her ticket as instructed, she was told she could not have it till the date of her departure was known. Finally at 9:00 o'clock one morning she was told that she must be at the airport at 11:00 a.m., but must first collect her ticket in another part of Berlin. No transport was provided for her, but she managed somehow to get to the airport on time, only to be told she must wait until evening. When she asked if she might eat something, she was told, "No. No Germans are allowed in the airport restaurant." When she begged to be allowed to telephone to her husband to bring her some food, she was told Germans were not allowed to use the telephone. Nor was she allowed to leave the airport.

When she arrived at the Rhine-Main airport late on a cold and rainy night in February, without having eaten anything all day, she was refused transport to Frankfurt fifteen miles away, and any accommodation for the night. After standing in the road a long time she managed to thumb a ride.

Although she had been told in Berlin that the Military Government would look after her on arrival in Frankfurt, she had luckily had her doubts and had reserved a room in a German hotel.

Next morning she reported at the Western Airline office in Frankfurt as instructed, but no one there knew anything about her. Furious by now, she telephoned the Military Government in Berlin at her own expense and said she was coming home. Thereupon action was finally taken and after a few days she was sent to Bremerhaven by train.

The Berlin authorities who had arranged her trip to America had assured her that, once she joined the other women delegates from the Western zones, everything would be all right and they would all be properly looked after. But when the seven German women specially selected by the Military Government on account of their anti-Nazi record to "study democracy" in the United States, boarded the ship on which they were to sail, they found themselves confined to the hold next to the stokers' quarters, but in worse accommodations. The one small "cabin" into which they were all crammed was icy cold and they had to pass through the Negro crew's sleeping quarters to reach the washroom and lavatory which they were permitted to use.

Nora Melle next day managed to persuade the purser to assign them two cabins, still on E deck but warmer and further away from the propellers which had kept them awake all night.

Two of the German women were sixty years old and were ill throughout the voyage. But their companions were forbidden to carry any food to them, and were themselves fed from the leftovers of the American passengers after the latter had finished eating. They had their food dumped down on dirty tables and were allowed only the napkins already used by the non-German passengers. The only alleviation of the misery of the sick women was provided by sympathetic Negro members of the crew who surreptitiously brought them food and ice water.

The German "guests of Military Government" were also strictly forbidden by the captain of the ship to enter the covered portions of the deck or the passengers' recreation room. This Captain Nelson of the Army transport *Henry Gibbins* was thought to be mainly accountable for their treatment. No doubt he was a spiritual brother of the Nazis who would have treated Jews in exactly the same way as he treated these German women, several of whom had been in prison under Hitler's rule.

As one of the German women delegates said to me: "If the hatred of Germans is so great that we had to be subjected to such treatment no Germans should be invited to visit America, or the Military Government should have selected Nazis to come who deserved such treatment as we have received."

The stupidity of this kind of thing is all the greater because of the very different treatment given by the Russians to the Germans they try to win over to the antidemocratic cause. The Berlin women who accept invitations to visit the Soviet Union are treated as honored guests. Automobiles are sent to fetch them from their homes; they travel first class and, far from being subjected to indignities and privations, they are showered with attentions.

Yet such is the steadfast loyalty of the German democrats to our cause and theirs that I found the women so wretchedly treated by the American Army reluctant to have their experiences published because this would give ammunition to the Communists in their propaganda against the democracies.

Moreover, as Nora Melle said to me, they had been treated in the most friendly fashion in the United States, and they understood that their treatment on the voyage was not the fault of the Military Government. I have written about it to show the legacy of the original Roosevelt-Morgenthau directives which still poison our relations with the Germans, and too frequently hamper the sincere endeavor of the higher Military Government authorities to encourage the German democrats.

The friendly behavior of the Negro crew of the Army transport *Henry Gibbins* toward the ill-treated German "guests of Military Government" was not exceptional. In the United States zone I found that the Negro soldiers of America have won the affection and respect of many Germans. The children of Negroes and German women, far from being treated as outcasts were accepted into the community and admired for their good looks, according both to what I was told and my own observations when traveling in German coaches.

Either because they are naturally kinder and more polite than white people, or because they are accustomed to treating all white people with respect, or because they sympathize with the Germans who are subject to the same insulting discrimination in their country as they themselves suffer in America, the Negro soldiers seem to have behaved more chivalrously than most white Americans.

The cynical and the racially prejudiced say that the Germans who consort with the negro GI's are thinking only of their PX cards, and that the Negroes are only interested in the opportunity to have sexual intercourse with white women. But there is certainly more to it than this. The colonial soldiers whose cruel lusts were given free license by the French in the early days of the occupation are still regarded with fear and loathing by the Germans. It seemed from what the Germans told me that the colored United States soldiers had taken less advantage of their position as conquerors than the white GI's and officers.

Like other Americans, colored soldiers appreciate the qualities of German women; their loyalty and readiness to give as well as take. Driving from Nuremberg to Frankfurt with a Negro corporal as my driver, and a young white American as my fellow passenger, I listened with interest to the two of them discussing the reasons why American soldiers and officers who had "fraternized" with German girls so often fell in love with them and married them. Both said it was because American women were so spoiled and selfish that no one who had had a love affair with a German woman would ever again be satisfied with what passes for love in the States. The astonishing thing to me was that the young colored corporal criticized the women of his own race in the States for the same shortcomings as white women in America: that they wanted you to entertain them all the time and spend all your money on them; whereas German girls were not spenders and were quite happy to sit quietly at home with you; that American women never thought that you might be tired after a hard day's work, whereas German women would attend to your comfort and give you peace and rest.

These sentiments, of course, reflected the natural liking of the male for women who were ready to serve and wait instead of demanding and dominating. While listening to this conversation as we rushed through the night, I remembered Nietzsche's dictum that the function of women is to give pleasure to the warrior, and reflected that their experiences as conquerors was hardly likely to fit the men of the occupation forces, white or colored, for married life in the United States.

My Negro driver did not confine his conversation to the qualities of German women. He disserted at length and in graphic fashion on the absence of a color bar in Germany which made it so much happier a place for colored people than the United States. That was why there were so many reenlistments, and why men ordered home had been known to commit suicide or desert. It was, he said, a funny thing that the Germans, whom Americans had been taught to believe were the most brutally race-conscious people in the world, had proved to be just the opposite.

I told him that I had learned years ago in China that most Germans had far less of the inbred "white man's" superiority toward the colored races than the British and Americans and had consequently been the most popular foreigners in China before Hitler came to power. I also said that this was no doubt due to the fact that the Germans had never possessed extensive African or Asiatic colonial empires or any Negro slaves, so that they had not needed to create the kind of race theory required to justify the oppression and exploitation of colored races. Hitler had invented the myth of Aryan superiority in order to provide an "ethical" basis for the conquest of Europe, just as the Anglo-Saxons had subscribed to the myth of white superiority to justify colonial empire and Negro slavery. So it was only natural that the Germans were comparatively free of prejudice against the Negroes, whom they had no reason to hate or despise, while regarding Poles and Russians as inferior races. To each his own prejudices according to his interests.

While on the subject of race prejudice, it should be noted that anti-Semitism in Germany before Hitler came to power was no worse than, if as bad as, it is in America today. The Nazis were able to whip up anti-Semitism into a destructive and cruel passion, and carry out their pogroms only by making the Jews the scapegoats for German economic distress.

Unfortunately for the future, the revengeful attitude of some Military Government officials who were Jews, the fact that Morgenthau gave his name to the policy of genocide underwritten by President Roosevelt, and the abuse by many non-German Jews of their privileged position as DP's have converted more Germans to anti-Semitism than Hitler's racial laws and propaganda. Under the Nazis many, if not most, Germans sympathized with the Jews and were ashamed of the atrocities committed by the Nazis. But according to what I was told by German Jews, since the defeat of Germany and the Allied occupation more and more Germans formerly free of anti-Semitic prejudice are saying that after all Hitler was right: the Jews are the cause of German misery and the unjust treatment Germans receive at the hands of the victorious democracies.

Personally, it has always seemed to me that the Communists and their sympathizers were the main influence which inspired our inhuman treatment of the Germans during the first years of the occupation. But the fact that many of the Communists and their fellow travelers, given leading positions in the Military Government, and acting as investigators and prosecutors in the Nuremberg and Dachau trials, were also Jews, has naturally added fuel to the fire of anti-Semitic prejudice.

Jeanette Wolff, the intrepid Jewish Social-Democratic leader to whom I have already referred in the chapter on Berlin, told me that it was tragic for the German Jews that the behavior of many American Jews and DP's was giving legitimate grounds for anti-Semitism in Germany, and would redound against the German Jews who were not in the least responsible for America's oppression of the German people, and had themselves been treated little if at all better than other Germans by the Military Government.

Jeanette Wolff's views were not exceptional. Whereas hatred of the German people too often drives out all pity and sense of justice among those Jews who escaped from Germany in the thirties or never lived in Germany, the German Jews who stayed at home and suffered under Hitler's terror, whose relatives and friends were murdered, and who themselves endured the horrors of the concentration camps, are for the most part without hatred of the German *people*, and still feel themselves to be Germans. It is the American Jews (often of Polish or Russian origin) and the returned exiles who seem determined to avenge the agony of the Jewish people in Hitler's Reich by punishing the whole German people.

I suppose the explanation lies in the fact that the Jews who stayed in Germany know from experience that the German people as a whole were not responsible for Nazi crimes. Many of them owe their survival to the risks taken by plain ordinary Germans to save them by hiding them or feeding them. And the Jews who emerged alive from the concentration camps know that many Germans suffered the same hunger and torture as the Jews because they opposed the tyranny of the Nazis and spoke out against the persecution of the Jews. But the foreign Jews, and those who escaped from Germany after the Nazis came to power, know only about the concentration camps, the tortures and the gas chambers, and being unaware of the facts of the German resistance to Hitler, are incapable of distinguishing the trees from the wood.

As Hans Rothfels points out in his book, *The German Opposition to Hitler*,[30] when the unbelievable horrors of the concentration camps were revealed at the war's end, little was heard about the large number of German victims of Nazi bestiality. He writes:

In no official report has the American public been told that there were practically no foreigners in Buchenwald until the summer of 1943, and that among the 20,000 survivors (51,000 having been killed), there were still 2,000 Germans of the Reich. Obviously the Gestapo was not of the opinion that all Germans were Nazis, or because of the war, were solidly behind the regime.

According to a United States Seventh Army pamphlet the majority of prisoners at Dachau before the war were also Germans. There are estimated to have been half a million Germans before the war who were, or had been, in the concentration camps for opposition to the Nazis.

Whereas in the early days of the Nazi regime no one much cared about the horrors committed in the concentration camps because the

---

[30] Henry Regnery Company, 1948, p. 14.

victims were mainly Germans, knowledge of the German resistance to Hitler seems to have been intentionally withheld from the American public during and since the war. Presumably it was felt that knowledge of the number of Germans who had lost their lives or their liberty in combating the Nazi regime might weaken the hatred of the German people which it was the aim of the Administration and most of the press to inspire.

So anxious was Washington to hide the facts, that the OWI went so far as to report Hitler's version of the July 20, 1944 plot to assassinate him, repeating the Führer's lie that only a very small "clique" of ambitious officers was involved.[31] Even after the war the subject of the German opposition was tabu in the American press and also censored in Germany by the Military Government.

According to Dr. Rothfels, American correspondents were forbidden to give out any news of specific resistance to Hitler, and one American had von Schlabrendorff's book on the resistance taken from him by the Military Government as forbidden literature inside Germany. Rothfels quotes Germans as saying that in the eyes of some Allied military personnel it was better to have been a Nazi than a survivor of the July 20 plot, because the conspirators were considered to have "tried to cheat us out of our victory."

It is not only totalitarian governments which poison the minds of their subjects by false propaganda. By more subtle and clever methods the citizens of the Western democracies are too frequently prevented from knowing the truth and taught to believe untruths.

I was forcibly struck by the contrast between the attitude of Mr. Fishbein, the American who represented the American Joint Distribution Committee in Berlin, and Jeanette Wolff and her daughter who had spent six years in Hitler's concentration camps. Mr. Fishbein so hated the Germans that he would not even admit that the Berliners were displaying remarkable courage in defense of democracy and said sneeringly that they had just chosen our side because we were the stronger. Jeanette Wolff told

---

[31] *Ibid.*, p. 20.

me that the Jewish Relief Agency had refused to give assistance to *German* Jews in Berlin and left them starving and ragged while supplying only Polish and other East European Jews.

I am not in a position to judge whether this accusation could be substantiated, or whether it was true, as she also said, that the Jewish DP camp in Berlin was the center for huge black-market operations, and that many relief shipments from America were illegally sold instead of being distributed. It is, however, a known fact that, when the Jewish DP's were evacuated from Berlin in the summer of 1948, huge stocks of shoes and clothing and a very large sum of money were found in the camp by Military Government authorities.

Black-marketing was, in any case, the main occupation of many DP's of all nations, for their privileged status made it impossible for the German police to cope with their illegal activities.

The complaint of the Germans that they are *rechtlos* (without rights or the protection of law) is amply borne out by the regulations in force concerning Allied nationals and displaced persons.

The German police have no right to interfere with any nationals of the victor countries. They are not permitted even to enter the DP camps, much less interfere with the black-market operations carried on from these "extraterritorial" settlements outside the jurisdiction of the German authorities. Our "master race" regulations are carried so far that a German policeman is not permitted to protect German nationals from violence on the part of the conquerors or DP's. When I asked a Military Government official in Berlin concerned with legal matters, whether a German policeman could arrest an American if he saw him murdering someone, the answer was: "No; he would have to find a military policeman."

A particularly unpleasant feature of our laws for Germans is the punishment meted out to children for minor offenses. I visited the Jugend Hof in Berlin where some hundreds of ragged, hungry kids, many of whom were only ten to twelve years old, were incarcerated in a former concentration camp. Some were awaiting trial, while others had been condemned to six months' or a year's imprisonment for petty thievery, begging from Americans outside the PX stores, or selling on the black market. Two of the boys were in for six months for having been found playing with an old pair of boxing gloves which they said they had found in a disused schoolroom—it was American Army property, so the crime was a serious one.

The attitude of the United States military police appeared to differ greatly in various places. In Berlin and Frankfurt they co-operated with the German police to maintain law and order, but in Munich, for instance, Germans told me they could expect no protection or redress against unlawful acts committed by the occupation forces. I shall long remember my old taxi driver in Munich who told me how often he had been cheated of his fare by American soldiers, and how useless it was to appeal to the military police who beat and abused you, if you approached them. "They just yell, 'You Sherman people' or 'dirty Kraut' if you claim your rights," said this old man.

No doubt much depends on the attitude of the general in command in each area. Naturally when the latter is a German hater, who thinks that the prestige of America is enhanced by treating the "natives" like the worst Southerners treat Negroes, some soldiers under his command are overbearing and brutal toward the Germans who are completely defenseless. But the higher Army authorities have endeavored during the past year or so to teach democratic behavior to the occupation forces. My air-lift pilot from Chicago, Lieutenant A. D. Porter, told me about the excellent indoctrination courses now being given to new arrivals in Germany at Marburg. Whereas in the old days the indoctrination courses he had attended when he was a bomber pilot had been intended "to harden the boys" by teaching them to hate all Germans, the major now giving instruction in the Army courses was saying to his classes:

"We've been kicking the Germans around for three years. It is now time to treat them like men. You shouldn't say 'Fritz' or 'you damned Kraut,' but address them as 'Mister' and remember they are persons like yourself whose human dignity should be respected."

This United States major, Lieutenant Porter said, also tells the young American soldiers to remember that the sooner Germany is reconstructed, the sooner they can go home and devote their services to their own country.

These new style indoctrination courses no doubt help to change the behavior of the United States occupation forces, but the pattern of behavior originally laid down for them lingers on.

It is moreover inevitable that many Americans should be demoralized by their privileged status in Germany. You can't put most young men in a position to disregard law, conscience, and training without spoiling them. It is to the credit of America that Washington's directives have not succeeded in Nazifying the American Army, but naturally many soldiers and officers have followed the totalitarian liberals among the civilian officials of Military Government in their disregard of democratic principles in the treatment of the conquered. Nor can the great improvement in the behavior of the occupation forces during the past two years expunge the record of brutality and lawlessness during the first years of the occupation. German disillusionment with America is all the greater because so much had been expected from her. Over and over again I was told:

"We expected Russian lawlessness, and we knew what to expect from the British who aim to eliminate Germany as a competitor, but we once believed the Americans were different."

Many Germans had listened to the American radio which assured them that Germany would not be destroyed. The harshness of our occupation policies; dismantlement which makes whole communities fear the loss of their livelihood; the robbery of individual German homes by American officers who carted off pictures, silver and furniture; the refusal of compensation to Germans whose homes were wrecked or despoiled, and other lawless acts, made some say, "It couldn't be worse under the Russians."

"The tragedy is," one German said to me, "that although the Americans have helped us, the behavior of their occupation forces has spoiled the effect. Even your gifts of food are spoiled by the manner of the giving. Whenever we complain of an injustice you say to us, 'What! You are daring to complain of what we do! you should just be thankful that we don't let you starve!'"

It is natural that a German who finally got his home back after it has been lived in by Americans for years, and found every bit of furniture and linen and his household utensils and books stolen is not satisfied to be told he ought to be grateful for his food ration and keep quiet. It is even less likely that a family condemned to live in a cellar for an indefinite period while Americans occupy their home, or keep it empty and refuse to return it to them, should love democracy.

Americans have certainly given more to the defeated Germans than they have taken from them, but the acts of individual members of the occupation forces often destroy any sense of gratitude.

Nor can everything be measured in economic terms. The "master race" attitude which the Military Government formerly prescribed for the occupation forces has aroused resentments which prevent much, if any, feeling of gratitude for American generosity.

Thus one finds many southern Germans who, although they recognize that France has despoiled Germany to a greater degree than the other Western powers, feel less hostile to the French than to the Americans and British, because in their personal relations with the Germans the French are more civil and friendly. Whereas America's national attitude is the best, and France's policy the most hostile, the behavior of individual Frenchmen is often far better than that of individual Americans.

The occupiers in Germany are demoralized not only by the opportunities given them to behave in a lawless manner and to insult and browbeat the defenseless. It is also far too easy in Germany to feel virtuous. The gift of a packet of cigarettes or a bar of chocolate, a kind word, or merely normally polite behavior toward the vanquished give you a sense of moral well-being. It is just too easy to be good in Germany. Generosity is not generosity if it costs you nothing, and you are in continual danger of considering yourself an exceptionally virtuous human being if you merely refrain from being a brute. I was often ashamed in Germany at the warm gratitude and appreciation evoked not only by a small gift, but by the smallest token of human sympathy.

One of the hardest things the Germans have to bear is deprivation of the right to represent their own case, and refute the many untruths told about them in the American press. Not only have they no government to speak for them and no diplomatic or other representatives abroad; the majority of American correspondents in Germany don't speak the language, and being ignorant of European history have swallowed all the propaganda about the wickedness of the German people. Their reporting is at best superficial and at worst extremely prejudiced. Moreover, some are still suffering from the hangover produced by the orgy of pro-Soviet and proCommunist propaganda in which the American press indulged during and immediately after the war. One of the most honest, and Soviet-disillusioned correspondents in Berlin said to me that although his mind accepted the necessity of treating the Germans as allies in the Cold War, his heart rejected this thesis, because he hated the Germans and had a great affection for the Russians.

Most newspapers and news agencies still treat Germany as if it were a theater of war in which news is to be obtained from the military authorities, and in which no knowledge of the language or its people is required. There was hardly a correspondent in Germany who had lived there before the war, and most of them had so little knowledge of the historical background that they really believed that the Germans knew nothing about democratic institutions except what they were now being taught.

During my first visit to Berlin I happened to go down to a big demonstration outside the Reichstag with the correspondents of two of the leading news agencies. Neither one of them spoke a word of German and they had no interpreter. They not only were unable to understand the speeches or the remarks of the crowd; one of them asked me, while Mayor Reuter was speaking "Who is that character?"

Since only a few of the largest dailies have their own correspondents in Germany, the majority of Americans get their news of Germany from such young men as these.

The worst effect of war propaganda is the aftereffects of the poison. Most Americans today sincerely believe that Germany has never known democracy or a rule of law, and has been the most aggressive of all European nations. So it is natural that American correspondents are for the most part psychologically as well as technically unqualified to report the news from Germany. The few correspondents who have no race prejudices and have cleared their minds of the war propaganda which taught that the Germans were devils, and the cause of all aggression in the world, find it difficult to break away from the closed-in circle in which the occupation forces live. If they were living with German families or in German hotels; if they had to make their own arrangements for housing and food and transport, if they had to exchange their dollars for marks at the official rate and, in general were flung from their backstream existence into the flood of German life, they would be able to report real news. As things are, most American correspondents live a life as removed from that of the mass of the people, as that of the Americans and British in Shanghai and Hong Kong. Some of them know a few Germans, just as in China some correspondents are friendly with some Chinese. But their lives are lived for the most part in the privileged, protected, and insulated surroundings of the conquerors. So with rare exceptions they naturally reflect the views of the Military Government, and have little sympathy for the German people and no disposition to report their grievances. Few of them seem to realize any better than the Military Government that you can't teach democracy unless you practice it, and that no people is going to embrace democracy if all it means is submission to the superior power of a conqueror. Instead, they continue to insist that our failure in Germany is due to the German character and tradition.

The sad thing is that it is precisely those who call themselves "liberals" who pursue the most illiberal line of thought and action. The very same people who would insist at home in America that juvenile delinquency and adult crime are a result either of being underprivileged or of an unhappy childhood and that criminals should be psychoanalyzed and reformed, not starved, reviled, and imprisoned, want to continue punishing the whole German people for their past.

I recently read an article in *Harper's* by a certain Mr. Bernard Tafer, who had been with the Military Government in Germany for three years.

In it he told the story of the Württemberg town of Schwäbisch-Gmünd, which in 1948 elected a former Nazi, Franz Konrad, as its mayor, and rejected the incumbent, the half-Jewish Franz Czisch. The author admits that in 1945, when Czisch had been elected, "a fresh breeze" had seemed to blow through Germany; the people had then been ready to believe in democracy. But instead of recognizing that the change which had occurred by 1948, not only in Schwäbisch-Gmünd, but "throughout the zone" was due to *our* behavior which had almost completely discredited democracy, Mr. Tafer blames the entire German personality and the German creed of "unthinking obedience to authority." He does not perceive the contradiction. If the Germans were, in fact, so innately "obedient to authority" as he thinks, they would today all obey Military Government, and would not have dared to show their defiance of its "overwhelming authority" by rejecting its German collaborators.

The author of the article admits that the German democrats are inseparably associated in German minds with "the present conditions of disorder and disgrace," but he fails to see that it is we, the occupying powers, who are responsible for this identification of democracy with disorder, misery, and injustice. The sad truth revealed by Mr. Tafer's article is that an idealistic and fair-minded liberal such as Franz Czisch had been discredited by having been associated with us.

Mr. Tafer saw nothing wrong with Governor LaFollette's decision to annul the election which had given Konrad three-quarters of the votes. Reading his article I was reminded of the story about one of Napoleon's generals who, having occupied a Belgian town, assembled all the inhabitants in the marketplace and announced: "I bring you liberty; anyone who moves without permission will be shot immediately."

The article in *Harper's*, which I mention, is not important in itself. But it is typical of thousands of other articles, news dispatches, and radio comments. So-called liberals and progressives dominate United States news media, and it is perhaps the gravest symptom of the weakness of democracy that "liberalism" is today identified with hatred, vengeance, the perpetuation of the schism in Western civilization, and, frequently even today, a sneaking fondness for the Communists.

During the past two years the "totalitarian liberals" in the Military Government have to a large extent been replaced by Americans who would like to practice what we preach, and who have done much to counteract the effect on the Germans of our actions and behavior during the first years of the occupation. But however good their intentions, Military Government officials cannot escape from the contradiction between authoritarian rule over a conquered people and the establishment of democratic government. Democratic government means government by consent of the people, and there can never be such consent in a country ruled by a foreign power which claims absolute authority and the right to intervene at any point in the conquered country's internal administrative affairs, and to control its economy, its laws, and its political life.

Military Government still regulates currency, banking and credit, foreign and domestic trade, the structure of industry, and economic and social policy, not to speak of reparations and requisitions. The German states were not even allowed to draw up their own constitutions. In General Clay's own words, addressed to the Bavarians in October 1946 and quoted by Governor von Wagoner on August 18, 1948:

"The approval which Military Government gives to this Constitution must, of course, be subject to the international agreements to which the United States Government is a party, to quadripartite legislation, and to the powers which Military Government must reserve in order to effectuate the basic policies of the occupation."

Thus the constitutions of the German states, not only had to conform to American ideas, but were subject to the approval of Soviet Russia. And even today, when there is no longer a quadripartite control council in existence, because the Russians walked out of it, France is able to act for the Soviet Union in preventing the formation of a viable West-German state. After conferring for months at Bonn and drawing up a democratic constitution for Western Germany according to Anglo-American directives, the leaders of Germany's democratic parties early in 1949 were told in effect that their labors had gone for nothing, on account of French objections. I shall consider this subject in Chapter 10, for here I am only concerned with the absurdity of trying to teach democracy to the Germans while denying them the freedom to govern themselves.

It would have been far less harmful to the cause of democracy to tell the Germans that they were to be subject to a military dictatorship for an indefinite period, than to pretend that we are out to establish democratic government.

As things are, we make a mockery of democracy and discredit Germany's democratic leaders by giving them responsibility without power. They are put up to bear the brunt of German dissatisfaction, and to act as buffers or scapegoats. As Dr. Alexander Boeker remarked in an article in the *New Leader*:[32]

"To give German democratic leaders the shadow of power without its substance merely serves to discredit democracy. There can be puppet dictators, but there is no such thing as a puppet democracy."

Not only are the German democrats placed in the unenviable position of scapegoats for Allied policies. They are continually subjected to indignities, reprimands and scoldings which undermine their authority, and emphasize their puppet status. Their recommendations are ignored unless they suit the wishes of the Military Government, but when disaster strikes they are held responsible. This was notably the case in the terrible winter and spring of 1947-48, when the population of the Ruhr was reduced to a famine ration of 800 calories.

Dr. Johannes Semmler, who was then Chairman of the German Economic Council, had approached the Bipartite Control Office in Frankfurt early in December 1947, to insist that something must be done to avert the threatening famine in the Ruhr. He made proposals concerning the use of the funds accumulating in the hands of JEIA[33] for the import of food and raw materials. But he was rebuffed and not even permitted to write to Generals Clay and Robertson, much less discuss the situation with the Military Governors.

When, on January 8, 1948, Generals Clay and Robertson met the Presidents of the *Länder* (States) to discuss the formation of a Western state, Dr. Semmler was not admitted to the conference because the

---

[32] March 26, 1949
[33] The Joint Export and Import Agency of Military Government.

Military Governors refused to permit economic questions to be discussed, in spite of the desperate food situation.

On January 4, at a meeting of the CDU in Bavaria, when asked to report on the economic situation, Semmler, thinking himself among friends, let himself go and voiced strong criticism of the Military Government's attitude toward the famine in the Ruhr, and refusal to use the proceeds of exports to import food to avert it. He thought he was speaking off the record, but his remarks were reported to the Military Government. That evening he went to Frankfurt to confer with the Presidents of the *Länder*, and was finally admitted to the Military Governors' conference as an "observer." Meanwhile a Military Government spokesman had announced on the radio that Semmler was "a damned liar." At the end of the Frankfurt conference Clay and Robertson called Semmler in, and Clay expressed his resentment at the remarks reported to have been made by Semmler, seeing that he, General Clay, had himself made representations to Congress concerning the food shortage. Semmler insisted that his remarks had been inadequately reported.

Finally, without waiting to see the written report he had been asked to submit concerning what he had actually said, the Military Government removed Semmler from his post as Chairman of the German Economic Council, to which he had been elected. Subsequently he was held for questioning by the United States Military Government while his house and office were searched and his papers and files taken away. The excuse made was that Semmler was under suspicion of black-marketeering, and the fact that a pound and a half of coffee and a dozen bottles of wine were found in his home was given as evidence.

Of course Semmler's treatment at the hands of the American Military Government made the Germans say: "Look, anyone who speaks the truth is removed from office and persecuted. Only quislings are able to hold office under the United States Military Government."

Semmler, according to the Swiss press, became the most popular man in Germany. Even the Social Democrats who had formerly criticized him for his conservative views and policies refrained from criticizing him after he had been made a martyr by the United States Military Government.

Dr. Semmler, whom I interviewed in Munich, said that he saw no sense in leading a German opposition to America, in spite of the fact that we continued to persecute him by controlling his movements, censoring his correspondence, and listening in on his telephone conversations. He had hopes of the Marshall Plan and had refused both British and French offers of a high position if he would leave the American zone. He considered that it was only a small clique of Americans which is responsible for the treatment he received, and he even gave General Clay the benefit of the doubt, saying that he had probably been misinformed. Dr. Semmler impressed me by his sincerity in wishing to bring Germany back into the Western community of nations. His regret was only that we made it so difficult for him and others with like views to orientate Germany toward the democracies. I could not but agree with him that unless criticism was permitted by the Military Government, Germany's democratic politicians would lose the confidence and respect of the people, and must appear as quislings. Only the Communists and die-hard Nazis now allied to them could reap any benefit from the Military Government's contemptuous treatment of German democratic leaders.

Just before I left Germany a State Department representative said to me: "If we succeed in Germany it will be in spite of, not because of, what we do and the way we behave."

"There are," he continued, "precious few Americans who deign to work with the Germans. It's much easier to issue decrees or send out anonymous communications telling the German authorities what they must do, than helping them to do it in the difficult situation in which they are placed."

One can hardly maintain that we are teaching the Germans democracy when we order their elected representatives to produce a law within a couple of weeks which would require months of debate and discussion in a democratically administered country. But that is precisely what the Military Government does.

Instead of sitting down with the Germans to thresh out solutions of the many and difficult problems which face them and the Military Government, there is long-distance criticism, denunciation, charges and counter charges. Far from endeavoring to inspire respect among the Germans for their elected representatives, the Military Government tends to ignore or humiliate them by treating them as puppets dependent on its favor, not on popular support, for the retention of office.

It is not only in the political sphere that the United States Military Government has discredited democracy. Its policies have been no less destructive of free enterprise, and no less fatal to the establishment of conditions in which honesty and endeavor are rewarded, and dishonesty and disobedience to the laws punished. It is hardly an exaggeration to say that the worst features of both a capitalist and a regimented economy have been combined in Germany.

Until the currency reform of June 1948, the United States Military Government preserved the regimented economy inherited from the Nazis, without allowing the German authorities the power to make it work. The result was naturally an era of lawlessness, in which only black-marketeers could make profits.

The industrialists and legitimate traders could sell only at controlled prices which produced less than the costs of production or of purchase. But the black-marketeers, who consisted of a strange conglomeration of former Nazis precluded from earning an honest living by the denazification law, DP's protected from interference by Military Government which forbade the German police to enter their residences, and other declassed elements whose treatment either by the Nazis, or by the victorious democracies, had taught them to disrespect the law, and have regard for nothing but their own self-preservation.

In the regime of acute scarcities of food, clothing, housing, and other necessities of life, which resulted in part from Germany's defeat and in part from Allied directives to do nothing to get the German economy back in working order, it was inevitable that the laws and regulations of Nazi war economy should be retained. But it was the height of folly or of callous disregard of the needs of the German people to refuse them the power to enforce the controls which would at least have secured a fair distribution of the food and other necessities left to be divided. As Gustav Stolper wrote:[34]

"As scarcities and distress grew, the rigidities of the war economy were not eased but tightened. But beneath the suffocating web of bureaucratic activities, exercised either by members of the occupying forces, or to a much larger extent by Germans in the services of these forces, the life of the people in its limitless variety of activities tries to go on. Resistance stiffens with the pressure, the directions become second nature with the increase of the unnatural pressure, demoralization spreads with orders which run against the normal moral faculties of their objects. A planned economy of hunger requires a society of saints to whom mortification is a moral aim in itself.

"The Military Government started out by freezing the status as they found it—prices, incomes and rations. What they froze was already a relationship full of discrepancies and maladjustments.

This freezing, the international mainstay of a war economy, worked during the war about as well in Germany as in the United States and Britain.

"But much has changed in the meantime. Rations (following Germany's defeat) have fallen way below minimum nutritional standards, and the worker works half-time, if he works at all. Thus he has to draw on his savings if they still exist to buy in the black market some additional food to keep himself and his family alive.

In January 1947 the occupying powers made up a cost-of-living index. It told the German public that living costs were only about 25 per cent above 1938, and about 15 per cent above 1945.

"Everybody in Germany was bitterly amused at this ingenious product of statistical witchcraft. Everybody knew that to mend an old suit or coat, or even have alterations made would cost more than a new suit or

---

[34] *German Realities* (Reynal & Hitchcock, New York, 1948, p. 76)

coat before the war. Or a patch on the sole of his shoe would cost more than a pair of new shoes had cost not long ago."

The new shoes or coat being unobtainable and the rations purchased at no more than a quarter above the former price being inadequate to sustain life, these statistics had no validity.

Moreover, the income of the average worker hardly covered the cost of the rationed foods. Only such industrialists who could procure extra food for their workers, or who produced goods which they could give them to sell on the black market, could continue to operate their factories successfully.

Inflation of the currency, started by the Nazis, but immensely increased by Military Government at the beginning of the occupation, when it handed over to the Russians the plates to print unlimited quantities of marks, further increased the economic chaos in Germany.

Currency reform was delayed for years in the hope of coming to an agreement with the Russians. And when finally, in June 1948, it was instituted by the Western powers, it was carried out in as unjust a manner as could possibly have been conceived. All savings beyond a bare ten per cent were wiped out, and no provision was made for the widows and orphans and aged who had no other means of subsistence, or for the crippled veterans unable to work. A multitude of small industrial enterprises were ruined; the city and state administrations were deprived of the funds out of which they had paid a dole to the unemployed and the millions of expellees driven into Rump Germany. Charitable organizations lost practically all their funds and post-office savings were wiped out.

Currency reform, in fact, was like a drastic surgical operation performed by a doctor who was determined either that the patient should die, or recover the strength to cease being a pensioner of the Western powers. For a time the operation seemed to have been successful. The sick and the crippled, the unemployed and the unemployable were deprived of the means of existence. But the incentive to work was revived for a time, and manufacturers and merchants who had withheld their goods from the market so long as they could obtain no profit by selling them, brought them out now that they could be exchanged for money which had acquired real values. And the peasants and farmers who had hidden their produce, or consumed it, so long as it could not be exchanged for the manufactured goods they needed, brought food to the market, after the currency reform.

This happy development was however short-lived. The slack was soon taken up. Since Military Government failed to import sufficient raw materials to keep German industry producing, within a few months of currency reform hoarding began again, prices rose, and the workers found themselves worse off, or no better off, than before currency reform. Moreover, dismantlement, held in abeyance before currency reform, assumed disastrous proportions afterwards, so that the possibility of Western Germany producing and exporting the manufactured goods to pay for raw material imports, continually diminished.

German suspicions of the good faith of America in allowing the revival of private enterprise, and the possibility of the Germans working for their own support, were heightened by the current rumors that the proceeds of German exports were being used to liquidate the debt incurred by the United States Army at the beginning of the occupation when we not only allowed the Russians to print unlimited quantities of marks, but permitted American soldiers to exchange this paper (obtained by selling watches, cigarettes, chocolate, and other goods to the Russians) for American dollars.

Mr. Logan, the new chief of the Joint Export and Import Agency for Bizonia appointed in 1948, has to some extent re-established America's reputation for honesty in dealing with German assets. He is said to have insisted on an accounting of all JEIA funds, to have refused to use them to wipe out the American Army's debt, and to have insisted that we fulfill our pledge to utilize the proceeds of German exports for the importation of food and raw materials for the rehabilitation of Western Germany. But since Mr. Logan shares power with the British he is not in a position to prevent Allied control of Germany's foreign trade from being used to prevent German competition with Britain in the world market.

The Germans consider JEIA to be a gigantic Anglo-American commercial monopoly which prevents Germany from trading with her natural markets and suppliers and forces her to buy and sell in the British Empire and the United States. German exporters and importers under the foreign trade monopoly established by Britain and America are in fact only auxiliary agencies of an Anglo-American monopoly of German trade.

The Germans naturally consider that Anglo-American control of their foreign trade must preclude any possibility of their becoming self-supporting, and say that whenever they can offer goods at lower prices than the British, they are refused the right to export them. They also complain that since they are not permitted to send their own commercial representatives abroad, they have no possibility of developing export possibilities wherever Germans compete with their conquerors.

German exports formerly consisted of an infinite variety of articles adapted to specific requirements, and requiring detailed knowledge of markets. Naturally, therefore, a gigantic Anglo-American bureaucratic organization such as JEIA is not in a position to discover export possibilities even if it were not controlled by Germany's competitors on the world market. Of course, if Americans were as conscious of their national interest as the British, JEIA would endeavor to increase German exports even when these compete with those of the British. But as things are, the British are able to exert the whip hand in ordering what the Germans may or may not produce and export. Thus, for instance, on April 3, 1949, the *New York Times* published a dispatch from Berlin announcing that British and French representatives in London had "wrung a reluctant agreement out of the United States delegates" to destroy Germany's synthetic rubber, gas, and oil plants because of Britain's worry "about markets for her natural rubber resources."

"Economic experts in the United States Military Government," the dispatch continued, "wanted the industries retained in Germany and said that Congress might take a dim view of an agreement to prohibit those industries permanently."

The Germans, having already had all their patents robbed from them by the Allied Military Government, are also naturally suspicious of the possibility given to JEIA to ferret out and make use of new German inventions without compensation.

In this connection I must quote the remark made by a student at the University of Munich, who said in a public meeting that although the Americans expected Germans to be grateful for the food the United States was providing, the total value of this charity was less than that of the patents stolen from the German people by the American and British military governments.

At the end of 1948 JEIA relinquished some of its powers, and Military Government announced that export and import licenses would henceforth be granted by the Deutsche Bank. No German however believes that this means freedom, since the Deutsche Bank is under Military Government control.

The prevalent German belief that JEIA constitutes a joint Anglo-American system for preventing Germany from competing on the world market, was strengthened by the fixing of German exchange at the unreal rate of 30 cents to the dollar, and by the numerous instances in which German export orders have been held up pending investigation as to whether Britain could not supply the goods instead.

Early in 1949 the efforts of the United States Military Government to halt the drain on the German economy constituted by France's exports of currency and manufactures, and by the advantage taken by Americans and others of France's refusal to permit effective German customs control, resulted in a rise in the free-, or black-, market value of the mark. But so long as the German authorities are prevented by France from guarding their frontiers, and are not allowed by the Anglo-American authorities to decide what use is to be made of the proceeds accruing from German exports, a "free economy" cannot be expected to work in Germany.

It is also extremely doubtful whether in the present conditions of scarcity produced by the war and by Western occupation policies, Germany could in any case afford an uncontrolled economy. Britain with her very much larger national income would almost certainly find it impossible to re-establish a free economy even if the Conservatives instead of the Socialists won the next election.

It is useful in this connection to compare the situation of Western Germany and Britain today.

If you trace out the borders of Western Germany and Britain you find that not only their areas but even their shape are almost identical.

The population of Britain is 46 million as against Western Germany's 50 million.[35] Western Germany's arable area is slightly larger than Britain's but since it consists of less fertile land it produces 5.9 million tons of grain as against Britain's 6.3 million tons.

Thus Britain is today slightly more self-sufficient in food production than Western Germany, deprived by the Yalta and Potsdam agreements of its Eastern bread basket. Both countries must "export or die" but Western Germany's need to export is even greater than Britain's, not only because of her smaller production of breadstuffs but also because Britain still possesses colonial territories in Africa and Asia which produce a subsidy for the economy of the United Kingdom.

But, whereas British exports amount to $6,180,000,000, Germany's are valued at only $527,000.000; and whereas $5,384,000,000 of British exports consist of manufactured goods, $300,000,000 of Germany's $527,000,000 total consists of coal, timber, and other raw materials she needs for her own subsistence.

The consequence of this extreme disparity in income, combined with the much larger American subsidy paid to Britain under the Marshall Plan, is that the British population consumes 2,850 calories a day as against the German diet of 1,702; and that whereas the British get 82 pounds of meat and 33.8 pounds of fat a year, the Germans receive on an average only 11.6 pounds of meat and 18 pounds of fats.

---

[35] These figures and those in the nest paragraphs are taken from an article written by Dr. Fritz Baade, head of the Institute of World Economy at Kiel.

As regards clothing, housing and warmth, soap, and other necessities, the German situation is incomparably worse than that of the British.

Needing to export far more than the British, the Germans are being prevented by America, as well as by the British Government, from producing and exporting enough to pay for their minimum needs. Of course, it can be said that since Britain "won the war" this is only what the Germans deserve. But from the American standpoint, unless we are prepared to let millions of Germans die of starvation, it makes no sense either economically or politically to deprive the German "common man" of the opportunity to earn his living for the benefit of his English counterpart.

By deferring to British and French policy the United States is preventing the revival of a free economy not only in Germany but also in Western Europe.

By the fall of 1948 confidence in the new currency had already been undermined; hoarding had begun again; prices were continually rising, and the workers, finding themselves as badly or worse off than before currency reform and the removal of economic controls, were demanding that the advocates of free enterprise be removed from control of the German Economic Council.

The effort of German liberals and conservatives to institute free internal trade, and revive the profit motive, cannot prevail against the demand for a controlled economy because of the Allied policy which perpetuates scarcity and penalizes endeavor.

Our fundamental mistake was our failure to recognize the fact that a free economy cannot be instituted without the other freedoms. The Germans, still deprived of both liberty and responsibility, cannot make a free economy work, for it is impossible to institute a free economy when there is not enough of the necessities of life to go around. Furthermore, most people will evade taxes, hoard, and speculate if they consider themselves to be ruled by foreigners who exploit them. They feel no sense of responsibility under such conditions. And why should anyone work and display initiative and inventiveness if held down to a subsistence level of existence by Allied directives according to the Level of Industry Plan?

Besides holding the German economy in a straight-jacket by the continued implementation of a revised, but by no means abandoned, Morgenthau Plan, we burden the German economy with heavy occupation costs. General Clay has said that such costs are unimportant in view of the fact that America is supplying Germany with food and raw materials amounting to a greater sum. But the Germans have never been assured that such imports are a gift. For all they know they are a debt to be paid off in the future.

In any case these imports barely compensate the Germans for the loss of their Eastern bread basket to Russia and Poland, for which the Western powers are responsible.

In terms of the budgets of each of the *Länder* in Western Germany the costs of occupation constitute a crushing burden, precluding expenditures on the rebuilding of her bombed cities and on other necessary public works and desperately needed social services.

Occupation costs in the financial year 1947-48, according to German calculations, amounted to 1,651,000,000 marks in the American zone, and to 2,684,000,000 in the British zone, making a total of 4,335,000,000 marks for Bizonia. This sum constitutes 34 per cent of the tax revenues of the *Länder*. In the French zone the proportion is 60 per cent.

With respect to requisitions, housing, and other occupation costs neither America nor Britain has observed the requirements of international law as embodied in the Hague Convention. Individual Americans and British in the first months of the occupation looted on a scale unknown in recent European history. Since then we have imposed burdens on the German economy by requisitions and mandatory services which go far beyond what is permitted under international law.

Complete figures of occupation costs in Bizonia are not available. But an itemized account of the requisitions, mandatory services and other demands made by the British occupation forces is available for the State of North-Rhine Westphalia, which includes the Ruhr area. The report issued by the Minister of Finance of this State is in my possession, although it was suppressed by the British Military Government shortly after publication.

Although occupation costs in the United States zone are now considerably less than in the British zone, America bears part of the responsibility for the situation since the British and American zones have been merged.

The North-Rhine Westphalia report does not take into account either irregular requisitions by individual members of the occupying forces (looting), or reparations and restitutions, or multilateral deliveries, or timber felling, or the supplies of coal and electricity, steel, cement, and other raw materials delivered to the Allies, or the confiscation of German patents and assets abroad. It deals only with the requisitions and services supposedly demanded for the use of the occupation forces and included in the Emergency Budget of the State.

The figures given demonstrate not only the huge burden imposed on the German economy, but also the fact that far from decreasing their demands the British have increased them since the end of the war.

The following table shows the net total of occupation costs (i.e., requisitions and mandatory services less receipts and income from exports and imports under British control) as compared with revenue:

	Occupation Costs		Tax Revenue	
1946	374	million marks	3,027	million marks
1947	1,141	" "	3,539	" "

Thus occupation costs accounted for 12.4 per cent of revenue in 1946, and for 32.3 per cent in 1947.

As the Finance Minister's report says: "The enormous mandatory services rendered to the occupying Power were made at the expense of the last reserves at the disposal of trade and industry, and would have led to a complete collapse of the economic life and financial chaos, but for the intervention of the occupying Powers in the form of ERP and currency reform."

In other words the British, whose standard of life in Germany is much higher than at home, thanks to the demands they make on the German economy, enjoy a secondary subsidy from the Marshall Plan over and above what they receive direct under ERP appropriations to Britain.

The North-Rhine Westphalia report gives a mass of interesting details concerning the items included under requisitions, the waste of housing space, and the large number of Germans required to serve the needs and pleasures of the occupying forces.

Expenditures for the services of German employees and servants of the British Military Government (all paid for by the German economy) increased from 55,000,000 marks in the financial year 1945-46, to 185,000,000 in 1946-47, and 336,000,000 in 1947-48.

Among the many examples given of "conspicuous waste" is that of the Minden Club at Weser Klause where some seventy Germans are employed in two shifts to serve an average of five luncheon and twelve dinner guests.

The foreign consulates (including those of the Russian satellites) also employ a large number of Germans whose salaries are charged to occupation costs and have to be met out of the taxation revenue of the German states. Even the Dutch Red Cross which concerns itself only with Dutch nationals, has the salaries of its German employees charged to the North-Rhine Westphalia government. Sergeants and musicians as well as officers have servants whose wages are paid by the Germans.

The occupation burden which is most bitterly resented in Germany is the requisitioning of houses and apartments, and the refusal to hand them back to their owners even when they are vacant or only partly occupied. Bombing produced extreme overcrowding in all German cities, and since steel, cement, and wood have been denied for the reconstruction of houses and apartments, the continued occupation of the best undamaged housing in Germany for the use of the occupation forces constitutes an enduring grievance. The fact that the reduction in the size of both the American and British occupation forces has not led to any substantial increase in the living space allowed to the German population renders the sense of grievance all the greater.

The North-Rhine Westphalia report catalogues a very large number of houses, hotels, and apartments in various towns now practically unused, but which the British Military Government refuses to let the Germans reoccupy. The following are but a few typical examples:

A house of 12 rooms with 2,230 square feet of space at Herten occupied by three persons.

At Bad Oyenhausen, headquarters of the British Army of the Rhine, if 325 square feet of space were allocated to each officer and 130 square feet to each soldier, the total accommodation required would be 665,000 square feet. But the actual space requisitioned is 1,272,000 square feet.

In the town of Blomberg dwelling space was requisitioned for 1,700 DP's. The present number of DP's is 1,000, but no space has been released. Almost all these DP's are gainfully employed, but they pay no rent, nor anything for gas and electricity supplied by the German economy.

At Heiligenkirchen 4 houses and 2 hotels with 16,300 square feet of space are occupied by only 15 Allied personnel.

In Herford at 20 Kreishausstrasse, two houses with twelve rooms are occupied by "one male person." At Dortmund, a British captain occupies a villa of 14 rooms.

At Hamm, the Hotel Busch Kuhle comprising 35 rooms and 4 bathrooms is occupied by 4 women and 2 men of the British Red Cross.

These are not isolated examples but typical ones. The list of similar examples occupies many pages.

I myself in Bonn was shocked to find myself the sole occupant with the German staff of a huge villa reserved for the use of transient Allied guests. There were so few of the latter that this villa was to be given up—not to the Germans—but to a Belgian general who was to have the exclusive use of its 30-odd rooms.

The North-Rhine Westphalia report also catalogues the loss to the German economy through the occupation of industrial premises by the British and the Belgians who share with them the "duty" of occupation.

Even vegetable gardens and farms have been taken and the German owners deprived of the produce. In a number of cases productive fields have been converted into sports grounds although all the German sports grounds had already been requisitioned for the exclusive use of Allied personnel.

According to the Hague Convention, the occupying power "is responsible for damage caused by action of the members of their armed forces." But neither the British nor the Americans have observed international law in this respect any more than in others. They have instead shifted the burden of compensation onto the German State administrations. So if and when requisitioned premises are returned to their German owners who find that their furniture, linen, books and other property which they were forced to leave behind, have been removed or destroyed, they cannot claim damages from the occupying power.

The Germans suffer not only through the requisitioning of desperately needed housing space. As taxpayers they are also burdened with the rents and compensation for damage paid to the owners of requisitioned property. This compensation is small in comparison with the loss suffered by the owners of the requisitioned houses but it nevertheless constitutes a sufficient burden on the German State budgets to preclude any possibility of funds being available for reconstruction.

Since the British and Belgian occupation forces, and also the DP's pay nothing for electricity, gas, and water supplied by the German economy, there is naturally tremendous wastage. Lights are left burning day and night in spite of the Allied talk about the need to economize power consumption.

Lastly, it is necessary to refer briefly to "requisitions" other than buildings. The North-Rhine Westphalia report shows clearly that the huge quantities of goods supplied to the British occupation forces are far and away beyond their consumption requirements, and constitute in fact reparations out of current production.

The list of requisitions in North-Rhine Westphalia includes 116.6 million pounds of lump pitch, crude tar, and anthracite oil exported to Belgium, France and Holland; 23,000 gas ranges or cookers, coal and electric stoves, and kitchen ranges of all sorts. Hundreds of thousands of bath tubs, screws, nails, door locks and other ironware are also reported to have been regularly requisitioned and shipped to England. The list includes tens of thousands of flour boxes, hot-water cans, enameled wash basins, jugs, and toilet pails, children's bath tubs, aluminum cooking pots, spoons, forks and knives amounting to a total of nearly 3,000,000 marks. In addition, the British requisitioned 25,000 cruet stands and 42,000 napkin rings; 94,000 skillets and fish frying pans and 24,000 or more meat cutting machines, bread boxes, kettles, cooking pots, wine coolers, and other miscellaneous kitchen utensils.

They took 2.5 million pieces of porcelain from one German firm alone; 681,000 soap tablets; 500 ladies' umbrellas; cigars to the value of 23,000 marks; 659 Ford automobiles; 50 omnibuses; tens of thousands of electric bulbs delivered after currency reform and worth 134,000 marks; nearly 4,000 refrigerators; 8,000 fountain pens, 1,000 toy electric railways, 9,867 gymnastic appliances, 5,568 bicycles, 6.6 million pounds of varnish and paint, and a lot of other miscellaneous items which it would occupy too much space to list.

The list of furniture supplied without payment to the British occupation forces is also too long to reproduce in full. But the total, including armchairs, sofas, filing cabinets, bookcases, beds, sets of club furniture, washstands, tables, card tables, and so forth, amounts to 710,000 items. The list of requisitions also includes tens of thousands of carpets, shoes, trunks, and other leather manufactures.

The British also requisitioned some hundreds of thousands of ladies' dresses, blouses, and underwear; men's shirts, pants, morning coats, and children's clothing. Also on the huge list of manufactured goods requisitioned are 20,240 pull-overs and 2,000 pairs of trousers for boys, 16,000 pairs of children's stockings, 251,000 pairs of shoes, 12,000 children's coats, 110,000 napkins, and 70,000 layettes.

Finally, there is the list of alcoholic beverages which North-Rhine Westphalia had to deliver without payment to the British Army, either for its own consumption or for sale on the black market, or for export to England. This list includes 3.5 million bottles and 733 quarts of schnapps, and 910,000 bottles of dry gin.

According to the North-Rhine Westphalia report the Germans are also charged with the support of foreign businessmen and tourists. The latter pay for their accommodation, food, and transport, but the money is apparently pocketed by the Military Government while the German economy is charged for their maintenance. Thus, for instance, between July 1 and September 30, 1948, 316,000 marks, plus a few thousand more for taxi service, were charged to the North-Rhine Westphalia Emergency Budget for accommodations, services, and food supplied to Allied business men and tourists. "The increase in August 1948," says the report, "is due to the large number of British hotel guests on the occasion of the 700th anniversary of Cologne Cathedral."

The British even charge the Germans with the cost of repairing Allied ships and feeding Allied crews, the total in 1947 amounting to 2,000,000 marks.

There is, of course, no warrant in international law for requisitioning of goods and services for persons having no connection with the occupying power. But the North-Rhine Westphalia report charges that:

"No credit has been made so far for these items. Nor have any credits so far been received for foreign currency payments made by foreign consulates to British agencies for rents, for the salaries of German personnel, or for the many goods supplied. It is known that in the clubs and canteens run by NAAFI, Steinhäger [schnapps] and gin are sold to the occupation forces, and information received from Hamburg states that these spirits (requisitioned in Germany) are also shipped to British canteens abroad."

There is no doubt that the Germans are correct in stating that many of the items listed as requisitions for the use of the occupation forces are nothing of the kind, and constitute in fact reparations deliveries from current production. Nor can it be denied that the "increased demands of the British occupying powers for goods in short supply" contribute to the inflation which is nullifying the benefits of currency reform. So long as the German economy has to supply large quantities of goods which are not paid for, and also to allocate a great number of people to serve the occupiers without payment by the latter, Western Germany can never achieve economic stability.

In the British zone individuals appear to reap much of the benefit from the forced free delivery of goods and services to the occupation power. I was charged only twenty-five cents a day for my hotel room in Düsseldorf and food and drink were correspondingly cheap. In the United States zone, the Military Government takes the profit by charging foreign visitors and newspaper correspondents for their accommodation and for services without compensating the Germans who supply both. For instance, I discovered in Frankfurt that a rent of only 500 marks a month was being paid for the Park Hotel which has 90 or 100 bedrooms, although it charged the correspondents and others two dollars a day for rent and service. Presumably the wages of the chambermaids and waiters were paid for by the Germans.

In the case of the United States zone, although the Army makes a large profit out of the accommodations and services paid for by the Germans, the American taxpayer is contributing food and raw materials to a far greater amount. But in the case of the British zone the "hidden reparations" delivered as "occupation costs" are not compensated for by

British gifts to Germany. Apart from food shipments from America the United States, according to the North-Rhine Westphalia report, released large stocks from army stores for disposal on the German domestic market, thus to some extent compensating the German economy for the loss entailed by British requisitions of clothing.

Although the British have in general shown themselves less inclined than the United States to disregard international law and Anglo-Saxon law in the administration of their zone, they have taken advantage of the Nuremberg judgments to justify any acts required to advance their economic interests. According to the regulations in force in the British zone a German worker may not refuse to work for the Military Government, and cannot quit his job with the British under any circumstances. The Allied Control Council decree legitimizing forced labor has been a particular boon to the British who can thus compel the Germans to dismantle the factories.

In the Bochum case when several German workers were arrested and sentenced to prison for refusing to work on dismantlement, the defense argued that the Hague Convention forbids the occupying power to force anyone to act against his own country, and also that the use of forced labor was designated at Nuremberg as a "crime against humanity." But the British court replied that the Germans had no right to appeal to the provisions of the Hague Rules of Land Warfare, because it was decreed at Nuremberg that international law does not apply to Germans. When the German defense argued that it had been said at Nuremberg that everyone should act according to his conscience and refuse to obey superior orders if these went against conscience, the British court replied that no German had the right under any circumstances to disobey Military Government which is the absolute authority.

In this respect as in so many others the British like the Americans have adopted in Germany the same principles as the defeated Nazis.

10

THE FRENCH RIDE HIGH

"IF IT WERE NOT FOR THE AID AND COMFORT FRANCE HAS GIVEN to the Soviet Union, we should have settled the Berlin crisis long ago."

The American officer who said this to me was referring to the French refusal to agree to a stronger stand being taken against Soviet Russia at the beginning of the blockade, and to France's desire to abandon Berlin whatever the cost to Western Europe and America. But his remark, which expressed the exasperation of the American Army at being hobbled by French timidity and Communist influence in France, could be applied to the whole international situation.

France today is like a dead weight hanging around the neck of the free world. Partly because of their concern with the extinct menace of German aggression, partly because of their hope of avoiding war with Soviet Russia by appeasement, and partly because of Communist influence, France prevents the implementation of an American policy designed both to rehabilitate Western Europe and to ensure its defense. At every turn and on every issue, French stalling succeeds in nullifying the American effort to make Europe self-supporting and secure. On the question of reparations, on the Occupation Statute, and on the Ruhr, as in the case of the defense of Berlin, France's short-sighted policy weakens the Western world. If ruled by the Communists, France could not have done a better job in keeping Europe divided, weak, and powerless, and bringing near the day when America will either go bankrupt or revert to an isolationist policy.

The politicians who rule France today, like the Bourbons, seem to have learned nothing and forgotten nothing. Just as in the twenties they insisted on implementation of a policy of revenge and retribution which destroyed Germany and gave power to Hitler, so now, once again, they are dragging Europe toward the abyss.

It is one of the curious phenomena of the modern world that the French nation, which prides itself on being the most rational of peoples, acts like an hysterical woman in international affairs. Perhaps the explanation is that given me by an American officer who had participated in the negotiations with the French in Berlin. "The French," he said, "have lost their pride. If they had put up a brave fight against the Germans and kept their self-respect, they would not now be so revengeful and stupid. The British who suffered much more than the French came out of the war with their heads up because of their courage, but the French came out of it with nothing but shame and fear."

The very fact that so many French collaborated with the Germans during the occupation now makes them the foremost exponents of a ruthless policy toward Germany. They seek to expunge the record of their past acceptance of German domination by wanting to kick the conquered Germans harder than those who brought about their defeat.

Talking to this American officer in Berlin, I was reminded of what General Robert E. Wood had said to me years ago. He told me how his grandfather, who was a general in the Civil War, had said to him: "Brave men don't hate their enemies; they respect them. They leave the hating to the women and the preachers."

Unfortunately for the future of the free world, the United States treats France like a beloved mistress, or a weak and foolish wife who must be indulged. Whether it is because of the reverence for French culture, inspired in Americans at school, where French is often the only language taught, or the belief that France still stands for liberty, equality, and fraternity, or simply the attraction of the Paris flesh pots, the State Department, the ECA, and most American newspapermen and authors just love France. Paris is chosen as the headquarters for ECA; Paris is where American trade-union leaders meet their European comrades; Paris is where the United Nations meets when it leaves Lake Success; Paris is the place where all good journalists hope to go.

France, which lacks the will to work or to fight, and has neither the intelligence nor the vision nor the strength to be the leader of Europe, is still regarded in America as the capital of Europe. So the poisonous French atmosphere of corruption, prejudice, weakness, and hate is chosen for the settlement of European problems.

As the *New York Times* correspondent in Berlin, Sydney Gruson, reported on April 18, 1949:

Military Government officials who share in General Clay's annoyance with ECA's stand on Germany claim that the Marshall Plan administration operates under a definitely French orientation. Among Americans in Germany that is a serious charge, since the French are always considered at fault for delays and troubles in evolving a threepower policy for Germany due to their intense fears of German resurgence.

The occasion for this despatch was ECA's stalling on General Clay's request for the release of 200,000,000 D marks from the counterpart funds for the purchase of rolling stock and equipment for the German railways. General Clay had also apparently been incensed by the refusal of the ECA authorities to permit part of the 5 per cent counterpart fund earmarked for the use of the American and British military governments, to be used to finance RIAS—the excellent radio station in Berlin which beams anti-Communist propaganda to the Russian zone—and for the Voice of America in its Berlin operations.

The impression that ECA is unduly influenced by the French Government is heightened by the fact that Paul Hoffman and his deputies spend much of their time in Paris and only pay flying visits to other European countries. But it is the special favor shown to France in the allocation of ECA funds and the failure of Paul Hoffman to stop dismantlement by exerting pressure on France and Britain which prove his insufficient regard for the United States taxpayer and the long-term objectives of the Marshall Plan.

As I have already noted in Chapter 3, the ECA did not even try to save most of the factories scheduled for dismantlement, and the State

Department went even further than Paul Hoffman's organization in appeasing France and Britain.

The outstanding example of the cost to the American taxpayer of Dean Acheson's readiness to allow France to continue destroying Germany's assets, is the April 1949 agreement to let France tear down part of the great works at Oppau producing nitrogen fertilizers.

The Oppau plant, which is the largest synthetic nitrogen plant in Europe, has the capacity to produce 730 tons of pure nitrogen a day. Its capacity is to be reduced to 410 tons, which means an annual loss of 100,000 tons of nitrogen fertilizer without any corresponding gain in French production. Most of the dismantled equipment will be nothing but scrap, the residual value being calculated as worth only a million dollars, as against the four and a half million dollars originally invested in the plant.

According to the calculations made by Dr. Fritz Baade of the Kiel Institute of World Economy, the nitrogen fertilizer which will have to be imported into Germany to compensate for this loss will cost $300 a ton, or a total of $36,000,000 to pay for the 100,000 tons of production lost through dismantlement.

Thus every dollar which France may eventually gain will cost the American taxpayer thirty-six dollars. Should the loss to the world of the Oppau plant's production result in such a shortage that nitrogen fertilizers cannot be supplied to German agriculture by America, the cost will be even higher. If extra grain has to be imported into Germany as a result of the French dismantlement of Oppau, then each dollar gained by France will cost America two hundred dollars.

If Western Germany is ever to become self-supporting, it requires not less, but more nitrogen fertilizers than before the war. It should be permitted to produce enough to bring its nitrogen fertilizer consumption up to the Dutch-Belgian level of fifty pounds an acre. This would require more than the total original capacity of the Oppau plant. Instead, we are allowing the French to destroy any possibility of German agriculture being supplied with its minimum prewar needs.

Up to now, the French have allowed Oppau to produce only 80,000 tons as against its 200,000 ton capacity, and after delivering two-thirds of this production to the farmers in the French zone, they have exported the rest for France's profit.

Everyone by now knows that the Russians, by refusing to treat Germany as an economic unit, have imposed a crushing burden on the American taxpayer. But few Americans are aware that France is also responsible for the high taxes they have to pay. According to Dr. Baade the refusal of the French to allow Oppau to provide fertilizers for Bizonia has entailed a loss of two million tons grain value a year, which is comparable to the amount lost by Russian intransigeance and the Polish sequestration of former German territory east of the Oder-Neisse line.

Oppau is only one example of the manner in which French policy is weakening Europe and burdening the American economy.

The French in their zone of Germany have acted in a manner comparable only with that of the Russians. They have stripped it of machinery and food to such an extent that only American subsidies are now keeping the German population there alive.

The French have refused to take any of the German expellees from the East, so that their zone, which includes fertile lands, should be self-sustaining. But French looting produced actual starvation until ECA began to give aid in 1948. Today the United States, besides directly subsidizing the French economy to the tune of $875,000,000 a year, is also providing the French zone with $155,000,000 to compensate for what France takes out of it in the way of food, timber, manufactures, and machinery.

The French did not wait upon any Allied agreement to exact reparations. At the beginning of their occupation they started to seize factory equipment and other German assets, so that by the time the Allied dismantlement list was announced, France had already reduced her zone to a productive capacity well below the 1936 level.

The French, who claim that the Germans removed some 60,000 machines from France during the occupation (and take no account of the

40,000 machines which the Germans claim to have delivered to France in the same period) had already taken 45,000 machines from their zone alone when the dismantlement list for all three Western zones was published in 1947. These machines, taken to France as *prélèvements*, a polite name for looting, do not even figure on the reparations account. And although the Germans in the French zone were told that the official dismantlement program to come afterwards would be modified accordingly, this promise was not kept. Two hundred and thirty-four enterprises were scheduled for dismantlement in October 1947, only thirty-four of which could be regarded as war industries, and most of which belonged to the light-industry categories supposed to be expanded according to the Revised Level of Industry Plan. In Württemberg, for instance, the textile industry has been deprived of all its modern interlock, round knitting, and weaving machinery, and thus precluded from any possibility of exporting. South Baden similarly lost some two thousand textile machines. The factories producing agricultural machinery were similarly dismantled. The machine-tool industry in the Württemberg area was left with only 55 per cent of its capacity after the first French removals, although according to the Level of Industry Plan, it was supposed to be left with 83 per cent. Yet further removals of machinery are now taking place according to the official Allied dismantlement program.

The leather, wood processing, and building industries have been similarly shorn of equipment. The fine mechanics and optics industry, is supposed under the Level of Industry Plan to be allowed a capacity 38 per cent higher than in 1936, but in South Baden the French, by February 1947, had already reduced production to half of the 1936 figure by the removal of 2,155 expensive machines, and have since still further reduced its productive capacity.

Worst of all is the case of the watch and clock industry already referred to in Chapter 3. By their preliminary and subsequent removals of machinery the French have crippled this old industry, which once supplied the livelihood of thousands of people in the Black Forest area.

In the statement it released on April 13, 1949, the ECA office of information in Washington gives a list of "French Voluntary Retentions" in their zone of the whole or part of forty plants, included on the list of

381 examined by the Humphrey Committee. But neither in this report, nor in the Humphrey Committee Report[36] is any account taken of the huge quantity of factory equipment France has taken out of her zone without reference to the Inter-Allied Reparations Authority, and without making any report to ECA. One of the many injustices to which the German people are now becoming accustomed is that the ECA has recommended the release as reparations of the equipment of many factories producing peacetime goods, because they had already been allocated to recipient nations, but took no account of France's and Britain's removals of machinery not on the dismantlement list, and not figuring as reparations.

The reasons given by the ECA for its decision not to retain in Germany the plants already allocated, rouses a suspicion that even today Washington has not completely abandoned its former policy of appeasing Russia, or was impelled by France and Britain not to annoy Stalin; for in the preamble to the Humphrey Committee report it is stated:

The problem of the political implications involved in a further change of the reparations program, which had already been scaled down previously, was strongly urged upon us by both the British and the French, as well as by the President of IARA. The fact that, of the nineteen nations entitled to reparations, only nine of them are beneficiaries of the European Recovery Program further complicated that issue. This was particularly important in affecting our decisions with respect to plants that had already been allocated to IARA for reparations and also those which had been additionally sub-allocated by IARA to recipient countries. The complications ensuing with respect to both the allocated and the sub-allocated plants were found to be so involved that, after careful consideration, we recommended to you the immediate release of all such plants.

In other words, Paul Hoffman's organization decided not to stop the dismantlement and shipment of the factory equipment allocated to Soviet Russia and her satellites. This is being done in spite of the "regret"

---

[36] Report on plants scheduled for removal as reparations from the three Western zones of Germany, January 1949. Industrial Advisory Committee, Economic Cooperation Administration.

with which the ECA decided "to acquiesce in the removal of some equipment from a number of small factories making articles useful for a peacetime economy."

The machinery released by ECA for shipment to the Communists is by no means only that taken from peacetime industries. It also includes precisely the types of heavy machinery regarded as "strategic goods," which the countries in receipt of Marshall Plan aid are forbidden to export to Russia. So we have the strange spectacle of ECA agreeing to deliver to the Communists from Germany precisely those items which are recognized as helping to increase the Soviet war potential.

All in all, dismantlement, even as modified by the recent agreement with the ECA authorities, will leave the French zone with no more than half the industrial capacity of 1936.

The ECA authorities did not, apparently, even try to save such specialized peacetime factories as the *Wafios* works near Tubingen which I visited. *Wafios* was one of the most modern factories in Germany and produced wire-working machinery for the production of paper clips, safety pins, bobby pins, wire netting, and upholstery springs. At the beginning of the occupation the French came and took away 200 machine tools from *Wafios* without so much as giving an official receipt. A few months later three French officers came and took another 34 machines for use in France. Next came "Section T" of the French Military Government which took another 70, saying, "This is final; we will not take anything more from you." When the owner of *Wafios* said he was left without enough machinery to carry on, he was told: "You can now learn to work in the primitive way without modern machinery." Finally in the summer of 1948 yet another French commission arrived and ordered 72 more machines to be dismantled, this time as regular reparations to be allocated by IAIA. This last lot of machinery was standing out in the open when I visited the *Wafios* plant and would presumably soon become scrap.

Wafios at the time of my visit had about a quarter of its original equipment, consisting of its oldest machinery. A family-owned enterprise, where the relations between workers and employer were similar to those which prevailed in Siegen, with the owner managing somehow or other to obtain cider and fat for his men to keep them from starving, *Wafios* was still working, although many operations had to be carried on by hand. The owner said to me: "I have traveled all over the world; now I sit here in this crazy madhouse, while the French, British, and American military missions come one after another. The world is now full of loafers in uniform and dollars will not save it until there are no more ignoramuses with military authority."

The French spoliation of German forests, which arouses more resentment and hatred than their looting of replaceable property, is also likely to have harmful and enduring consequences for Europe as a whole. Everywhere you go in the French zone you see huge stacks of logs by the roadside, or being carted along the roads. The Black Forest is still beautiful, but in many places the trees have been cut down and ugly stumps witness to the despoliation of one of the loveliest places in Europe.

The French, according to German reports, have already cut down three times as much timber as Germany took from the whole of France during the occupation.

The British have also severely depleted German timber resources. Timber fellings in the British zone were four times larger than the increment by growth in 1946, three and a half times larger in 1947, and more than twice as large in 1948. The British have decreased their demands year by year, but the French have increased them, so that in 1948 the percentage of trees they cut down as compared with increments was 379.

C. A. Schenck, the founder of the Biltmore Forest School, in a pamphlet published in New York in 1948, shows that the woodland area per capita of the population is only 0.33 acres in Germany in comparison with almost 4 acres in the United States, where there is, nevertheless, no longer any superabundance of timber.

Only 0.5 per cent of the timber area of the world is in Germany, and there is an annual shortage of timber of 290 million cubic feet which used to be imported. Yet 7 per cent of Germany's forest reserves have been listed for cutting since the occupation, and are being sent abroad.

As Mr. Schenck's pamphlet points out, the worst feature of the British and French cuttings is in their failure to observe the rules of silviculture in their cutting, and to replant the denuded areas. He writes:

In the French zone of the Black Forest 3,000 Italians are now employed by the French Military Government at clear cutting on a gigantic scale. The British are employing (notably in the Harz Mountains) 700 English colonial soldiers as lumberjacks. Naturally in these operations all time-honored rules of silviculture are omitted, since they are an impediment to logging.

The author also states that there were already 33,600 acres in the French zone crying for reforestation; 75,000 in North Rhineland in the British zone, and 41,000 in the United States zone.

The Germans have not only suffered a severe diminution of their forests through British and French cuttings and exports. The forced export of coal has also led to increased use by the Germans of wood as fuel for house heating.

The soil erosion which is resulting from the uneconomic exploitation of Germany's forests by her conquerors will seriously reduce the quantity of arable land. It is also likely to have a permanently harmful effect on the climate of Europe.

The Swiss are already concerned at the climatic effects of the French and British deforestation of Germany.

The German climate [a Swiss forestry expert wrote] is assuming steppe features. This danger ought to be taken seriously, not only in Germany itself but in all Europe. It is certain that as a consequence climatic changes will take place in Switzerland. Reforestation is not taken care of after the cuttings have been made, because of the lack of personnel, seeds and plants.[37]

---

[37] Cited by Hans Huth in *Report on the Present Situation of Nature Protection in the American, British and French Occupied Zones of Germany* (Chicago, June 1948).

An article in the forestry journal of the Food and Agriculture Organization of the United Nations (*Unasylva*, July-August 1947) stated: "Many countries view an excessive depletion of Germany's wood resources with grave anxiety as upsetting the whole economic structure and balance of Europe and as mortgaging the future with a problem it will take at least a hundred years to adjust."

As Edmund Burke said at the time of the French Revolution, you cannot indict a whole nation. It would be as unfair to account the whole French people responsible for the vindictive stupidity of present-day French policy as it is to regard all Germans as having been supporters of the Nazi regime. It is the French politicians of all parties who play upon national passions and hatreds for their own advantage who are responsible for the vendetta against the Germans which is weakening all Europe, and may succeed in delivering it to Stalin. For the strange thing today is that the French people, as distinct from their government, seem more friendly to the Germans than in the past. This is the impression gained by such Germans as Dr. Ernst Reuter and Annadore Leber who have visited France recently; it was also my own.

During the two weeks I spent in Paris in the summer of 1948 I made a point of asking every Frenchman I met how it had been under the German occupation. And the answer I received was almost always the same, whether I spoke to the waiters in restaurants, to workers or small shop keepers, to servants or porters: A shrug of the shoulders and the remark, "Well, we ate a little better then than now." And the last man I spoke to, who was the porter who carried my bag to the train on which I was returning to Germany, said, "If only we French could get together with the German people, everything would be better; that would be something. We might then enjoy peace and a decent living."

It seemed in France that it was the rich, not the poor, who hated the Germans, for the latter during the occupation had at least ensured an equitable distribution of the food and goods available, whereas in Liberated France the rich got richer and the poor poorer every day.

On my way from England to Germany via Ostende at the beginning of August 1948 I had a conversation which throws some light on the discrepancy between the attitude of the French and Belgian governments and press and the sentiments of many French and Belgian citizens of the middle and lower classes. I was traveling second-class as I usually do, not only for reasons of economy, but because people are more inclined to speak freely to strangers on long train journeys than in any other circumstances. If you travel in comfort in an international sleeping car the chances are that you will speak little or not at all to your fellow passengers, and that most of them will be foreigners like yourself. But in the second and third-class carriages where you sit up all night the hours pass more quickly if you talk. So I have often had intimate conversations with strangers whom I would never meet again and who for that reason feel secure in revealing their true sentiments.

On this occasion four people including myself occupied the carriage. Opposite me there was an Englishman with whom I soon got involved in a friendly argument about Germany. At one point in our discussion he turned to the lady sitting at his side and, after giving her a summary of our discussion in French, said: "Madame will certainly agree with me since her people suffered under the German occupation." The lady, who was remarkably pretty, replied: "No, Monsieur, I agree entirely with Madame. I am very sorry for the German people today, and besides I see no sense in the present policy of keeping them in such miserable conditions that they may be driven to side with Russia against us."

The man next to me, who turned out to be a Belgian businessman on his way to Prague, broke in and said: "We simply cannot understand the American policy of destroying Germany so that there is no barrier between us and Soviet Russia. It is we who will suffer the results of Anglo-American stupidity when the Russians sweep across Europe."

The Englishman said he was very astonished that my views instead of his should be finding support, since this could hardly be the general sentiment of the Belgian population. Thereupon the young Belgian lady said to him: "Monsieur, you should not believe everything which is said to you in public. Many people will not tell you their real opinion. Today there is a black market in ideas."

This seemed to me a penetrating observation. In such countries as France and Belgium where lynch law was applied to collaborators after the liberation, fear of showing friendliness to the German people has not yet died down. And even in the freest countries people often say what is expected of them, expressing the sentiments considered as orthodox and respectable, although they may have quite different views "under the counter." Just as free trade in many European countries is now called black-marketeering, so in the realm of politics and international affairs, common sense, logic, humanity, and reasonableness are too often considered as evidence of depravity or reaction.

The influence of what is regarded as public opinion, because it is the view expressed in the newspapers and in the statements of politicians, is almost as potent as a Gestapo or a GPU in silencing "dangerous thoughts."

The Belgian lady made it clear to me, however, that it was not only the fear of not being considered respectable which led many people to demand revenge, although they actually had no hatred for the German people and knew that Allied policy toward Germany hurt them as much as the Germans. After I had given her a copy of an article of mine pleading for a rational and humane attitude toward the Germans, she expressed great astonishment. "Is it really possible to say such things in the United States?" she said. "Why, here in Belgium, you would be sent to prison if you published such an article as the one you have shown me."

The article in question was one I had written for the Washington newsletter, *Human Events*, in which I had contrasted the barbarism of our present-day policy toward the defeated with the greater humanity and intelligence of conquerors in past ages, when chivalry or rational self-interest had restrained the victors from wreaking all-out vengeance on the vanquished. The Belgian lady told me how a friend of hers had been arrested in the winter of 1947-48 and kept in prison without food for three days, for having dared to protest against the Allied policy of starving the Germans.

Three months later, when I traveled through the French zone, I was struck by the contrast between the attitude of the French soldiers I talked to and that of their government and the occupation authorities.

I visited the French zone three times, but the longest time I spent there was when I drove from Siegen to the Black Forest in October with Helmuth Weber, his sister Margarita, and her French husband René. The two men had business to do in the French zone and I took the opportunity to go with them in the old Mercedes. I had already learned how difficult it is to find out anything if one comes to the French zone as an American journalist, because the German factory owners are forbidden on pain of imprisonment to tell Americans about the French seizures of machinery or to admit them to their factories.

Traveling with both Helmuth and René I had the advantage of getting both the Germans and the French to talk to me with little constraint. When we visited German factories René remained in the background, and when I went into *cafés* and barracks to talk to the French, Helmuth usually stayed behind in the automobile. However, there were also many occasions when we all got together with both Germans and French and I found that neither had any personal hostility toward the other. Indeed I was struck by the friendliness displayed by the French *poilus* (GI's) toward the German people. Moreover, unlike the Paris politicians, they were hoping that the Germans would fight with them if Russia attacked, instead of fearing, or pretending to fear, German aggression.

Poor René, who was anxious to convince me that the French were not so bad as I imagined, was delighted when the French soldiers, junior officers, and workers we talked to echoed his own chivalrous and intelligent views. But the trouble with the French, as Carlo Schmidt had said to me, is that individually they are reasonable, but once they become part of the bureaucratic apparatus, they are impossible.

There were a considerable number of French workers in the zone, mechanics and lumberjacks, some of whom I spoke to at Alpirsbach, a tiny village in the Black Forest where we spent two nights. Although they were working for the French capitalists, denuding Germany of her timber, they were themselves paid so little that they were little better off than the Germans their employers were robbing.

Most of the French soldiers and workers look as poor as, and are usually dirtier and more unkempt than, the Germans, so that it is difficult to regard them as a master race, or as exploiters and oppressors of the subject German people. There is, moreover, no such social and economic barrier between the French "common man" and his German counterpart, such as that which divides the Americans from the conquered.

The French, let it be said to their credit, have not inculcated their soldiers and civilians with any doctrine of national superiority, and they have observed the old and honorable rules of warfare at least with regard to the billeting of their occupation forces. French officers and soldiers live in German homes without throwing the owners into the street as the British and Americans have done. The owners in some cases are relegated to the cellar or the attic, and many Germans complain of the destruction and neglect of their houses by the French, but at least they are still permitted to find shelter in their own homes.

Thus, in the French zone there is a curious contrast between the great hatred of the French occupation authorities who have fleeced the people, confiscated their cattle and grain and machines, starved them, and sent them to prison for protesting against French oppression and looting, and the day-to-day, if not friendly, at least equalitarian, relations between many individual French and German people.

The impression I received in Germany was that whereas on the governmental level the Americans are regarded as the most humane and rational of the occupying powers, in personal contact the French are somewhat less disliked than the Americans and the British.

The same contrast is to some extent true of the Russians. In Berlin I was often told that General Sokolovsky and his staff treated the Germans with whom they came in contact with far greater friendliness, politeness, and consideration than the Americans or the British. If French policy and actions matched the personal behavior of the French occupation forces, there is no doubt that they would be better liked than the Americans.

The French, again like the Russians, have made a point of conciliating the former ruling classes in Germany while oppressing the

German workers, capitalists, and peasants. In the French zone, as in the Soviet zone, former Nazis are regarded as valuable allies if they will carry out French wishes; and neither the Russians nor the French have condemned the German officer class to the pauper status to which they are relegated in the United States zone. Whereas we accept or reject the cooperation of Germans according to their social or economic origins or class status, the French like the Russians are uninterested in a man's antecedents providing he is ready to collaborate.

The French, like the Russians, seek to win over the intelligentsia, whereas in the American zone professors, students, and writers are placed in the lowest category when it comes to food rations, and find it almost impossible to exist. For instance, the French have restored the University of Freiburg and refounded the ancient University of Mayence closed for over a century, whereas the Americans occupy most of the university buildings at Heidelberg for their own use and have kept students in the lowest category for food rations. While the American Military Government has cold-shouldered any German intellectuals of independent views, the French have welcomed them and tried to conciliate them.

In Germany I was often reminded of the observations made by my brother who sailed the Pacific for several years before he died in the Fiji Islands where he had settled down to practice as a doctor in 1934. In his letters he had contrasted the wonderful hospital at Fiji, and the sanitation and medical services provided by the British, with the severe exploitation of the native peoples by the French, but the latter's better individual behavior toward the natives.

The British, he had said, did the right thing but looked down on the natives and refused to mix with them socially. The French on the other hand, squeezed all they could out of the native population of their islands and provided few of the amenities of civilization in return, but they put up no color bar in their social intercourse with the natives. It seemed as if the same was true in Germany. The German "upper classes," excluding the industrialists ruined by the French, were on better terms with their conquerors than the same elements in the United States and British zone. But the German workers, factory owners, and peasants hated France who robbed them and deprived them of their livelihood.

The French were also playing a clever game in representing themselves as having a common interest with the Germans in opposition to the United States. I cannot vouch for the truth of all the stories I heard, but it seemed that the French were trying to persuade the Germans to make common cause with them against America. For instance, I was told that the French authorities in 1948 had proposed a secret deal which would have allowed the Germans to keep all their machinery over fifteen years old, irrespective of the dismantlement list, if they would turn over to the French all the new machinery they obtained from the Americans or the United States zone of Germany. I was also told that French officers were saying to the Germans they were not really so hostile and revengeful as they seemed, but it was necessary for France to take this line in order to get maximum aid from America; that only insistence on French fears of Germany could enable them to obtain large subsidies from America.

As I have already said, I have no proof of the truth of such assertions, but there seemed little doubt that the French were playing a very devious game. Like the Russians they offer jobs to Germans penalized by the United States Military Government or offended by the cavalier treatment they have received at American hands. And like the Russians they offer privileges to anyone ready to support their policy.

In the economic sphere the corruption which is the characteristic of French internal politics has free play in Germany. Factory owners were told they could save their machinery if they would give bribes to French officials, and German industrial corporations were offered the choice of having their enterprises taken as reparations, or allowing the French a controlling interest as majority stockholders.

Generally speaking, it seemed that the French, in their own small way, limited as they were by their lack of military power, were playing much the same game as the Russians. They offered material benefits, privileges, and forgiveness for former Nazi affiliations, to all who would serve their interests today. They expropriated, penalized, or sent to prison the honest liberals and conservatives who opposed them, while asking no questions concerning the past of those ready to collaborate with them. It was therefore not surprising to find great hatred of the French among both the liberal socialists and conservative capitalists, but considerable amity for the French among reactionary Bavarian monarchists and separatists, and among the German officer class which was treated with greater respect and justice by the French than by the Americans. General Koenig, the French military governor, in contrast to Generals Clay and Robertson, allowed German officers and their widows to receive their pensions. For, as General Speidel's wife said to me in Freudenstadt, "the French have at least a sense of honor." Perhaps honor does not entirely explain it; it would seem that the French, like the Communists, try to take advantage of the resentment caused by American policy in Germany, while using all their influence to impel the United States to get itself hated by the Germans. In this, as in so many other respects, the French play the Communist game, although they imagine they are playing their own hand.

The seeming contradictions in France's policy are explained by her old aim of dividing Germany by fostering separatist tendencies, and her hope of incorporating the Rhineland territories into a Greater France. Having succeeded this time in detaching the Saar from Germany by threatening to dismantle its industries and ruin its people unless they voted to join France, the French no doubt still hope to be equally successful in the rest of their zone by means of intimidation and bribery.

"A good German," in French eyes, is a German prepared to sacrifice his country's interests in order to save his own. Any German prepared to do so can enjoy a "happy life" whether or not he was formerly a Nazi and whatever his present political sympathies. The French care not at all whether a man is a democrat; he only needs to be pro-French or to be ready to serve French interests. Thus French policy is the very antithesis of American: we refuse to be friends even with those most anxious to collaborate with us unless we are sure their past is irreproachable.

One German I talked to in the French zone had been offered a huge income by the French Military Governor if he would accept the position of head of an "independent" palatinate.

The atmosphere in the French zone is in many respects like that under the Soviet terror. There are no concentration camps, but the *Sûreté* is regarded by the Germans as another Gestapo, and people are imprisoned for no other offense than that of complaining against the occupation authorities, or protesting the seizure of their property.

A current joke I heard expresses the feelings of the German people. French trucks and automobiles are all labeled TOA, the letters standing for *Transport Occupation Allemagne*. But the Germans say TOA stands for "Terror Ohne (Without) Adolf!"

The sullen faces of the people, their extreme poverty, and the difficulty we experienced in buying any food except potatoes, witnessed to the omnipresent fear of the French and the manner in which they have stripped their zone of food and goods. The French live off the land like the Russians, and again like the Russians they employ huge numbers of people to force the peasants to give up their milk, eggs and live stock, vegetables, and even grain.

In Baden Baden where General Koenig lives in state like a Viceroy of India, there are more French people than Germans— 40,000 against 30,000, according to the calculations of the Ministry of Economics for Württemberg-Hohenzollern. France uses her zone as a training ground for her conscript army and the French occupation forces not only bring in their wives and children, but also their grandmothers, aunts, sisters, and cousins. Besides all these people living off the German economy, there are the children and invalids brought from France for holidays or cures, who have to be supplied with huge quantities of milk, butter, and eggs. Until 1948 many Germans in the French zone were literally starving, but since last summer, American ECA appropriations to the French zone have somewhat ameliorated their condition.

A German doctor and his wife whom I visited at Wissen, in the French zone adjoining Siegen, told me that after being without any fat ration for months, they had received a pound of butter in August, thanks to America. They now had some hopes of being able to save their little boy, who, like so many other German children in the French zone, had developed tuberculosis because French requisitions left no milk or fats for German consumption. They and everyone else I talked to were wondering whether America would really force the French to stop their locustlike activities, or whether United States aid to the French zone would be drained off by France for her own use.

Of course, some of the peasants manage to hide their food from the French as I discovered at a little inn in a village in the lovely countryside above the Rhine Valley. On this occasion I was returning from a drive to Altenkirchen. We stopped to drink a glass of wine at the inn and, thanks to Otto who is the type of person who jokes and gets friendly with everyone, we soon had the landlady sitting with us and talking freely. I drew her out about the French, and she told us how they had come into the farmhouses and taken away the linen and even the furniture, as well as all the food they could find. They took all the milk, confiscated the live stock and slaughtered it for their own use, and in general left the Germans almost nothing to eat. However, she ended up by asking us if we would like to taste some Westphalian ham. Of course we said we would be delighted and, laughing, she took me with her to her bedroom and showed me the ham hidden in a box under her bed.

The ham was delicious and while we were eating it two men came in who might have posed for pictures symbolizing country and town, peasant and worker, in occupied Germany. The first one was a giant of a young man, red-haired, blue-eyed and ruddy faced, handsome and strong, and fit from his appearance to star as a Wagnerian hero. The other was small and emaciated, greyfaced and sad, and dressed in patched cotton overalls. The first was a peasant and the other a metal worker earning only 75 pfennigs an hour, since the factories in the French zone pay the lowest wages. Incidentally, this worker was one of the very few people I met in Germany who not only admitted he had been a Nazi, but said he still was one in sentiment. In his view the workers had "never had it so good" as under Hitler, and he was very bitter at the Allied confiscation of the Labor Front's security funds, hospitals, and sanitariums. He had consumption and said that he would formerly have been aided, but now he could get no medical aid.

I hoped that it was only in the French zone that workers were being driven back to Nazism by their miserable conditions of life; but I fear it is also true in Bizonia.

The young peasant, for his part, had no interest in politics. When I asked him how he lived, he laughed and said, "We peasants always manage; the French aren't smart enough to find everything."

Of course, it is the townspeople who suffer most when, as in the French zone, the peasants can only sell at a profit on the black market, and deliver food at the prices the French pay only under compulsion.

The number of people required to force peasants to give up food in exchange for low fixed prices makes the whole proceeding uneconomic. For instance, at a small farm I visited in a clearing in the depths of the Black Forest far away from any town or village, I was told that the French periodically sent three men to collect what was demanded. The farm was worked by a woman and her three sons, two other sons having fallen in the war, and the youngest being a prisoner of war in Russia. They had four cows, and three bullocks, some pigs and chickens, sufficient arable land to produce enough grain for their own bread and animal fodder and a large vegetable garden. They had to deliver 700 liters of milk per cow per year, although only the best cows, they said, gave as much as 2,000 liters a year. The French also took so many pigs out of each litter, so many eggs per hen, 43 hundredweight of potatoes, a certain quantity of grain, and so on. The largest of the three bullocks was to be taken the following week.

Whether or not the French were justified in taking as much as they did, the point which struck me was the waste of labor involved in this forcible collection from thousands of little farms, of what, in sum, amounted to a small quantity of food. The sustenance of the inspectors employed must have eaten up most of the supplies thus obtained. The Soviets discovered long ago that the only way to force the agrarian population to give up the fruits of its labor for nothing, or for a price far below its value, is to herd the peasants into collective farms and treat them like factory workers. It simply can't be done except at a prohibitive cost so long as individual farmers cultivate the land.

The family I visited in the Black Forest were not actually badly off in spite of their resentment against the French. But this was because their most profitable activity was the manufacture of *Kirsch*, the spirit made out of cherries which is the specialty of the region. They kept their stills in the forest where the French were unable to find them and did a thriving black-market trade in Germany and across the French border near Strasbourg. All they needed to do was to give some of their liquor to the French sentries.

It is, of course, the French themselves who profit most from the denial to the Germans of customs control at the borders of the French zone. Professor Karl Brandt of Stanford University, who was spending his sabbatical year teaching at Heidelberg University, took me over into Switzerland in his automobile so that I could see for myself what goes on at the frontier. When our automobile arrived at the customs barrier at Basel, two French sergeants examined our passports but did not even inquire whether we had any German currency or goods to declare. The two German customs officials at the barrier were not allowed to come near our automobile, much less inspect our luggage.

It was thus very easy for any Allied nationals to export anything they pleased from Germany via the French zone, and the French were largely responsible for the fall in value of the new D mark caused by the illegal export by black-marketeers of goods needed in Germany. Dr. Brandt and I calculated how quickly a fortune could be made by, for instance, bringing cognac into Germany from France, selling it on the black market at a profit of several hundred per cent, using the marks thus obtained to buy German manufactured goods, and then running them into Switzerland for re-export. Alternatively, any Allied national could take his marks into Switzerland and sell them there to a Swiss bank, which could dispose of them at a tenth of their official value to those who wished to buy goods in Germany. All this illegal trade naturally stimulated the production of luxury goods in Germany for illegal export, in place of necessities. So whereas, for instance, shoes are very high priced and scarce on the German market, great quantities of leather are used to make ladies' purses and other fancy goods.

The Russians in Berlin were similarly doing "good business" in undermining the German currency. Following currency reform the French had already reaped a huge exchange profit without any effort on their part. Out of a total of 5,000,000,000 marks, which was the original new currency issue in June 1948, the British took 266,000,000, the Americans

255,000,000, and the French 250,000,000, for their own use. The total drain on the German economy thus came to over three-quarters of a billion, or 15 per cent of the money in circulation. The French share being disproportionately large, in view of the small size of their zone, they allowed their nationals to exchange practically unlimited amounts at par, whereas the Germans were allowed a maximum of forty marks a head at the exchange rate of ten old marks for one D mark. Consequently, the French before currency reform busied themselves acquiring all the old marks they could lay their hands upon, by fair means or foul. In some cases they went to German friends and made a deal, in other cases they sought the good will of their German servants by offering to exchange the latter's savings for them at par, and in some known instances the French surrounded whole villages and confiscated all the money of the inhabitants. One way or another, the French acquired huge quantities of the new currency and proceeded to export it to Switzerland where there is a free exchange. When this racket subsided they renewed their profits by the export of marks obtained by black-market dealings, or by fresh confiscations of German property.

As I have already related, General Clay tried to induce the French to stop the leak of marks and goods across the frontiers of their zone, but the State Department gave way to the French, and the Occupation Statute denies effective customs control to the proposed Western German government. As usual, the French are being allowed to undermine the German economy while the United States taxpayers supply funds for its support.

American GI's and the pilots of the air lift evidently do not share the State Department's predilection for the French, but their views do not, of course, affect United States policy.

On my first flight out of Berlin on the air lift the United States pilot said to me: "The British are doing a swell job, but do you know, the French aren't helping at all to supply Berlin? They only fly in cognac for sale on the black-market or to Americans." And the sergeant mechanic said:

"Do you know that those b—— in Paris won't let you into the best hotels unless you are an officer?"

Another pilot, who flies a United States staff plane, said to me:

"I always know when I have left Germany. When I look down and see uncultivated fields with no one working in sight I know I am over France. Those guys needn't work since they have us Americans to work for them."

These sentiments are, of course, also prejudiced. But it is a fact that the French, if they worked as they once did, and did not so mismanage their economy and finance, should have had no need of American food subsidies except during the 1946-47 drought. The land of France is fertile and she is not overpopulated.

In Paris one is shocked by the abundant luxury displayed in food and clothing in contrast to the poverty of the French workers and British austerity. The number of waiters, hotel servants, and others catering to the luxury trades would surely allow France to dispense with a large part of her ECA appropriation if they were set to work producing necessities and exports. In a word, the French upper classes are still enjoying a far easier and pleasanter life than most of the American taxpayers supporting the French economy.

But France, apparently, has only to ask to receive. No one demands anything of her but a smile and her good will. So France goes on talking about her war losses, although her looting in Germany, combined with reparations and American gifts, have more than compensated for the material damage she suffered during the war and the occupation.

Whereas the manner in which the British dispose of American aid is examined and subject to criticism, like those of a wife, France is treated by the United States like a mistress whose favors are uncertain and whose extravagances are not questioned.

It would not matter much if all that was involved was the pensioning of "La Belle France" by generous Uncle Sam, or the maintenance of Paris as a city of pleasure for the delectation of State Department and ECA officials, and American newspapermen. The danger lies in the influence which France exerts on American policy—an influence which is likely to increase rather than diminish once the State Department takes over the administration of Germany. The Army has to be realistic, since it has to fight the wars which poor diplomacy brings about. And the Army's view of the value of the French is summarized in the remark made to me by a member of General Clay's staff: "The French won't fight. Period."

"Why then," I asked, "does so much consideration have to be given to the French point of view? Why, if the French are of no value as allies, must we continually give way to France, on dismantlement, on the Ruhr and just about everything else?"

The answer I received was to the effect that America could not go ahead with the rehabilitation of Western Europe and with plans for its defense with active opposition in the rear, in France; that the French tell the Americans that if they get involved in war with Russia, as for instance over Berlin, they, the French, will stay out of it and refuse bases to the United States. The French, in effect, blackmail the United States, saying they will be neutral in any war with Russia, unless America concedes everything they want regarding Germany.

The French tell the Americans that in their concern over the danger of a third world war, they must prepare to win it in such a way as to prepare the way for a fourth one; that America must not make use of Germany to help defeat Soviet Russia, because the end result would be German supremacy in Europe. In answer to this the American Army authorities say: "Well, if you won't permit the Germans to defend themselves against Russia, are you yourselves prepared to defend her?" And, of course, the French then throw up their hands in horror and cry, "*What!* We defend Germany? Are you crazy?"

The net result of French intransigeance is that the United States is expected to defend Europe, and to pursue a policy toward Germany which not only renders her defenseless, but would endanger the American Army's security in war by creating hatred of the United States among the German population.

In these difficult circumstances General Clay and the Department of the Army appear to have endeavored to steer a middle course. They have made every possible concession to the French point of view, but have refused to agree to the complete ruin of Germany demanded by France. They have gone on hoping that if the American taxpayer continued to make up the losses resulting from the concessions made to the French on dismantlement and the Ruhr, Western Europe including Germany will eventually be federated and all its resources and manpower mobilized for defense against the Soviet menace. This hope is based on the belief that in time French fears can be allayed and France will then allow Germany and Europe to recover economic prosperity and be made strong enough to resist Communist pressure. But this hope must disappear if the French continue to miss their opportunity to become as strong as a free Germany.

Many as are the criticisms which can be leveled at the United States Military Government, the American Army must be given the credit for seeing things straight and seeing them whole. Since they bear the responsibility for the defense of Western Europe as well as of the United States, the Military cannot afford to live in the cloud cuckoo land inhabited by many of the civilians who determine Administration policy. The Army was, therefore, naturally incensed at what it regarded as France's "sabotage"[38] of the June 1948 London agreement to set up a West German state and of other measures designed to stem the Communist tide.

When the discussions on the Occupation Statute (which according to the London agreement was to be negotiated by the military governors) were referred back to the British, French, and American governments, the *New York Herald Tribune* reported:

It is an open secret that the French, who consider General Clay a hardboiled American, prefer to shift everything possible to the governmental level, where they have frequently been able to obtain concessions they were unable to get from the American Military

---

[38] See the *New York Times* dispatch from Paris on March 18, 1949.

Government. Many officials here [in Germany] believe that in negotiations at the governmental level the French and British deal with Americans who know the German problem far less intimately than does General Clay's staff. The results were described this way by an American official in Berlin: "Sometimes it seems to us that the American negotiators at the higher level—not really acquainted with the full details and history of each issue—*do not know the importance of what they are giving away.*"

Unfortunately for the security of Europe and the peace of the world, the State Department is now assuming control of America's German policy. This means, now that Dean Acheson is Secretary of State, that America is giving way to France on the most vital issues, annulling the effects of Marshall Plan assistance to Europe, and jeopardizing the peace of the world. For nothing can be more certain than that, if France's hysterical, or simulated, fear of Germany, combined with her desire to appease Russia, continue to determine United States policy, Europe will be so weakened and the Communists so strengthened, that Stalin will be emboldened to attack the Western world.

The influence of France was most clearly displayed when the Occupation Statute was presented to the Germans on April 10, 1949. Instead of allowing the Germans the self-government promised a year ago, all real power is reserved to the occupation authorities.

This statute can most fitly be compared to the old Japanese constitution and the present Soviet constitution, which similarly take away in one paragraph the liberties and rights granted in another. While pretending to give the Western Germans the right to rule themselves, the Occupation Statute gives them responsibility without power: an overriding veto is imposed on the legislative, judicial, administrative, and economic powers of the proposed West German government.

It is necessary to examine this spurious document in some detail to appreciate the conditions of servitude we have offered to the German people under the veneer of liberty.

The Occupation Statute "specifically reserves" to the occupying powers not only powers over disarmament, reparations, and restitutions, but also over all the following fields: scientific research, restrictions on industry, prohibition of civil aviation, decartelization and deconcentration of industry, nondiscrimination in trade, foreign interests in Germany, foreign affairs and foreign trade, displaced persons and admission of refugees. Nor is this by any means all. The occupation powers not only continue to control Germany's foreign trade for their own benefit. They are to continue to control internal German economic policy and the use Germany makes of her imports. Paragraph 2(e) is the real joker, since it can be interpreted to mean just anything and everything. For it says that the occupation authorities reserve to themselves all the powers necessary for the "protection, prestige and security of Allied forces, dependents, employees and their representatives, their immunities and satisfaction of occupation costs and their other requirements."

Nor are the Germans to be permitted to enjoy the protection of law, *habeas corpus*, or other civil liberties. "The civil rights of every person," according to paragraph 6, "to be protected against arbitrary arrest, search or seizure, to be represented by counsel, to be admitted to bail as circumstances warrant, to communicate with relatives, and to have a fair and prompt trial," are all "subject to the requirements of the security of the occupation authorities."

The "German Federal Government" is not even to be permitted to pass any laws without first notifying the occupation authorities, who can veto any legislation "inconsistent with decisions or actions taken by the occupation authorities themselves."

Finally the conquerors reserve the right to annul, at any moment, even the extremely limited powers granted to the puppet government they want to establish. Paragraph 3 of the Occupation Statute says: "The occupation authorities reserve the right to resume, in whole or in part, the exercise of full authority if they consider that to do so is essential to security or to preserve democratic (sic) government in Germany, or in pursuance of the international obligations of their governments."

India, before she gained her independence, was a freer country than Germany under the colonial status laid down for her in the Occupation Statute. In this connection it is worth mentioning a conversation I had in

Düsseldorf with the correspondent of several Indian newspapers. I had said to him that Germany now seemed to have been relegated to the same status as nineteenth-century India, and he replied: "Yes, I always say to my German friends, 'We had it, and now you have it; we are now free, but you have become the subjects of America, Britain, and France, and you have fewer rights than we had before we gained our independence, for at least the British instituted a rule of law in India, whereas in Germany there is no such thing.'"

Not only does the Occupation Statute deny to the Germans those elementary human rights which Mrs. Roosevelt and other American delegates to UNESCO are so fond of talking about. It also is obviously designed to prevent Germany from competing on the world market. Both her foreign trade and her scientific research are to be controlled by her conquerors and competitors. Thus Germany is to be handicapped in the development of new techniques, or forced to let her competitors derive the benefit of the future inventions of her scientists and technicians.

This proviso in the Occupation Statute is the most disastrous of all its clauses from the point of view of European recovery. For Europe cannot hope to live without American subsidies unless it can develop new technical processes and overcome its lack of natural resources through scientific discoveries and the development of its chemical industries. The Germans, as everyone knows, have led the world in the invention of substitutes through chemical processes. They are now to be kept from utilizing their brains, inventiveness, and capacity for painstaking research for their own and Europe's benefit. It is as if the brightest and most industrious boy in the class were forbidden to study and work.

Dean Acheson's bland statement that there is "no foundation" for the contention of the German newspapers that these clauses in the Occupation Statute are motivated by fear of German competition, is hardly likely to inspire confidence in the honesty and truthfulness of the United States Secretary of State.

The Occupation Statute is bad enough in itself, but there might be some hope that it will be interpreted in a liberal spirit were it not for the veto power given to each of the three Western occupation powers by the intergovernmental agreement signed in Washington on April 8, 1949, and made public on April 26. "Unanimous agreement" is required on all important questions embracing: disarmament and demilitarization *including related fields of scientific research*, prohibitions and restrictions on industry and civil aviation; and controls in regard to the Ruhr, restitutions, reparations, decartelizations, deconcentration, nondiscrimination in trade matters, foreign interests in Germany and claims against Germany.

No one can doubt that the vast field over which the veto power reigns will enable Britain and France to refuse any modification in the Level of Industry Plan, or any other relaxation of the controls which now prevent Germany's paying her own way and contributing her full quota to the needs of European reconstruction. The United States Secretary of State has in fact given Britain and France the right to perpetuate Germany's economic servitude, whatever the present cost to the American taxpayer, and the future cost in lives if and when war comes. The time is apparently long since past when the Senate of the United States claimed its right to sanction what are in fact treaties with foreign powers, so this "agreement" with Britain and France is likely to go unchallenged.

The Occupation Statute constitutes a grave retrogression in United States policy. For although great concessions have been made to the French point of view in drawing up the Ruhr Statute, which regularizes the colonial status of Germany's main industrial area, the United States Military Government had at least provided therein that the limitation on German steel production was to be temporary. But now the State Department has put France in a position to exercise a veto power over German and European recovery similar to that which Russia exercises in the United Nations to the detriment of the world, and likely to be used as unscrupulously.

The French have even succeeded in preventing the new German state from acquiring the right to maintain a federal police force for the detection and suppression of subversive activities. The Communists are to be allowed even greater freedom than they enjoy in France to destroy democracy from within.

As was to be expected, in view of the colonial status prescribed for them under the Occupation Statute, the German democratic parties have not been permitted to decide upon the Constitution of the new Western German state. After the parliamentary council at Bonn had spent months drawing up a constitution, and the Christian Democrats (CDU) and Social Democrats (SDP) had at last reached a compromise agreement on such disputed questions as the division of fiscal and economic powers between the central government and the *Länder*, and the balance of legislative powers between the upper and lower houses of the federal legislature. The military governors intervened to amend the constitution in favor of the CDU which favors a weak central government.

The French objections to the establishment of a viable WestGerman state, and their desire to permit only a loose federation of states was allowed to prevail. The United States supported France by similarly favoring the reactionary separatist forces in Bavaria and the Rhineland, as against the SDR supported by the British.

In respect to the foundation of the West-German state, the British have in fact shown far greater political intelligence than the United States and France. Under their Labour Government, their political genius and the enlightened attitude they formerly adopted towards their vanquished foes have been obscured by the frantic desire of the Labour party to become independent of America through the acquisition of dollars by any means, fair or foul. But with regard to the political future of Germany the British showed themselves to be incomparably more enlightened than the French. They went so far as to reveal to the Social Democrats that the Western powers had secretly agreed to allow somewhat greater legislative and fiscal powers to the proposed central government, should the Germans balk at the harsh terms originally presented. The British thus enabled the Social Democrats to obtain a little more power for the future government of Western Germany than would otherwise have been the case. At the time of writing it is not yet decided whether the German Social Democrats will have the courage and political wisdom to follow the lead of Kurt Schumacher and Carlo Schmidt, who have advised against collaboration with the Western conquerors in setting up a German state denied any real authority.

The weak brothers among the German democrats may give way to superior force and accept the quisling status offered them. But one thing is certain. The German politicians who accept the Occupation Statute as the basis for a "democratic" government will be regarded as puppets and traitors by the majority of their countrymen. It is therefore to be hoped that the liberal elements in Germany will keep their reputations clean by refusing to form a West-German government under the terms of servitude offered to them by the Western occupation powers acting under French influence. If they accept, there will be little hope for democracy in Germany now or in the future.

Unfortunately for the future of democracy in Germany and Europe as a whole, the blackmailing tactics adopted by the United States may force the SDP and other German democrats to accept the terms offered them by the Western powers. For the military governors are insisting that the German leaders who refuse to set up the impotent Western state they are being urged to establish are playing into Russia's hands.

It is both tragic and short-sighted for the United States to confront the German democrats with such an inescapable dilemma: if they collaborate in setting up a West-German state without power, they are likely to lose the support of the German people who will regard them as quislings; if they refuse, they will be accused of helping the Communists.

In fact, the German democratic leaders were in a position for once to do a little blackmailing themselves. For the Western powers, having committed themselves to a four-power conference on Germany if Soviet Russia would lift the Berlin blockade, were desperately anxious to reach an agreement with the German democratic parties in time to set up a West-German state before Stalin offered to lift the blockade.

But, to judge from their past history, the German democratic politicians are unlikely to take advantage of their opportunity to force real concessions from the Western powers. They are more likely to pursue their straightforward course and let their conquerors turn the tables on them. On the other hand, it is possible that the pressure brought to bear on the Germans by the United States Military Government was inspired by General Clay's fears that the State Department might make a deal with

Russia as well as with France to prevent the formation of the Western state, unless the new German state were set up before the secret Washington-Moscow negotiations resulted in agreement. It is more than a little suspicious that knowledge of the negotiations with Russia, initiated by Dean Acheson in February 1949, was withheld from both the Germans and the American public until April 25 when Tass reported it.

Now that negotiations with Soviet Russia are once again in prospect, the veto power which the Western powers have reserved to themselves under the Occupation Statute, must preclude any agreement which does not permit Russia, as well as France, to sabotage all American plans for the recovery of Germany or Europe. We shall in all probability be faced with the choice of withdrawing all troops from Germany and granting the Germans full liberty at the risk of leaving them defenseless before the armed might of Soviet Russia and her German hirelings, or dishonoring our own promise to give the Western Germans a limited right to self-government.

For obviously no Four Power agreement is possible unless Russia obtains the same veto powers as America, France, and Britain; and no one can doubt that a German administration subject in all its acts to a Russian veto would be unable to govern unless it followed the Communist Party line.

It is impossible to say whether Dean Acheson, in jeopardizing all Europe and weakening America by the concessions he has made to France, was activated by the belief that the military support of France is worth the price, or by his former affiliation with the group once known as "Frankfurter's Hot Dogs," which included Algernon Hiss. Acheson's friendship with Felix Frankfurter is no secret, nor is there any doubt that Judge Frankfurter was one of the most influential sponsors of the fateful "unconditional surrender" formula and the Morgenthau Plan. Thus it seems probable that the 1949 retrogression in American policy is at least to some extent inspired by those who have no such aversion for Stalin's dictatorship as they had for Hitler's, and are still more concerned with punishing the Germans than stopping the Communists.

Dean Acheson is also supposed to have a British orientation, but the British, although as short-sighted as the French with regard to dismantlement, have thrown their weight on the side of the German Social Democrats who insist that if a Western German government is to be formed it must be allowed sufficient power to govern. So once again it would appear to be French influence, which is impelling the United States to give right of way to the Communists.

As after the first World War, so again today, France is stifling German democracy. Once again she is preventing the implementation of a policy which could win the mass of the German people to our side. Once again she is strengthening the totalitarian forces which nearly destroyed her in the last war and are certain to defeat her next time.

As Carlo Schmidt is reported to have said in April 1949:

Whether any of us likes it or not one thing is true in Europe today—its future depends on the workers of Germany. Russia cannot win them yet—but the West can lose them. If they should ever desert the West and slide into Bolshevism, then you need no longer worry about what France's workers will do. Then you can have all the Atlantic Pacts you can write. Stalin will need no Molotov or Vishinsky, no Cominform, not a single tank. Bolshevism will be everywhere.[39]

At the war's end France had an opportunity that is never likely to recur, to assume the lead in Europe, not by conquest, but by acting according to the great principles of the French Revolution. But instead of uniting Europe on the basis of liberty, equality, and fraternity, France has displayed only a mean desire to appease the strong, bully the vanquished, and beg from the rich. Were she the great and intelligent nation which many Americans believe her to be, she would have been magnanimous in the hour of Germany's total defeat, and thus have ended the long and tragic epic of aggression and counteraggression by bringing victor and vanquished alike into a free federated Europe. Instead, she has taken the lead in perpetuating old feuds, dividing Europe, and preparing the way for

---

[39] *Time*, April 4, 1949.

Communist conquest. So long as France influences American policy, there can be little hope for peace, security, or prosperity in Europe, or an end to the subsidies which Americans are supplying to the Old World.

11

CONCLUSION

THE REPORTING OF NEWS FROM GERMANY HAS BEEN INADEQUATE ever since her surrender. It is so colored by anti-German prejudice and ignorance that the American public, even today, is uninformed about the facts and unaware of the consequences of our German policy. So in appealing for justice and compassion for the vanquished and endeavoring to show the American people the moral and material price they are paying for revenge, I know that I am not only laying myself open to the charge of being pro-German. I am also likely to be told that the picture is no longer so dark as the one I have painted. For the American press as a whole has concentrated during the past year on reporting only the high lights of economic recovery and has ignored the basic problems which palliatives such as currency reform and Marshall aid cannot solve.

To those who accuse me of being pro-German I cannot do better than cite the words of Tom Paine, who said: "Where liberty is not, there is my country." Since the Germans have been deprived by their conquerors of freedom and elementary human rights and reduced to the status of colonials ruled by four sets of masters, it seems to me to be the function of men and women of good will and liberal sentiment to espouse their cause.

Some of my readers may think that I have given undue weight to the German point of view. If this is true, my contribution constitutes only a drop in the ocean compared to the continuous, and somewhat monotonous, spate of books, articles, newspaper reports, and radio comment which have by now established an accepted legend.

Germans are not permitted to speak for themselves except in accents of humility pleasing to their conquerors, so no one knows today what they are thinking and feeling. I do not pretend to have done more than penetrate a little below the surface of the uniformity and submissiveness imposed on Germany, but I have endeavored to "speak for the silent."

I shall also, no doubt, be accused in some quarters, of partiality because I have not given space to the record of Nazi crimes. This omission is not due to my failure to recognize Hitler's responsibility for the material and moral wreckage in Europe, and the decline of Western civilization. The reason why I have not repeated the ofttold tale of Nazi crimes against humanity is that it is already familiar to every American. It is our own record which is not known, and it seems high time that the victors began to search their own consciences.

The roles of oppressors and oppressed change with the times. Yesterday's arrogant victor is today's vanquished, and those who fought for liberty now deprive others of freedom. It seems as true today as when Thucydides wrote his history of the Peloponnesian War that "right as the world goes is only a question between equals in power, while the strong do what they can and the weak suffer what they must."

Evil begets evil and injustice breeds more injustice. Revenge creates an overwhelming desire for counterrevenge; nations deprived of liberty become pathologically nationalist. If "Europe's interminable wars," which now threaten to destroy Western civilization are ever to end, and Communism with its creed of hatred is not to overwhelm us, the cycle must be broken. We must finally abjure the belief that two wrongs make a right.

I should not wish, however, to do the least injustice to the good intentions and considerable achievements of the United States Military Government. The United States Army is, I think, least to blame for the shortcomings, errors, injustices, and failures dealt with in this book. In spite of the orders they originally received from Washington to do nothing to rehabilitate Germany, the Army authorities averted a complete collapse at the beginning of the occupation. Public utilities were put back into operation, the streets were cleared of rubble, some industries were helped to start working again, and mass starvation and epidemics were averted by the use of Army funds to import food and alleviate acute distress. In general, it can be said that the Military Government, soon after it took over the administration of the ruined, hungry, and morally shattered land it occupied, pursued as enlightened a policy as was possible within the limits set by the executive authorities in Washington.

The United States Military Government under General Clay has had a clearer perception of the Communist danger than the Administration. Every Army officer concerned with the security of the United States and aware of the extent of the obligations we have undertaken in Europe, is aware of the fact that unless the German people are included in the North Atlantic Pact and armed for their own defense and that of Europe, Soviet Russia will be able to sweep us and our Western allies at least as far as the Pyrenees. But no one dares to say in public that unless Germany becomes our full-fledged ally, America must either abandon Europe to Communism as soon as Stalin has prepared his subjects for war, or be prepared to sacrifice so many American lives to defend it that the losses of World War II will appear insignificant.

Although born English, I have chosen to be an American because in America I have found more equality and social justice, less nationalist prejudice, and more regard for the rights and claims of other peoples than anywhere else in the world. The tragedy is that all the good will of the American people, their generosity and sincere desire to extend the benefits of their civilization to less fortunate nations, are to a large extent nullified by their lack of knowledge of past history and present realities in Europe.

America's ignorance of Germany is a dangerous thing. One can recall the fact that when the Allied armies entered Germany, the OWI and other war agencies claiming to have expert knowledge of German sentiment predicted that a Nazi sniper would be found behind every bush, and in every attic and cellar, and that there were bands of "werewolves" ready to murder our occupation forces. Events proved instead that millions of Germans were prepared to greet us as liberators, but were rebuffed, and that there were too few convinced Nazis left in Germany to cause any serious difficulties to our occupation forces.

The tragedy was that we refused to collaborate with the Germans who had braved the Nazi horror and would have been capable of reorientating Germany. Instead, we revived the Nazi ideology by refusing to separate the sheep from the goats when we took over the administration of our part of the shattered Third Reich. The same ignorance today of the real sentiments of the German people is leading us to ignore the danger of Germany's throwing in her lot with Soviet Russia, not because the German people have an inborn aversion to democracy, but because many of them no longer have any hope that the West will accord them either freedom, or the right to work, or the possibility of defending themselves against Soviet Russia.

Having been convinced by war propaganda that the Germans are innately more aggressive and cruel than other peoples, most Americans are unable to realize that the punishment of the German people only serves to strengthen the Soviet aggressors.

The most important influence in America furthering Communist aims would seem to be the refusal of the New Dealers to admit that President Roosevelt's policies were fundamentally mistaken. They must continue to believe that the German people are the fount of all iniquity, and a continuing menace to the peace of the world, if they are to preserve their veneration for the late President. Most of them lack the courage to admit that their revered leader was mistaken in believing that all that was necessary for the establishment of lasting peace was the crushing out of existence of the German nation, and that this aim justified close collaboration with Stalin. Some New Dealers, or so-called progressives, like Wallace even today turn the same blind eye on Soviet "crimes against humanity," as Roosevelt and his wife during the war. Others, who are too intelligent or decent to ignore the evidence, nevertheless persist in demanding that the full pound of flesh be exacted from defeated Germany. They all lack the moral courage to admit that President Roosevelt's policies were fundamentally wrong and have proved a colossal failure. To sustain their faith in their dead leader they continue to demand the implementation of his German policy, long after the assumptions on which it was based have been proven false. They want Germany to be kept impotent even at the cost of rendering Europe incapable of self-defense. They are prepared to run the risk of driving the Germans to side with Russia by denying them freedom and equality and the possibility of earning their living so long as they remain on our side of the Iron Curtain.

The Republicans, having subscribed to a bipartisan foreign policy, are similarly held the prisoners of past errors. They too cannot face the political consequences of admitting they were mistaken. With rare exceptions the Republicans have followed the Democratic lead in throwing good money after bad rather than cut losses and start on a fresh and enlightened foreign policy. They too must be held guilty for the failure of the United States to make a clean break with the past.

Nor is it easy for the American people as a whole to accept the sad truth that for the second time in a quarter of a century they have sacrificed their sons and husbands in foreign wars to no good purpose. Far from "making the world safe for democracy," both wars have diminished the area of freedom, and the last one has merely substituted one totalitarian dictatorship for another. But it is difficult for those who have lost their loved ones to admit that they died in vain.

The reluctance of the human mind to face unpalatable truths, the inability of politicians to admit their mistakes, the aftermath of war propaganda, and the sinful pride which inspires us all, play into the hands of the Communists.

It is conducive to spiritual satisfaction and self-respect to view past or present enemies as the only transgressors against the laws of God and man. To admit that the capacity for evil is inherent in all mankind would destroy our sense of superiority. So we have gone far toward the adoption of the Nazi theory of "racial" differences, and have ourselves assumed the position of a superior or master race.

Worst of all we have been seduced by the Nazi-Communist theory that justice means the collective punishment of the many for the sins of a few.

In the second century A.D. Emperor Trajan enunciated the principle that it is better for many guilty persons to escape punishment than for one innocent person to be wrongly condemned. The Communists have reversed this principle. They say that it is better for a thousand innocent people to be condemned than for one guilty person to escape.

In our treatment of the Germans we have adopted the Communists' principle instead of that of the civilized Western world.

Those who indict the whole German nation for the crimes of the Nazis put themselves in the same category as the Bolsheviks, who murdered millions of people for the "crime" of belonging to "the capitalist class" (in which the Communists included the more prosperous peasants called "kulaks"); and of the Nazis who exterminated millions of Jews and other "inferior" races such as the Poles and Russians.

By treating all Germans as criminals or pariahs, and punishing them all by our policies, we deny the very essence both of Christian civilization and of rational liberalism: belief in individual responsibility; the rule of law, not of men; and the equality of all peoples irrespective of class, race, nation, or creed.

As I complete the writing of this book, the battle for Berlin is ending and the struggle for Germany is beginning. If, as seems probable, the Communists have learned that they cannot win Germany by force and terror and are preparing to reverse their tactics, we shall no longer be able to count upon Stalin's cruelties and blunders to keep the Germans on our side. There is a limit to endurance and sanity when there is no hope. If democracy continues to offer not bread but a stone, the German people will be driven once again to repudiate Western civilization. If Soviet Russia offers the freedom and unity which the West cannot, or will not, give them, the Germans may combine with Russia to destroy us together with themselves.

The West could easily have won the hearts and minds of the German people at the beginning of the occupation by offering them liberty, a rule of law, hope, and protection from the renewal of totalitarian tyranny imposed by Russia. We chose instead to make a mockery of democracy, not only by punishing all Germans for the sins of the Nazis, but also by our equation of communism with democracy until Soviet Russia started to menace us. We condoned every atrocity formerly committed by Hitler when it was committed by Stalin, and demonstrated our readiness to get along with the Soviet dictator even after it became evident that he had taken Hitler's place as the scourge of Europe.

The Germans have observed that every concession we have made to their demand to be allowed to work and eat and govern themselves has been made only as the result of our growing awareness of the menace which Communism constitutes to our own freedom. They consider our rule as a lesser evil than that of Communist Russia, but few of them any longer believe that we will ever allow them the same liberties and rights as we claim for ourselves.

Most Germans have no illusions about Communism. But many of them will never forget the brutal and unjust treatment they received at our hands before we realized that Soviet Russia is our enemy as well as theirs. Whether they were democrats emerging from long years of hiding or released from concentration camps; or young men and women who had obeyed Hitler from a mistaken, but sincere, conviction that no patriot could fail to follow his leader; or workers driven desperate by long years of unemployment which had rendered them incapable of resisting the demagogic propaganda of the Nazis; or the defeated men of the German army who bore little or no responsibility for Nazi atrocities, but had fought bravely to save their country from the Communist terror only to find themselves branded as criminals by their Western conquerors and kept as slave laborers in France and England as well as in Russia, none of them have cause to "love democracy."

The legacy of the past now constitutes an acute danger. If Stalin should propose that all the victors withdraw their forces from Germany and allow her to become united and free of control by Military Government, he may yet win the battle for Germany. The fact that the Red Army is close enough to impose Russia's will at any moment, and the existence of a well-armed "police force" in the Eastern zone under Communist control, would make such freedom fictitious. But the temptation will be great so long as we continue to forbid the Germans to produce to the limit of their capacity, and deny them the right to export their manufactures on equal terms with the British and French, while also insisting on Western Germany's unilateral disarmament. Moreover, thanks to our foolish agreements at Yalta and Potsdam, and our short-sighted strategy, only Soviet Russia can restore her lost territories to Germany, give her unity, and open up the markets of Eastern Europe which are essential to the German economy. If we continue to control Germany's foreign trade in the interests of her British and French competitors, sooner or later the Germans will be driven by economic compulsions to make a deal with the Soviet Union.

Stalin can also rest assured that France will continue to play into his hands. He can now safely make his gesture to obtain German good will, secure in the knowledge that the West will reject his proposal to set Germany free and that we will take upon ourselves the onus of continuing to occupy her.

The only peace which can endure and is worth the sacrifices of war is one founded on justice. Unless we recognize our own transgressions against law and humanity, and seek to implement the principles for which Americans have gone to war twice in a generation, there can be no hope for the salvation of Western civilization. All the atom bombs we can manufacture will not save us if we lose our self-respect and the trust and esteem of the peoples of the world, including the conquered and powerless.

Most Americans, being still isolationist at heart, have felt that one of the rewards of victory was freedom to dismiss the whole subject of Germany from their minds. Thus they gave right of way to the minority of fanatics, professional anti-Germans, and Communist sympathizers, who led the chorus of hatred in the years of tension and passion engendered by war, and have been successful in perpetuating their influence by smearing all dissidents. This harmful minority has succeeded in widening the abyss which separates us from the nation for whose fate we made ourselves responsible by the demand for unconditional surrender.

Only very recently has the American public become aware of the fact that total victory burdens the United States for good or ill with total responsibility, not only for the fate of the German people but for the destiny of Europe. The terrible responsibility they had unknowingly assumed was realized only after Soviet aggression and intransigeance and Stalin's openly declared hostility toward the United States had awakened the Americans from the pipe dream induced by Administration propaganda and the ignorant or servile journalists who spread the same lies. The mirage of a United Nations organization in which the lion and the lamb were to lie down together and the victor nations were to remain friends forever is now dispelled. But the poison instilled into the veins of the American people by the apostles of hatred and vengeance still distorts their vision and prevents them from adopting the totally new policy which alone can ensure that the world shall not succumb to Stalin in spite of President Roosevelt's errors of judgment and sacrifices of principle.

The task which the United States undertook in Germany, that of persuading a brave people with old traditions and a high level of culture, to adopt the democratic faith and institutions of their Western conquerors, was perhaps in any case an impossible one. It required tact, understanding, and sympathy, and was certainly incompatible with the behavior prescribed for the occupying forces. Obviously we could not both "teach democracy" to the Germans and ourselves behave as conquerors or as a "master race." We could only succeed by following the high principles of the American tradition, but these, together with the Atlantic Charter, were in fact repudiated in our dealings with the German people. And even though we have since turned over a new leaf, begun to restore the German economy, and given the German people some hope of eventually being admitted as equals into a European federation, our policy still lacks the warmth and humanity which are necessary to overcome the memory of past injury and bitterness on both sides. Fruitful cooperation between peoples is impossible without trust, fair dealing, and equality, and these require a complete change in our approach to Germany.

The political and military consequences of vengeance may prove disastrous to the Western world. Europe cannot be defended militarily, or "made safe for democracy" politically, unless Germany is brought into the community of free nations as an equal partner.

I am convinced that not only the dictates of reason, common sense, and self-interest, but also the call of conscience and belief in a justice which transcends national boundaries, will impel a radical change in United States policy once the American people are made aware of the facts which have for so long been withheld from them.

OTHER TITLES

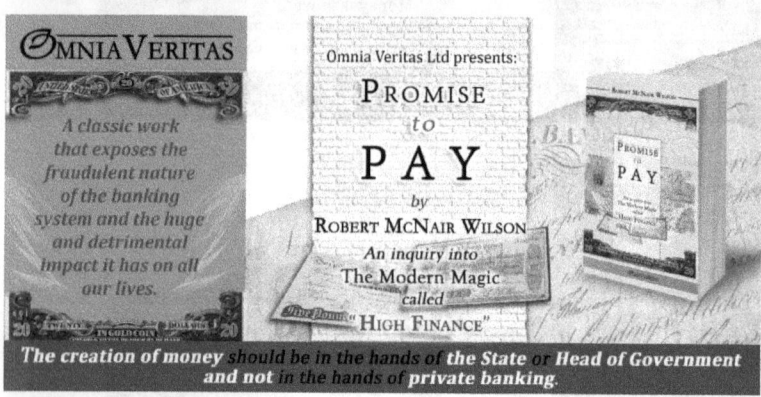

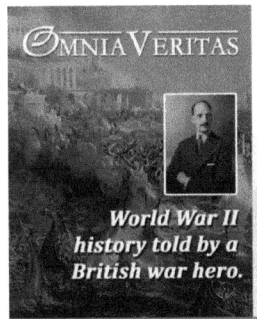

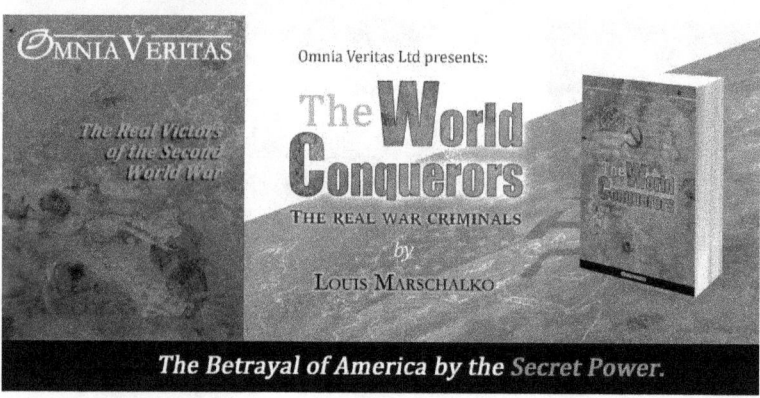

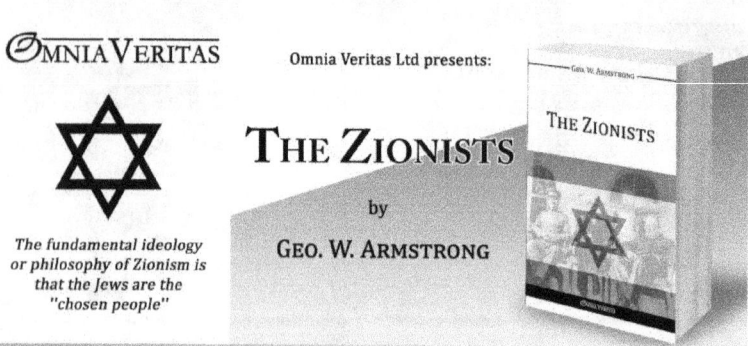

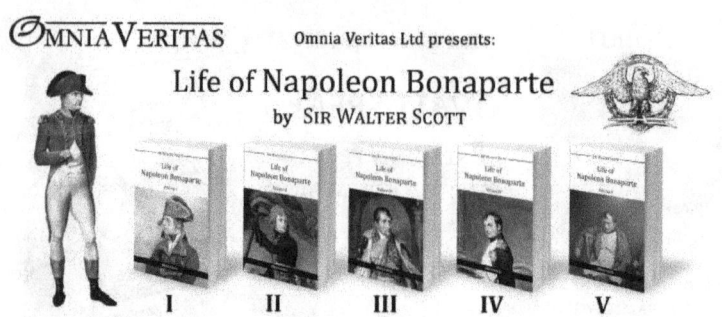

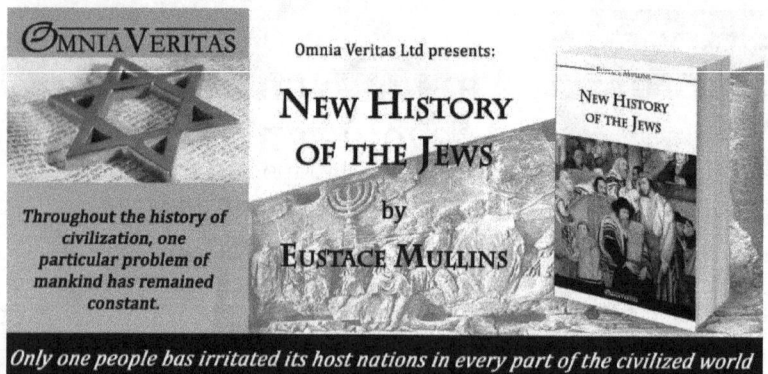

www.omnia-veritas.com

www.ingramcontent.com/pod-product-compliance
Lightning Source LLC
Chambersburg PA
CBHW050122170426
43197CB00011B/1681